CIVIL LIABILITY FOR ANIMALS

CIVIL LIABILITY FOR ANIMALS

SIR PETER NORTH
CBE, QC, DCL, FBA

OXFORD
UNIVERSITY PRESS

OXFORD
UNIVERSITY PRESS

Great Clarendon Street, Oxford OX2 6DP

Oxford University Press is a department of the University of Oxford.
It furthers the University's objective of excellence in research, scholarship,
and education by publishing worldwide in

Oxford New York

Auckland Cape Town Dar es Salaam Hong Kong Karachi
Kuala Lumpur Madrid Melbourne Mexico City Nairobi
New Delhi Shanghai Taipei Toronto

With offices in

Argentina Austria Brazil Chile Czech Republic France Greece
Guatemala Hungary Italy Japan Poland Portugal Singapore
South Korea Switzerland Thailand Turkey Ukraine Vietnam

Published in the United States
by Oxford University Press Inc., New York

First published 2012

British Library Cataloguing-in-Publication Data
Data available

Library of Congress Cataloging in Publication Data
Data available

Typeset by Cenveo, Bangalore, India
Printed in Great Britain
by Ashford Colour
Press Ltd, Gosport, Hampshire

ISBN 978–0–19–960081–6

1 3 5 7 9 10 8 6 4 2

For Henry, Ollie, Stella, Maisie and Trinity

PREFACE

My earlier book, *The Modern Law of Animals*, was published 40 years ago at the time of the passing of the Animals Act 1971. This book is, in essence, a second edition of that book, but the passage of time has indicated that a different title might now be more appropriate. I should express my gratitude, at the outset, to those judges and others who suggested to me a few years ago that there might be value in the reworking of my earlier book. There are, I believe, a number of reasons for this. There have been 40 years of decisions on the application and interpretation of the 1971 Act, with, in recent times, a substantial increase in the number of useful and interesting decisions which are now accessible, though not to be found in regular series of Law Reports. The most striking of the decisions on the 1971 Act is that of the House of Lords in 2003 in *Mirvahedy v Henley*, which, although it settled conflicts as to how the provisions of the Act on liability for animals of a non-dangerous species are to be interpreted, has in its wake spawned a movement for legislative amendment of the 1971 Act. Account has also had to be taken of varied developments in other areas of the law of torts that impinge on civil liability for harm done by animals. It is also the case that the reforms of this area of the law which culminated in the 1971 Act have been followed in a range of other common law jurisdictions, often in rather differing ways; and these throw light on the state of the law in this country. I have, where appropriate, referred to decisions in these other jurisdictions, and indeed, to English common law decisions preceding the passage of the 1971 Act, where these may be thought helpful in illustrating the operation of the provisions of the Act.

I should express my gratitude to Professor Martin Matthews and to a number of officials in the Department for Environment, Food and Rural Affairs for their assistance in investigating proposals for reform of the 1971 Act. I am grateful to Oxford University Press for agreeing to publish this 'second edition', and particularly for the support that I have received from Vicky Pittman, Jessica Huntley, and their colleagues at the Press for taking this project through its various stages so efficiently. As ever, I am most grateful for the support of my wife in bearing with such fortitude the intrusions of this project on a so-called life of retirement.

Peter North
Oxford
June 2011

CONTENTS

TABLE OF CASES

TABLE OF LEGISLATION

TABLE OF SECONDARY LEGISLATION

1

INTRODUCTION

1. The Common Law

'The law of torts has grown up historically in separate compartments and . . . beasts have travelled in a compartment of their own.'[1]

While you might find a few animals in the other compartments of the torts train, it is undoubtedly true that since mediaeval times specialized rules of liability have been developed to deal with the question of harm done by animals.[2] Not only was liability imposed for such harm under the general application of the torts of nuisance, negligence, trespass, and the like, but two common law actions, the *scienter* action and cattle trespass, and one statutory head of liability, under the Dogs Acts 1906–1928, existed to provide redress for a person who, or whose property, was injured by assorted animals. **1.01**

The general common law position was described as: **1.02**

> a pot-pourri of specialised rules of mediaeval origin. These special rules, for the most part, are such as to give rights of action which are additional to the rights of action which, in modern times, lie in respect of damage generally (that is, whether or not the damage was caused by an animal). A person who has suffered damage caused by an animal can frame his action for redress on modern principles—for example, in negligence; or he can frame it under the special rules which are peculiar to liability for

[1] *Read v J Lyons & Co Ltd* [1947] AC 156, 182.

[2] For a discussion of these rules, see G Williams, *Liability for Animals* (1939), *passim* (hereafter referred to as Williams); Delany (1953) 10 NILQ 135; Davis (1964) 1 NZULR 206.

damage done by animals; or he can, by including separate causes of action in the one proceeding, get the better of both worlds—modern and mediaeval.[3]

2. The Movement for Reform

1.03 By the middle of the twentieth century, dissatisfaction with these mediaeval rules, or aspects of them, as well as with the decision[4] not to apply the law of negligence in cases of harm caused by animals straying onto the highway became evident. There were two general complaints made of the law; they were that it was uncertain and obscure, and that the development of fine distinctions had led to 'excessive complexity and sometimes quite unreasonable results'.[5] A special committee was established in 1951, under the chairmanship of Lord Goddard CJ, which reported in 1953 on the Law of Civil Liability for Damage done by Animals;[6] the Law Reform Committee for Scotland reported on the same topic in 1963;[7] and the Law Commission reported in 1967 on Civil Liability for Animals,[8] their report[9] containing draft legislation which has been substantially implemented in the Animals Act 1971.[10] There had also been varied attempts to introduce Private Member's Bills to amend the law of negligence relating to animals straying onto the highway.[11]

3. The Four Problem Areas

1.04 One might ask what was so wrong with the common law that it provoked so much reforming activity in the course of 20 years. It is proposed to examine briefly the different areas of liability for harm done by animals and to consider the various recommendations for their improvement which were made.

(1) Liability for dangerous animals: the *scienter* action

1.05 The keeper of an animal was liable without proof of fault if the animal caused any injury to person or property provided the animal either belonged to the class of wild animals, animals *ferae naturae*, or, if it was a tame animal, *mansuetae naturae*,

[3] Report of the New South Wales Law Reform Commission on Civil Liability for Animals (1970) LRC 8, para 5.

[4] *Searle v Wallbank* [1947] AC 341.

[5] 795 HC Deb (1970) c 510.

[6] Cmnd 8746 (1953). Lord Goddard had, in fact, recommended the establishment of such a committee a decade earlier: *Hughes v Williams* [1943] KB 574, 580.

[7] Twelfth Report of the Law Reform Committee for Scotland, Cmnd 2185 (1963).

[8] Law Com No 13; see Roberts (1968) 31 MLR 683.

[9] The movement for reform in other jurisdictions is considered below, paras 1.24–1.27.

[10] The Act came into force on 1 October 1971; see Animals Act 1971, s 13(3). The Act applies to England and Wales, but not to Scotland or Northern Ireland: s 13(4).

[11] North (1966) Conv (NS) 44.

provided it had a vicious propensity known to the keeper. Another way of expressing this would be to say that the keeper was only liable where he knew of his animal's vicious propensity, but that such knowledge was irrebuttably presumed in the case of wild animals.

Among the problems with the developed *scienter* action were the difficulty and inflexibility of deciding whether an animal belonged to a species *ferae naturae*, the fact that that decision was made with regard to the species and not to the particular animal, and that danger to mankind was the sole criterion of 'wildness', without any reference to danger to property. When one turns to liability for harm done by animals *mansuetae naturae*, the common law suffered from a further variety of complexities and uncertainties. The defendant had to have knowledge of his animal's vicious propensity; it was not enough that he had the means of knowing this or that he ought to have known this. It was debatable whether there was liability for damage inflicted other than by an 'attack', or for injuries caused by a natural propensity of the animal. It was unclear whether the animal had to have escaped from his keeper's control, whether there was strict liability as between employer and employee, and what was the scope of the defences to the action, particularly whether act of a third party was a defence. **1.06**

Given all these varied defects, reform appeared inevitable, but it posed a fundamental choice. **1.07**

> Reform may take one of two general courses. It may modify or replace these special rules which are collateral to the general body of the law; or it may take the bolder course of sweeping aside these special rules, thereby leading to the result that liability for damage done by animals will be determined exclusively by the same principles which pertain in respect of damage otherwise caused.[12]

The majority of the bodies which reported on liability under the *scienter* action preferred the bolder, more fundamental, course. The Goddard Committee recommended that the *scienter* action should be abolished and: **1.08**

> that (subject to the law of cattle trespass . . .) liability for the acts of every class of animal should be based upon negligence. This need not result in any practical diminution of an owner's responsibility for a dangerous animal because the degree of care which must be exercised in the keeping of an animal will depend upon its nature and will obviously be far higher in the case of a tiger than of a dog.[13]

The one qualification of this general liability was the further recommendation relating to burden of proof that:

> it should be for the defendant to show that he acted without negligence and not for the plaintiff to adduce affirmative proof that negligence existed.[14]

[12] Report of the New South Wales Law Reform Commission on Civil Liability for Animals (1970) LRC 8, para 6.

[13] Report of the Goddard Committee (1953) para 2.

[14] Ibid, para 6.

The basic recommendation of the Law Reform Committee for Scotland was similar, though with no suggestion for the reversal of the burden of proof.

> We recommend that liability for injury caused by animals should . . . depend on whether there has been a failure to exercise reasonable care to prevent the animal causing the injury. We believe that this simple principle could be effectively applied in all cases and that it is flexible enough to allow the court to have regard to all the circumstances of a particular case.[15]

1.09 However, the Law Commission took a different view, proposing the formal abolition of the *scienter* action and its replacement by a similar statutory liability for dangerous animals; and this has been implemented in the Animals Act 1971.[16] They agreed that the common law as to *scienter* was antiquated and complex, but considered that that was an argument 'for its simplification rather than for the abandonment of its underlying principle'.[17] This presupposes that there was some fundamental principle contained therein which would be abandoned with the abandonment of strict liability. The one such principle given was that:

> With regard to animals we see a great deal of common sense in the broad distinction which the law makes between dangerous and non-dangerous animals. It does not seem unreasonable that the keeper of a dangerous animal should bear the special risk which is created by keeping it; moreover, it is a risk against which he can more conveniently insure than can the potential victim.[18]

1.10 While many would accept the force of the latter part of this reasoning, it does not necessarily indicate that liability should be strict. The whole point of the recommendations of the Goddard Committee[19] was that the standard of care expected of the keeper varied according to the type of animal. If it is wild and dangerous a far higher degree of care would be expected than if it is tame and docile. A flexible test based on negligence would enable liability to depend on less rigid and illogical factors than the legal distinctions between different classes of animal.

1.11 Having accepted, however, that the common law of *scienter* should be simplified rather than abandoned, the Law Commission made recommendations for such simplification. These took the form of the abolition of the common law action and its replacement with a new, but very similar, statutory action of strict liability based on a classification of animals into dangerous and non-dangerous categories, with liability in the latter depending on the keeper's knowledge of the animal's abnormal characteristics. Their specific recommendations were that:

> (i) Strict liability at common law for animals *ferae naturae* and for animals with known fierce propensities should be abolished.

[15] Twelfth Report of the Law Reform Committee for Scotland Cmnd 2185 (1963), para 11. Similar measures were proposed in Australia and New Zealand; see below, para 1.27.

[16] See ch 2.

[17] Law Commission Report, para 14.

[18] Ibid.

[19] Report of the Goddard Committee (1953), para 6.

(ii) Strict liability should be imposed in respect of any injury or damage done by animals belonging to a species which presents a special danger to persons or property. A species presents a special danger when animals belonging to it are likely to cause damage or any damage which they may cause is likely to be severe.

(iii) The question whether an animal belongs to such a species should depend as at present on a test prescribed by law; in determining this question a court should regard as the decisive consideration the risk to persons or property in the circumstances of this country. A species of animals which is generally domesticated in the British Isles should not be regarded in law as dangerous, but with regard to other species their domesticated or non-domesticated character abroad should be taken into account only to the extent that this factor may be relevant to the degree of risk which such species present in the circumstances of this country.

(iv) Strict liability should also be imposed in respect of injury or damage of any kind done by an animal which does not belong to a dangerous species, if the particular animal had dangerous characteristics known[20] to its keeper[21] which made it likely that injury or damage of that kind would occur or that any injury or damage of that kind which might occur would be severe. Such characteristics should be capable of giving rise to strict liability even if they are shared by other animals within the species, whether at a particular age, at certain times of the year or in certain conditions.

(v) Strict liability in respect of either of the two above categories should not depend on escape from control.

(vi) The fact that the plaintiff by reason of his negligence was solely responsible for the injury or damage, his voluntary assumption of the risk, and, to the extent that it contributed to the injury or damage, contributory negligence should be defences. But liability should not be restricted between employer and employee on the ground of voluntary assumption of risk. It should also be a defence that the plaintiff was at the time of the injury or damage a trespasser on the property where the animal was kept and, where the animal does not belong to a dangerous species, it was not kept there to cause damage to trespassers and, where the animal belongs to a dangerous species, it was not kept there to deter or cause damage to trespassers.[22]

[20] As to the requirement of knowledge, the Law Commission recommended, Report, para 97, that: 'Knowledge of dangerous characteristics of an animal should be imputed to a person in the following cases: (i) Where a servant of his who has charge of the animal knows of its dangerous characteristics. (ii) Where a member of his household under the age of sixteen who is a keeper of the animal knows of its dangerous characteristics.' See now Animals Act 1971, s 2(2)(c).

[21] The Law Commission Report, para 96, recommended that strict liability for injury or damage caused by an animal should be imposed on 'in the case of an action brought to enforce strict liability for animals of a dangerous species or with known dangerous characteristics, as well as for injury by dogs to livestock, the "keeper"—i.e. the owner or possessor of the animal—and a person a member of whose household under the age of sixteen is a keeper. If at any time the animal ceases to have a keeper a person who immediately before that time was a keeper should continue to bear responsibility for the animal until some other person becomes the keeper. But a person who takes in an animal to prevent it causing damage or to restore it to its owner should not be regarded as a keeper for this purpose.' See now Animals Act 1971, s 6(3).

[22] Law Commission Report, para 91.

1.12 In substance, all of these recommendations were implemented by the Animals Act 1971.[23] Whether this implementation may be said to remedy all the defects of the old law depends on whether one accepts that they can be remedied within the framework of specialized rules of strict liability. Undoubtedly, many anomalies have gone, but fine distinctions remain, especially in relation to liabilities for dangerous animals.[24]

(2) Straying animals: cattle trespass

1.13 The second special area, at common law, was the tort of cattle trespass. The owner of animals which fell within the legal definition of 'cattle', which encompassed most domestic animals but excluded cats and dogs, was strictly liable if his animals trespassed on another's land. He was liable whether they injured the land, the occupier's chattels, or the occupier himself.

1.14 There were two basic areas of discontent with this tort of cattle trespass. First, its detailed rules produced anomalies and, second, the incidence of strict liability for trespassing cattle required justification at a time when other forms of trespass were coming to be based on proof of fault,[25] especially in the light of the more recent extension of cattle trespass to include liability for personal injuries inflicted on the occupier of the land trespassed upon.[26] It was anomalous that, if cattle trespassed onto a man's land and injured both him and his employee, the former but not the latter could claim in cattle trespass, for only the former had sufficient interest in the land to maintain trespass to land, of which cattle trespass was a specialized derivative. An allied anomaly was that there was a right to detain trespassing cattle under the law of distress damage feasant, but the detainer had no real power of sale or disposal of the cattle. There was also uncertainty as to the meaning of 'cattle' and as to the scope of the defences to cattle trespass.

1.15 The most fundamental issue was whether strict liability for cattle trespass in any form could be justified. The Law Commission[27] took the view that there was no case for substantial change, on the basis that 'those bodies in touch with the farming community wish to retain strict liability for cattle trespass'.[28] Nevertheless, the anomalies and uncertainties had to be dealt with, and so the Law Commission recommended that cattle trespass, as such, should be abolished, to be replaced by a new form of statutory strict liability to provide a clear rule of liability which would

---

23 Animals Act 1971, ss 1, 2, 5, 6, 10.

24 See ch 2.

25 *Fowler v Lanning* [1959] 1 QB 426.

26 *Wormald v Cole* [1954] 1 QB 614.

27 Following the approach of the Report of the Goddard Committee (1953), para 25.

28 Law Commission Report, para 62. This might be compared with the view of the New South Wales Law Reform Commission, who thought that the anomalies of cattle trespass destroyed any case for its survival: Report on Civil Liability for Animals (1970) LRC 8, para 25.

enable disputes to be settled between neighbours without recourse to litigation. Their recommendations were that:

(i) The present rules of strict liability for cattle trespass should be abolished, and a new form of strict liability for straying livestock should be provided.

(ii) The straying of livestock should only be actionable upon proof of actual damage; this should cover reasonable expenses incurred in detaining the livestock where there is a right to do so or in finding the person to whom it belongs, but should otherwise be limited to damage to land and chattels.

(iii) Normally the occupier of the land strayed upon should be the only person to rely upon this strict rule of liability.[29] However, an owner of land out of possession whose interest in the land or in chattels thereon is damaged should also be able to do so.

(iv) The following should be defences to a claim under this rule of strict liability:

(a) The fact that the plaintiff by reason of his negligence was wholly responsible for the damage and, to the extent that it contributed to the damage, the partial defence of his contributory negligence. But neither of these defences should be available by reason only that the plaintiff could have prevented the straying by fencing, unless the straying would not have occurred but for the breach of a duty to fence by a person other than the defendant having an interest in the land upon which the livestock strayed.

(b) The fact that the livestock had strayed from a highway where it lawfully was.[30]

Recommendations to replace the law of distress damage feasant were also made, as follows:

(i) The right of distress damage feasant in respect of animals should be abolished. In its place there should be provided a new remedy whereby a person finding livestock which has strayed on to land in his occupation may detain it as security against payment of compensation for the damage which he has suffered and certain reasonable expenses.

(ii) The new remedy should be on the lines suggested by the Goddard Committee,[31] but should be elaborated, modified and extended in certain respects, in particular to give a power of sale to the detainer to cover not only the cost of detaining the animal, but also the damage which it has caused.[32]

These various recommendations were carried into effect by the Animals Act 1971, **1.16** both as to cattle trespass[33] and as to distress damage feasant.[34] Undoubtedly the statutory rules are better than the old common law, although areas, particularly in relation to the defences, are of a complexity such that they can hardly provide for

[29] The person to be held liable is the possessor of the livestock: Law Commission Report, para 96(ii).

[30] Law Commission Report, para 93.

[31] Report of the Goddard Committee (1953), para 9.

[32] Law Commission Report, para 94.

[33] Animals Act 1971, ss 1, 4, 5, 10.

[34] Ibid, s 7.

the settlement of disputes between farmers without the intervention of legal advisers. One general critical comment is that the reforms appear to have been designed on the advice of the farming community and with them in contemplation, even though, as decisions have shown,[35] a farmer's domestic animals may stray into gardens as well as into adjoining fields. This is seen especially in the context of the right to detain such animals. It is quite unrealistic to expect an ordinary householder to detain an errant sheep or cow for 14 days before selling it,[36] although a farmer well might and could.

(3) Special rules relating to dogs

1.17 Legislation was introduced in the nineteenth century to make special provision for liability for injuries done by dogs. This culminated in the Dogs Acts 1906–1928. Under these Acts, the owner of a dog was held strictly liable for any injury done by his dog to cattle or poultry, these being defined to include most domesticated animals. By and large, this legislation appeared to work quite well, but the Goddard Committee recommended[37] that liability should be extended to the keeper of the dog as well as the owner, and that new provision should be made for the imposition of liability on a person in whose household a dog is kept. The Dogs Acts 1906–1928 had unduly complex provisions on this matter. These recommendations were accepted by the Law Commission,[38] who also chose to propose the resolution of a number of doubts as to the scope and existence of the various defences to liability under the Dogs Acts 1906–1928. Again, their recommendations took the form of the abolition of the old remedy to be replaced by a new, but similar, statutory remedy. They recommended that:

> The strict liability at present imposed by the Dogs Acts 1906 to 1928 for injury by dogs to cattle or poultry should be retained but the principles of the liability should be restated in new legislative provisions. The fact that the plaintiff was by reason of his negligence the sole cause of the injury and, to the extent that it contributed to the injury, his contributory negligence, should be defences to an action brought under this form of strict liability. It should also be a defence that the livestock were straying on the land where they were attacked by the dog and the dog belonged to the occupier of the land or its presence there was authorised by him.[39]

1.18 While these wholly desirable recommendations found legislative effect in the Animals Act 1971,[40] the form in which they were drafted contains the seeds

---

[35] See below, para 3.47.
[36] Animals Act 1971, s 7(4), below, paras 3.52, 3.60.
[37] Report of the Goddard Committee (1953), para 6.
[38] And by the Law Reform Committee for Scotland: Twelfth Report Cmnd 2185 (1963), para 15.
[39] Law Commission Report, para 95. Liability should be imposed on a newly defined 'keeper' of the dog: see Law Commission Report, para 96, quoted above, para 1.11.
[40] Animals Act 1971, ss 1, 3, 5, 6, 10, 13.

of difficulties other than those which they were intended to cure. For example, instead of discussing the liability of the keeper of a dog which kills or injures livestock, liability is imposed for causing 'damage by killing or injuring livestock',[41] which raises, for example, the question of whether there is strict liability for damage other than the death of or injury to the livestock.[42]

It might be asked why special legislation is justified in the case of injuries by dogs. **1.19**
Although dogs have such physical attributes as enable them to inflict serious injuries on persons and property and have a natural tendency to chase and worry other animals, there are other animals which have a potential for causing even greater damage. Why should dogs be singled out for the imposition of strict liability on their keepers? The answer would appear to be that:

> what places dogs in a special position is that despite their canine characteristics and the rapidly increasing urbanisation of our society it is still popularly accepted that, broadly speaking, dogs are privileged to roam and that, in ordinary circumstances, the owner of a dog does not act unreasonably towards others in permitting it to do so. No like privilege is conceded to any other animal which is as likely as is a dog to inflict serious injury.[43] The position of dogs is special; and this warrants the imposition of special liability in respect of them.[44]

Cogent though this argument is, it either proves too much or points to a defect in the English law as to strict liability for dogs. The two characteristics of dogs which, combined with their special place in society, justify the imposition of special rules of liability are their characteristic of attacking, worrying, and chasing other animals and their characteristic of occasionally attacking people, with the ability to inflict severe injury. This latter would support the imposition of strict liability for personal injuries which was lacking in the Dogs Acts 1906–1928 and is similarly lacking in the Animals Act 1971, for liability there is based on the killing or injuring of livestock. It is as true of the Animals Act as it was of the Dogs Acts that: 'Parliament thought that sheep require more protection than human beings.'[45]

Allied to the question of liability for harm done by dogs is that of the measures **1.20**
which an occupier of land may take against dogs roaming on his land where his animals are put in jeopardy by their presence, and, especially, the circumstances in which such dogs may be shot. There is no doubt that a serious social problem is involved here, with thousands of sheep, cattle, and poultry being attacked by dogs each year. The common law position[46] was that a dog could be shot if it was actually attacking farm animals or was likely to renew an attack so that the animals were in

[41] Ibid, s 3.
[42] Discussed below, paras 7.04–7.08.
[43] A similar, if not wider, privilege is afforded to cats; but they have far less potential for causing substantial injury or damage.
[44] Report of the New South Wales Reform Commission (1970) LRC 8, para 35.
[45] *Hughes v Williams* [1943] KB 574, 580.
[46] *Cresswell v Sirl* [1948] 1 KB 241.

real and imminent danger. Shooting had to be the only practicable means open to the farmer to protect his animals or it must have been reasonable to regard it as such. It was generally considered that the right to shoot trespassing dogs was unduly restricted by these rules, for they were inapplicable to the case of the dog making off after an attack nor did they apply to the dog which was about to attack for the first time.

1.21 While the Law Commission accepted that three factors had to be balanced, namely the interests of owners of livestock, the interests of dog owners, and the inherent dangers in the use of firearms, they did conclude that some extension of the law was called for.[47] Accordingly, they recommended that:

(i) With regard to measures taken in protection of livestock against dogs, the defence to a civil action arising out of injury to a dog which was recognized in *Cresswell v Sirl* should be extended to cover reasonable belief in the existence or imminence of an attack on livestock by a dog.

(ii) It should also be a defence to such an action, subject to certain specific safeguards, that the defendant injured the dog after it had, or he reasonably thought that it had, worried livestock. Among the safeguards in particular should be the requirements that the dog was not in the control of any person, and that there were no practicable means, or the defendant reasonably believed that there were no practicable means, of ascertaining to whom the dog belonged.[48]

Detailed implementation of these recommendations was provided by section 9 of the Animals Act 1971.[49]

(4) Negligence

1.22 A line of cases culminating in the decision of the House of Lords in *Searle v Wallbank*[50] decided that an occupier of land adjoining a highway owed no duty of care to prevent his animals escaping onto the highway. He could be as negligent as he liked, for he would incur no liability to users of the highway for injuries caused to them by such straying animals. This rule was subjected to continual and stringent criticism, primarily on the basis that it 'appears to be ill-adapted to modern conditions'.[51] Both the Goddard Committee[52] and the Law Commission[53] took the view that the case for change was overwhelming[54] and that the rule in *Searle v*

---

47 Similar views had been put forward in the Report of the Goddard Committee, para 7 and in the Twelfth Report of the Law Reform Committee for Scotland Cmnd 2185 (1963), para 16.

48 Law Commission Report, para 98.

49 Discussed below, paras 7.34–7.45.

50 [1947] AC 341.

51 *Hughes v Williams* [1943] KB 574, 576; *Gomberg v Smith* [1963] 1 QB 25, 31, 40; *Ellis v Johnstone* [1963] 2 QB 8, 27.

52 Report of the Goddard Committee (1953), para 5.

53 Law Commission Report, para 40.

54 The Law Reform Committee for Scotland had taken a similar view in its Twelfth Report Cmnd 2185 (1963), para 8, but judicial activity in Scotland later rendered legislative action unnecessary: *Gardiner v Miller* 1967 SLT 29.

Wallbank should be abolished. The Law Commission's general recommendations on liability in negligence were:

(i) The general principles of the present law of negligence whereby the keeper of an animal is under a duty to prevent that animal causing injury or damage should not be disturbed.

(ii) The exception to this principle recognized by the House of Lords in *Searle v Wallbank* should be abolished, but in deciding whether the keeper of an animal has exercised reasonable care to prevent the animal causing damage by escaping on to the highway, regard should be had to a number of special considerations.

(iii) Notwithstanding (ii) above a person should not be regarded as committing a breach of the duty to take care by reason only of placing animals on any common land (within the meaning of the Commons Registration Act 1965) in any case where it is lawful for him to do so.[55]

Despite the history of criticism of the rule in *Searle v Wallbank*, these recommendations for its abolition proved to be the most controversial aspect of the Law Commission's Report, and of the Animals Act 1971 subsequent upon it, when the relevant section of the Act, section 8, was debated in Parliament. Two interests were ranged in opposition to each other—the farming interest, and that of the general public as users of the highway. The farming lobby was powerful and succeeded in having removed from the legislation the various special considerations referred to in the Law Commission's Report,[56] which had also been included in section 8 as originally drafted. However, these considerations[57] were intended merely as guidelines for a court faced with the issue of deciding whether a farmer had been negligent, and their removal from the Act does not appear to have had any direct effect on liability. They are factors which will be relevant to a determination of liability whether specifically mentioned or not.[58] **1.23**

4. Reform Elsewhere

The passage of the Animals Act 1971 was followed by a variety of reforming measures elsewhere in the common law world. In a number of instances, as in England, the legislation followed reports of law reform bodies; although the legislation has not always followed the proposals made by such bodies. The reform which followed **1.24**

[55] Law Commission Report, para 92.

[56] Ibid, para 92(ii).

[57] They were: '(a) the nature of the land and its situation in relation to the highway; (b) the use likely to be made of the highway at the time the damage was caused; (c) the obstacles, if any, to be overcome by animals in straying from the land on to the highway; (d) the extent to which users of the highway might be expected to be aware of and guard against the risks involved in the presence of animals on the highway; (e) the seriousness of any such risk and the steps that would have been necessary to avoid or reduce it.' Law Commission Draft Animals Bill, cl 8(2).

[58] See below, paras 5.09–5.17.

the 1971 Act most closely is that in Northern Ireland, namely the Animals (Northern Ireland) Order 1976.[59] Reference is made, in appropriate places, to decisions of the Northern Ireland courts relating to the Order.

1.25 In Scotland, although the common law and existing statutory position was noticeably different from that in England, there was strict liability for harm done by dangerous animals and by domestic animals, if the keeper had knowledge of the animal's propensity to cause harm, as well as statutory liability for harm done by 'straying beasts'[60] and by dogs.[61] Anxiety over the state of the law led to it being examined, first, by the Law Reform Committee for Scotland in 1963[62] and then, in 1985, by the Scottish Law Commission.[63] In their report, the Commission recommended replacement of the common law rules and the Winter Herding Act 1686 with a new rule of strict liability for special risks likely to cause serious injury to persons or animals, or material damage to property, with no need for the defender to know of the animal's dangerous characteristics. The Commission's draft Bill was carried into effect by the Animals (Scotland) Act 1987.[64] There have been few reported decisions on the 1987 Act. While a dog is presumed to fall into the category of animal likely to cause serious injury to person or property by 'attacking or harrying',[65] it has been held that that presumption does not extend to the causing of accidental damage by knocking into the pursuer;[66] although harrying can be of another dog where that leads to injury to the pursuer.[67]

1.26 In 1977, the Irish Law Reform Commission produced a substantial Working Paper on Civil Liability for Animals,[68] followed by a brief report in 1982.[69] These contained wide-ranging proposals for reform which followed the general pattern in England of providing statutory replacement of the common law rules on cattle trespass and the *scienter* action, coupled with abolition of the rule in *Searle v Wallbank*.[70] In the event, only this last proposal was given effect to in the Animals Act 1985.[71]

1.27 Rather greater reform was achieved in New Zealand. Proposals were made in 1975[72] for the replacement of the *scienter* action by the general law of negligence, the basic

[59] SI 1976/1040.

[60] Under the Winter Herding Act 1686.

[61] Under the Dogs Act 1906.

[62] Twelfth Annual Report Cmnd 2185 (1963).

[63] Scot Law Com No 97 (1985).

[64] See Carey Miller 1987 SLT (Notes) 229.

[65] See s 1(3)(a). The fact that cattle are deemed, by s 1(3)(b), to be likely to damage property does not carry any inference that they are likely to injure people: *Foskett v McClymont* 1998 SLT 892.

[66] *Fairlie v Carruthers* 1996 SLT (Sh Ct) 56; *Welsh v Brady* [2009] CSIH 60; 2009 SLT 747.

[67] *Flynn v Lothian and Borders Police* (2010) Unreported, 2 August.

[68] LRC Working Paper No 3 (1977).

[69] Report on Civil Liability for Animals: LC 2 (1982).

[70] [1947] AC 341.

[71] See s 2.

[72] Report of the Torts and General Law Reform Committee: The Law Relating to Liability for Animals (1975).

abolition of the rule in *Searle v Wallbank*, and the statutory reformulation of the tort of cattle trespass. In the event, the first two recommendations, but not the third, were substantially implemented by the Animals Law Reform Act 1989. In Australia, the most significant reforms have been in New South Wales,[73] South Australia,[74] and the Australian Capital Territory,[75] the first two following reports of law reform bodies.[76] In all three jurisdictions, the *scienter* action was replaced by the application of the general law of negligence, the action of cattle trespass was abandoned and dealt with under the general law of trespass, and the rule in *Searle v Wallbank* was abrogated.[77] In addition, in New South Wales, the rule in *Rylands v Fletcher* was disapplied to claims for damage done by animals.[78] There is a mixed picture of reform in Canada, with varied provincial legislation dealing with straying animals, as well as provisions which either alter the scope of,[79] or replace,[80] the *scienter* action.[81]

5. The Animals Act 1971

Looking back over 40 years, it is reasonable to ask how successful the Animals Act 1971, based as it is on a report from the Law Commission, has been in providing satisfactory solutions to the problems posed by harm done by animals. It is clear that neither the Report nor the Act when just passed had wholly favourable receptions. Of the report it was asked: 'Why is it that the Commission has concentrated its attention upon the details and preserved a general framework which has so little to commend it?'[82] The Animals Act 1971 has been described as 'a kind of mongrel **1.28**

[73] Animals Act 1977.

[74] Wrongs Act 1936, s 17(a), inserted by the Wrongs Act (Amendment) Act (No 2) 1983, s 10.

[75] Civil Law (Wrongs) Act 2002, ss 138–40, which consolidated the Civil Liability (Animals) Act 1984.

[76] Seventh Report of the Law Reform Committee of South Australia: Law Relating to Animals (1969); and the New South Wales Law Reform Commission Report on Civil Liability for Animals, LRC 8 (1970). Proposals for reform were also made in 1977 by the Queensland Law Reform Commission in a Working Paper which advocated reforms along the lines of the Animals Act 1971, but these suggestions have not been acted on.

[77] The rule in *Searle v Wallbank* has now been abandoned in all Australian jurisdictions except Queensland and the Northern Territory; see *Smith v Williams* [2006] Aus Torts Rep 81-863; F Trindade, P Cane, and M Lunney, *The Law of Torts in Australia*, 4th edn (2007), p 660.

[78] Animals Act 1977, s 9; although the High Court of Australia has since determined that the rule in *Rylands v Fletcher* no longer forms part of the law of Australia: *Burnie Port Authority v General Jones Pty Ltd* (1994) 179 CLR 520; and see below, para 6.10.

[79] eg in Ontario disapplying it to harm done by dogs: Dog Owners' Liability Act 1980, s 2(3).

[80] As in Manitoba, where the Animal Liability and Consequential Amendments Act 1998 abolished the *scienter* action but replaced it with statutory strict liability for damage to person or property; see ss 2, 4.

[81] See G Fridman, *The Law of Torts in Canada,* 4th edn (2002), pp 252–3, 265–7.

[82] Roberts (1968) 31 MLR 683, 684.

Bill';[83] as an Act parts of which 'bristle with practical difficulties';[84] and as one some of whose basic concepts are 'divorced from reality'.[85]

1.29 Undoubtedly, there were wholly desirable aspects to the report and the 1971 Act. The demise of *Searle v Wallbank*[86] was a beneficial measure,[87] which has caused no difficulty in practice. Equally useful and uncontroversial has been the recasting of the special rules relating to harm done by dogs.[88] The main criticism of the Act at the time was that it was fundamentally misconceived and, as a result, could not achieve its major objectives, namely to provide 'a new and clearer statement in statutory form of the law'[89] relating to animals, with the objective of removing anomalies and uncertainties and providing rules more suited to modern than mediaeval conditions. Many of the uncertainties and anomalies stemmed from the basic distinctions of the old law. Once the crucial decision was taken not to adopt the radical solution of abandoning the old categorization in favour of the flexible concept of negligence, but to retain different specialized categories of liability, the problems created by such categorization remain. Although the specialized categories of dangerous and non-dangerous animals are different from those under the *scienter* action, rigid distinctions still have to be drawn. Such distinctions have led to new uncertainties and new difficulties of interpretation. While it may often be inappropriate to refer to 'the old common law' for the purposes of interpreting the 1971 Act,[90] the Act has undoubtedly created new problems of interpretation to be addressed, not least in relation to the provisions relating to liability for dangerous animals,[91] where the criticisms of the legislation[92] have ranged from 'inept'[93] to 'obscure'.[94]

1.30 All in all, the Animals Act 1971 has done little to rid the law of complexity, as was vividly illustrated at the time of its passage.

> It is hardly a logical pattern to find liability as follows in these situations: (1) a cow escapes from farm A to farm B—strict liability; (2) a cow escapes from farm A onto the highway—negligence; (3) a cow escapes from common land onto the highway—no liability; (4) a cow escapes from the highway onto farm B—negligence.[95]

---

[83] 815 HC Deb (1971) c 612.
[84] Powell-Smith (1971) 121 NLJ 584.
[85] Samuels (1971) 34 MLR 550.
[86] [1947] AC 341.
[87] See s 8.
[88] See ss 3 and 9; and see ch 7.
[89] 795 HC Deb (1970) c 512.
[90] *Matthews v Wicks* (1987) CA, Unreported, 22 May; and see *Davies v Davies* [1975] QB 172, 179.
[91] s 2; see ch 2.
[92] See below, para 2.63.
[93] *Curtis v Betts* [1990] 1 WLR 459, 468.
[94] *Mirvahedy v Henley* [2003] UKHL 16, para 9; [2003] 2 AC 491.
[95] Samuels (1971) 34 MLR 550.

With the wisdom of hindsight, the approach adopted in New Zealand[96] and, especially, in New South Wales[97] of subsuming much of the specialized law on civil liability for harm done by animals into the law of negligence would have been a simpler, clearer approach and one which does not appear to have led to any difficulties or concerns in either jurisdiction.

[96] Animals Law Reform Act 1989; see above, para 1.27.
[97] Animals Act 1977; see above, para 1.27.

2

STRICT LIABILITY FOR DANGEROUS ANIMALS

1. Introduction

At common law, under the *scienter* action,[1] the keeper of an animal with a propensity to do harm was held strictly liable for any such injury caused. Such mischievous animals fell into two legal categories: animals *ferae naturae* and animals *mansuetae naturae*. It had long been established that the liability of the keeper varied according to such categorization and according to his knowledge of the animal's viciousness.[2] When the Law Commission came to examine this head of liability they approved the broad general distinction between liability for dangerous and non-dangerous 2.01

[1] On the development of this common law action, see G Williams, *Liability for Animals* (1939) (hereafter referred to as Williams), chs 15–21; Delany (1953) 10 NILQ 135, 135–7; Davis (1964) 1 NZULR 206, 222–3.

[2] 1 Hale PC 430–31; *R v Huggins* (1730) 2 Ld Raym 1574, 1583.

animals, especially as the keeper of a dangerous animal can more conveniently insure against the risk of its causing injury than can the claimant.[3] They concluded that such rules of strict liability should be amended and simplified, rather than abandoned.[4] This could best be done by abolishing the common law rules of the *scienter* action and replacing them by reformulated rules relating to strict liability for dangerous animals. This was done by the Animals Act 1971.[5]

2.02 Section 1 abolished the *scienter* action. It is provided by section 1(1)(a) that the provisions of the 1971 Act replace the rules of the common law imposing a strict liability in tort for damage done by an animal on the ground that the animal is regarded as *ferae naturae* or that its vicious or mischievous propensities are known or presumed to be known.

The replacement for the *scienter* action is to be found in section 2, as follows:

> (1) Where any damage is caused by an animal which belongs to a dangerous species, any person who is a keeper of the animal is liable for the damage, except as otherwise provided by this Act.
> (2) Where damage is caused by an animal which does not belong to a dangerous species, a keeper of the animal is liable for the damage, except as otherwise provided by this Act, if—
> (a) the damage is of a kind which the animal, unless restrained, was likely to cause or which, if caused by the animal, was likely to be severe; and
> (b) the likelihood of the damage or of its being severe was due to characteristics of the animal which are not normally found in animals of the same species or are not normally so found except at particular times or in particular circumstances; and
> (c) those characteristics were known to that keeper or were at any time known to a person who at that time had charge of the animal as that keeper's servant or, where that keeper is the head of a household, were known to another keeper of the animal who is a member of that household and under the age of sixteen.[6]

2.03 It will be obvious that the effect of section 2 is to define the liability of the keeper of a dangerous animal differently according to whether or not the animal belongs to a dangerous species. This means that any discussion of liability under section 2 must

---

[3] Law Commission Report, para 14.

[4] Ibid, para 18. Cf the Report of the Goddard Committee (1953), para 6, which recommended the abolition of the *scienter* action and the absorption of liability for dangerous animals into the law of negligence. In other jurisdictions, the *scienter* action has been abolished and simply replaced by liability at common law in negligence or nuisance; see, eg, the Animals Act 1977 (NSW), s 7; the Wrongs Act 1936 (SA), s 18, as inserted by the Wrongs Act Amendment Act (No 2) 1983 (SA), s 10; the Civil Law (Wrongs) Act 2002 (ACT), s 140; the Animals Law Reform Act 1989 (NZ), s 4; and see above, para 1.27.

[5] Almost identical provision has been made for Northern Ireland by the Animals (Northern Ireland) Order 1976, SI 1976/1040.

[6] And see the Animals (Northern Ireland) Order 1976, SI 1976/1040, Art 4.

be divided into a consideration, first, of liability for animals belonging to a dangerous species and then of the liability for other animals known to be dangerous. There are, however, various issues relating to liability under section 2 which are common to both types of cases. In discussing those issues, such as the question of what is an animal or who is the proper defendant to an action under section 2, it will not be necessary to distinguish between the two types of cases.

2. What is an Animal?

No general definition of 'animal' is provided in the Animals Act 1971, although there are definitions of 'livestock' and 'poultry' for the purposes of determining the scope of the provisions dealing with liability for injury done by dogs to livestock[7] and the right to kill or injure dogs worrying livestock,[8] and those dealing with liability for trespassing livestock[9] and the right to detain and sell such livestock.[10] It is suggested that the term 'animal' should include birds, reptiles, and insects,[11] but not bacteria and similar organisms.[12] This suggestion was approved in *Kane v McKenna*,[13] where the equivalent Northern Ireland provision[14] was applied to harm caused to a child by an attack by a bantam cockerel; although Carswell J did express some doubts as to whether 'game birds reared on the land' would be included. It is suggested that, if they have a keeper who can be identified, there is no justification for excluding them. **2.04**

3. What is a Species?

The determination of the meaning of the term 'species' arises under the 1971 Act both in determining whether an animal is a member of a 'dangerous species', under **2.05**

[7] Section 3, see below, para 7.04.

[8] Section 9, see below, paras 7.27–7.28.

[9] Section 4, see below, paras 3.04–3.06.

[10] Section 7, see below, para 3.48.

[11] Including bees: see *Stormer v Ingram* (1978) 21 SASR 93.

[12] In Scotland, there is a negative provision, in that, unless the context otherwise requires, 'animal' does not include 'viruses, bacteria, algae, fungi or protozoa': Animals (Scotland) Act 1987, s 7. In New Zealand, s 2 of the Animals Law Reform Act 1989 provides that the term 'animal' means any living member of the animal kingdom, and includes mammals, birds, fishes, and reptiles, but does not include human beings. It might be noted that no claim under the Animals Act 1971 was made in *D Pride and Partners v Institute of Animal Health* [2009] EWHC 685, which concerned various claims relating to the escape of foot and mouth disease virus from the defendants' premises which led to economic loss to the claimants because of prohibitions on the movement of livestock and the requirement to slaughter animals.

[13] (1991) 1 BNIL 105, appeal allowed on an issue of damages: (1992) 2 BNIL 125.

[14] Animals (Northern Ireland) Order 1976, SI 1976/1040, Art 4.

section 2(1),[15] and whether, if not dangerous, it has, under section 2(2)(b),[16] characteristics not normally found in animals of the same species. The only assistance in determining what constitutes a species is provided by section 11 of the Animals Act 1971, which states that '"species" includes sub-species and variety'.[17] This can be interpreted in two different ways. First, it can mean: 'Wherever the word "species" appears, the phrase "sub-species" may be substituted.' According to this interpretation one must examine the dangerousness of animals according to the sub-species to which they belong. Thus, if one sub-species of monkey is dangerous and another is not, the categorization of the particular monkey in question would depend on the sub-species to which it belonged. The other interpretation is quite the opposite: 'All sub-species and varieties of an animal have the same characterisation as dangerous or non-dangerous as is given to the species as a whole.' On this analysis, if elephants are classed, as a species, as dangerous, then no distinction can be based on the fact that a sub-species of elephant could be classed as non-dangerous.

2.06 This latter approach is certainly that which was favoured at common law, in relation to both elephants and monkeys. In *Behrens v Bertram Mills Circus Ltd*,[18] Devlin J was not prepared to distinguish between different varieties of elephants and he refused to hold that, while elephants generally are wild, Burmese elephants are not. He said that:

> Common knowledge about the ordinary course of nature will extend to a knowledge of the propensities of animals according to their different genera, but cannot be supposed to extend to the manner of behaviour of animals of the same genus in different parts of the world. Nor can one begin a process of inquiry which might lead in many directions (for example, I am told that female elephants are more docile than male, and that is why circus elephants are usually female) and be productive of minute subdivisions which would destroy the generality of the rule.[19]

Again, monkeys caused difficulties of classification in the *scienter* action. In *May v Burdett*,[20] the keeper of a monkey was held liable when it bit the claimant, but here the defendant was proved to have known of this particular monkey's vicious propensity so it did not matter how a monkey was classified. It has been argued since that 'ape or monkey'[21] does not include every species within the generic term

[15] See below, paras 2.34 et seq.

[16] See below, paras 2.61 et seq.

[17] Section 1(2) of the Animals (Scotland) Act 1987 contains a more extensive description of the term 'species', including 'a kind which is the product of hybridisation'; and the definition goes 'considerably beyond Linnaean classification': *Welsh v Brady* [2009] CSIH 60; 2009 SLT 747, 749. In particular, it allows for the sub-division of 'species' by reference, eg, to 'sex'; and it has been indicated that bulls can be regarded as a separate species from cows: *Foskett v McClymont* 1998 SC 96, 103.

[18] [1957] 2 QB 1.

[19] [1957] 2 QB 1, 16.

[20] (1846) 9 QB 101.

[21] Hale 1 PC 101.

'monkey' and that not all 'monkeys' are wild or dangerous by nature.[22] However, it does seem to have been assumed in Canada, at least, that some if not all monkeys are wild animals,[23] as also with chimpanzees in New Zealand.[24]

2.07 The problems of interpretation raised by section 11 might be illustrated further by the status of a cat. The cat is a commonly domesticated animal in the British Isles.[25] There is, however, also the case of the wild cat found in Scotland. It would seem very strange if the domesticated nature of the former should be held also to include the latter. A similar difficulty can be seen with domesticated and wild rabbits.[26] Do the former cause the latter to be classed as non-dangerous? Such problems might favour the first interpretation of the definition of 'species' given above. On the other hand, it is open to Devlin J's objection that it may lead to minute subdivisions of species and a variation of the legal rule dependent upon the categorization of the sub-species.

2.08 Although this question as to the meaning of 'species' has not yet arisen for consideration in the context of determining whether, under section 2(1) of the 1971 Act, an animal belongs to a 'dangerous species', it has arisen on a number of occasions in considering, under section 2(2)(b), whether the likelihood of damage or of its severity was due to characteristics found 'in animals of the same species'. It is quite clear that, in examining the issue of liability for harm caused by dogs, the first of the two possible interpretations considered above[27] has been adopted. In *Cummings v Granger*,[28] the Court of Appeal had to determine the liability of the keeper of an Alsatian guard dog. Ormrod LJ considered the statement, in section 11, that '"species" includes sub-species and variety', saying:

> These words have very much the ring of biological terms of art, and no doubt should be given that meaning. In other words, it would be very wrong to treat, say, a guard dog as being a variety of a species or sub-species for the purposes of the section. What we have to deal with here is a sub-species of dog or variety of dog called 'Alsatian'.[29]

2.09 This approach of considering different breeds of dog as sub-species of 'dog' has been followed on a number of occasions, not least in relation to Alsatian police dogs.[30]

---

22 *Brook v Cook* (1961) 105 Sol Jo 684; and see ibid, at pp 1094–5.

23 *Connor v The Princess Theatre* (1912) 27 OLR 466; and see *Andrew Baker's Case* cited by Hale 1 PC 430.

24 *James v Wellington City* [1972] NZLR 70, reversed on another ground [1972] NZLR 978.

25 Animals Act 1971, s 6(2)(a).

26 Rabbits may fall within s 6(2)(b) because they could be thought likely to cause severe damage to property.

27 Para 2.05.

28 [1977] QB 397.

29 Ibid, at pp 406–7; and see *Mirvahedy v Henley* [2003] UKHL 16, para 108; [2003] 2 AC 491.

30 *Gloster v Chief Constable of Greater Manchester Police* [2000] PIQR 114, 116, per Pill LJ; and see *Dhesi v Chief Constable of the West Midlands Police* [2000] Po LR 120. It is suggested that the comment by Lord Scott, in *Mirvahedy v Henley*, above, at para 126, that Pill LJ wrongly regarded 'trained police dog', rather than 'Alsation', as a sub-species is not borne out by Pill LJ's actual remarks, where he said

In the case of harm done by a Border Collie,[31] Pill J was clear that one had to compare the particular dog with the characteristic members of its breed:

> Where there is an identifiable breed of dog, a breed of long standing with acknowledged and identifiable characteristics, at least where it is a breed whose qualities are recognised as beneficial to man, the comparison should be with that breed or sub-species.[32]

Furthermore, in the case of dogs, the court has to consider the situation of an adult dog, rejecting the idea that puppies might be regarded as a sub-species.[33]

2.10 The issue remains as to whether the determination of the meaning of 'species' and 'sub-species' for the purposes of section 2(2)(b) necessarily applies to the interpretation of section 2(1). It is suggested that it should. There is no logical basis for interpreting such general terms differently as between two subsections of the same section.

4. Who is Liable?[34]

2.11 Liability under section 2 of the Animals Act 1971 is placed on the keeper of the dangerous animal in question and the issue of who is its keeper is dealt with by section 6, as follows:

> (3) Subject to subsection (4) of this section, a person is a keeper of an animal if—
>
> (a) he owns the animal or has it in his possession; or
>
> (b) he is the head of a household of which a member under the age of sixteen owns the animal or has it in his possession;
>
> and if at any time an animal ceases to be owned by or to be in the possession of a person, any person who immediately before that time was a keeper thereof by virtue of the preceding provisions of this subsection continues to be a keeper of the animal until another person becomes a keeper thereof by virtue of those provisions.
>
> (4) Where an animal is taken into and kept in possession for the purpose of preventing it from causing damage or of restoring it to its owner, a person is not a keeper of it by virtue only of that possession.[35]

---

that the ability to respond to training and instruction is a characteristic normally found in Alsatians, being 'the hallmark of the breed'.

[31] *Hunt v Wallis* [1994] PIQR 128.

[32] Ibid, at p 139; and see the similar approach in *Curtis v Betts* [1990] 1 WLR 459, 463, a case concerning a bull mastiff.

[33] *Mirvahedy v Henley*, above, para 108; although, in Scotland, bulls may be regarded as a separate species from cows: see above, para 2.05.

[34] This discussion is applicable also to the liability of the keeper of a dog, for injury done to livestock by that dog, under s 3 of the Animals Act 1971, below, paras 7.09–7.10.

[35] And see the Animals (Northern Ireland) Order 1976, SI 1976/1040, Art 4(2)(b) and (c).

The basic liability, under section 6(3)(a), is that of the owner or the possessor of the animal. The normal defendant, as at common law, will be the person who has control of and 'keeps'[36] the animal, ie the possessor of the animal.[37] The statutory liability in this context is the same as that at common law and the decisions thereunder remain relevant to an examination of who is a keeper within the meaning of section 6(3). The possessor is liable whether or not he is the owner of the animal. Thus, in *M'Kone v Wood*,[38] the defendant was held liable for injuries caused by a dog, known by him to be vicious, which had been left on his premises by a former employee of his. Lord Tenterden CJ said: **2.12**

> It is not material whether the defendant was the owner of the dog or not; if he kept it, that is sufficient; and the harbouring a dog about one's premises, or allowing him to be there or resort there, is a sufficient keeping of the dog to support this form of action.[39]

Undoubtedly, the person who harbours a dog in such circumstances will be held to have it in his possession for the purposes of section 6(3)(a). A less obvious case is that of merely allowing a dog to resort to one's premises and whether that will result necessarily in the conclusion that the dog is, thereby, in one's possession. Nevertheless, it was suggested at common law that 'if one out of charity harboured a dog and gave it food and it did mischief, then one was liable where there was evidence of *scienter*'.[40] Just such a situation can be illustrated by *Smith v Prendergast*.[41] Here the defendant was held liable for harm done by an Alsatian which had, three weeks earlier, strayed into his scrapyard and which he had fed so that it might act as a guard dog. Although the decision is based on common law negligence,[42] it is suggested that it would have been the same under the 1971 Act in terms of the links between the defendant and the dog. **2.13**

Liability was imposed at common law on the trainer of a horse kept in his stables by a third party for a weekly sum,[43] and would be imposed in similar circumstances under the 1971 Act.[44] Similarly, there was liability at common law where the defendant paid his foreman 1s per week for the use of the latter's dog to watch his premises.[45] **2.14**

On the other hand, the mere fact that the claimant has been injured by an animal on the defendant's premises does not necessarily impose liability on the defendant. **2.15**

---

36 eg *Jackson v Smithson* (1846) 15 M & W 563, 565; *May v Burdett* (1846) 9 QB 101, 110; *Knott v LCC* [1934] 1 KB 126, 143–4.

37 Cf *Breen v Slotin* [1948] 4 DLR 46.

38 (1831) 5 C & P 1.

39 Ibid, at p 2.

40 Ibid; and see *Judge v Cox* (1816) 1 Stark 285.

41 (1984) CA, Unreported, 16 October.

42 See below, paras 6.12–6.25.

43 *Walker v Hall* (1876) 40 JP 456.

44 *Fox v Kohn* (1995) CA, Unreported, 2 November; and see *Walsh v Connolly* [2006] NIQB 102.

45 *Bolton v Webster* (1895) 59 JP 571.

So, where a stray dog ran on to the defendants' station and, in the course of two hours, attacked a passenger, a cat, and then the claimant, there was no liability in the *scienter* action as there was no evidence that the defendants had any possession of the dog.[46] Again, where a school caretaker kept a dog on the premises, the school authority was not liable when the dog bit a cleaner, for they neither knew of the dog's existence nor of its vicious propensity and 'had neither property in nor possession of it and made no use of it'.[47] These common law decisions remain unaffected by the Animals Act 1971. Where the claimant's horse was injured by a third party's horse in circumstances where both horses were grazing in the defendants' field, under a grazing agreement, it was held that the defendants were not the keeper of the third party's horse.[48] There was no possession and so no liability under section 2. So, if, for example, an occupier of premises employs a security firm to guard his premises with dangerous dogs which are brought to the premises each night by their handler, the occupier of the premises will not be a keeper of the dogs as he is neither their owner nor their possessor. He will not, therefore, be strictly liable under section 2 for any injuries they cause, although he would be liable at common law if his conduct was in any way negligent towards an injured claimant.[49] The responsibility under section 2 rests in such a case solely on the security firm whose dogs they are.[50]

2.16 The interesting issue arose in *Flack v Hudson*[51] as to whether one keeper can sue another keeper for breach of the duty under section 2 of the 1971 Act. In this case, the claimant's wife was killed when she was exercising a horse at the request of the defendant who was held to be the owner, and a 'keeper', of the horse within the meaning of section 6(3). The trial judge found that, at the time of the accident, the claimant's wife was also a 'keeper' of the horse which she was riding. The Court of Appeal rejected the argument that one keeper could not sue another. Otton LJ said:

> I cannot see anything illogical in the interests of public policy which disentitles a bailee from maintaining an action against a bailor for damage attributable to a defect in the article which is the subject of the bailment. At common law (absent knowledge of the defect on the part of the bailee) the bailee has a clear and well established cause of action. There is nothing in the Act which expressly or by implication deprives the bailee of his cause of action or which limits the persons who can sue a keeper (ie owner or bailee) to third parties or strangers. If it had been the intention of Parliament to deny the right it would have expressly provided for this to happen.[52]

---

46 *Smith v Great Eastern Rail Co* (1866) LR 2 CP 4.

47 *Knott v LCC* [1934] 1 KB 126, 142.

48 *Doolan v EP Cornall & Sons* [2001] CLY 324.

49 The Guard Dogs Act 1975 does not confer a civil right of action; see below, para 7.21.

50 Unless the occupier might possibly be held liable for his independent contractors on the basis of the criticized 'extra-hazardous or dangerous operations doctrine': see M Jones and A Dugdale, *Clerk and Lindsell on Torts*, 20th edn (2010), para 6.67.

51 [2001] QB 698.

52 Ibid, at para 17.

Keene LJ also drew attention to the fact that, in cases such as this, the owner can draw protection from the fact that his knowledge of the dangerous characteristics of the animal must be proved in order to establish liability under section 2 of the Act.[53]

The second type of defendant to consider is the owner who has neither possession nor control of his dangerous animals. Varied dicta at common law suggested that such an owner would be liable for his dangerous animals, and Atkin LJ has asked: **2.17**

> Can the person who has acquired a tiger, so long as he remains its owner, relieve himself of responsibility by contracting with a third person for its custody?[54]

Nevertheless, an owner out of possession had never been held liable, at common law, at least where the animal was in the control of another person. However, section 6(3) is quite unequivocal. The owner of a dangerous animal is a keeper of it and is, therefore, subject to liability under section 2. It does not matter that he has neither possession nor control of it so long as the conditions of liability laid down in section 2 are satisfied.[55] When the owner sells the animal to another person, the latter is liable in the case of a dangerous species immediately title has passed. Where the animal does not belong to a dangerous species, even if the first owner knew of its dangerous characteristics, he will not be liable under section 2 once he has parted with title in and possession of the animal. It had been suggested[56] that the old owner should continue to be liable until the new owner becomes aware of the viciousness, thereby giving an incentive for the transferor to inform the transferee of the dangerous characteristics. There is no such provision in section 6(3) and the old owner's liability ceases immediately on there becoming a new keeper, ie a new owner. Of course, the new owner will not be liable under section 2 until he acquires knowledge of the dangerous characteristics,[57] and a seller will not be inclined to stress the dangerous nature of the animal he is selling.

In the case of the hire purchase of domestic farm animals,[58] the hire purchase company will, as owner, be a keeper of the animal within the meaning of section 6(3). It will, normally,[59] avoid liability under section 2, however, by reason of lack of knowledge of the dangerous characteristics of the animal: a state of ignorance **2.18**

[53] Ibid, at para 47.

[54] *Belvedere Fish Guano Co Ltd v Rainham Chemical Works Ltd* [1920] 2 KB 487, 504; and see *Brackenborough v Spalding UDC* [1942] AC 310, 324; *Knott v LCC* [1934] 1 KB 126, 141; though cf ibid, at p 140.

[55] See *Collings v Home Office* [2006] CLY 160.

[56] Williams, p 326.

[57] Section 2(2)(c).

[58] Hire purchase agreements relating to livestock are quite common: R Goode, *Hire Purchase Law and Practice*, 2nd edn (1970), p 41; and see, eg, *Tucker v Farm and General Investment Trust Ltd* [1966] 2 QB 421.

[59] Hire purchase of dangerous animals for a wildlife park will involve liability without any knowledge, under s 2(1).

which, no doubt, it will be anxious to perpetuate. If the animal is under the care and control of the owner's employee, neither at common law[60] nor under the Animals Act 1971 will this, in any way, relieve the owner from liability. Furthermore, the obligation of the owner would not appear to be delegable to an independent contractor.[61] On the other hand, merely to employ the keeper of a vicious monkey where the injury is done by the monkey neither on the defendant's premises nor in circumstances such as to give the defendant any control over the keeper or the monkey would not be sufficient to impose liability, under section 2 and section 6(3), on the defendant as a keeper.[62]

2.19 The third type of defendant to be considered is that best illustrated by the problem of the 'family pet'. It may well be that a child is the owner of a dangerous dog; the problem of liability for such an animal is dealt with in section 6(3)(b). A person is a keeper of an animal if 'he is the head of a household of which a member under the age of sixteen owns the animal or has it in his possession'. The liability of the head of the household under this subsection is dependent on the fact that he is not himself the owner or possessor of the animal, for otherwise he would be liable under section 6(3)(a). Furthermore, he is only liable if the member of his household who owns or possesses the animal is under the age of 16. These factors might be illustrated by the common law decision in *North v Wood*.[63] The defendant's 17-year-old daughter kept a bull terrier, known by the defendant to be dangerous, on the defendant's premises. The dog attacked and killed the claimant's dog. The defendant was held not liable at common law and he would not be liable under the Animals Act 1971, section 2. He was not in control or possession of the animal. It was in the possession of his daughter who both owned it and paid for its keep and so section 6(3)(a) is not satisfied so far as the defendant was concerned. Furthermore, the case does not fall within section 6(3)(b) because the daughter was over 15. On the other hand, there may well be cases[64] where the fact that a spouse or child over 15 owns the animal does not relieve from liability the other spouse or parent in whose house it is kept, especially in the case of a family pet. Such a pet may well not be in the exclusive possession of any one member of the family, and so the parent who occupies the house where it is kept may be liable as a possessor of it.[65] Such a conclusion in favour of possession may be the more likely if he exercises some control over it.[66] However, the mere fact that someone is the head of a household does not mean that he necessarily possesses all of the animals therein, hence the need for section 6(3)(b).

[60] *Baldwin v Casella* (1872) LR 7 Exch 325, below, para 2.110.
[61] *Pinn v Rew* (1916) 32 TLR 451, unless that case be restricted to liability for dangerous activities on or near a highway.
[62] cf *Connor v The Princess Theatre* (1912) 27 OLR 466.
[63] [1914] 1 KB 629; approved in *Knott v LCC* [1934] 1 KB 126.
[64] cf *Dawson v Warren* (1884) 2 NZLR 255; *Wood v Vaughan* (1889) 28 NBR 472, affirmed (1890) 18 SCR 703; *Stanford v Robertson* [1946] 3 DLR 313, affirmed, [1947] 1 DLR 493.
[65] *Stanford v Robertson*, above, at p 316.
[66] *Dawson v Warren*, above, at pp 260, 262.

Quite what constitutes a 'head of a household' within the meaning of section 6(3)(b) is none too clear,[67] particularly as many spouses and partners claim rights equal to those of the other spouse or partner in running the household;[68] although it may be improbable that we shall have many instances of a husband sheltering behind his wife's petticoats from liability for a child's pet by claiming that his wife is the head of the household.[69] Equally, it is unclear who are the members of a 'household'. It is assumed that parents and children living together are included; but it is debatable whether the head of a household is liable for injuries caused by the dangerous dog belonging to a 14-year-old friend of one of his children who is staying, with his dog, in the household for the weekend. Depending on the circumstances, the head of the household might be regarded as a keeper in his own right, but even then he would only be liable if the requirements of section 2 have been satisfied. **2.20**

The fourth class of possible 'keeper' to be considered is that of the owner or possessor of an animal that has escaped. Does his liability continue after the animal has escaped and, if so, for how long? This problem is dealt with in that part of section 6(3) of the Animals Act 1971, which provides that **2.21**

> if at any time an animal ceases to be owned or to be in the possession of a person, any person who immediately before that time was a keeper thereof by virtue of the preceding provisions of this subsection continues to be a keeper of the animal until another person becomes a keeper thereof by virtue of those provisions.

This provision needs to be examined in the context of the escape of three different types of animals. The first is the indigenous wild animal, such as a fox. It is not common for foxes to be kept as pets, but it does happen. It might also be said that foxes are a dangerous species because they are not 'commonly domesticated in the British Islands' and they are likely to cause severe damage to chickens.[70] The problem of the escaped fox was considered at common law as long ago as 1676 in *Mitchil v Alestree*,[71] where it was said by Twisden J: **2.22**

> if one hath kept a tame fox, which gets loose and grows wild, he that kept him before shall not answer for the damage the fox doth after he hath lost him, and he hath resumed his wild nature.[72]

[67] Who is the head of a household belonging to and run by two widowed sisters, with children under the age of 16? See 305 HL Deb (1969) cc 1436–7.

[68] Perhaps the answer is joint and several heads of the same household.

[69] In *Richardson v Dorn* [1937] 1 WWR 143, a husband kept a dangerous bull on his wife's farm and the wife was held not liable for injuries it caused, because it remained in the husband's control. Cf *Shaw v M'Creary* (1890) 19 OR 39, where a wife who allowed her husband to keep a bear on premises owned and occupied by him was held liable for harbouring the animal, although it is not clear how far the bear was not in the exclusive control and possession of the husband: Williams, p 325.

[70] See the discussion of the definition of a 'dangerous species', below, paras 2.35 et seq.

[71] (1676) 1 Vent 295; and see *Brady v Warren* [1900] 2 IR 632, 640.

[72] Ibid.

Liability seemed, therefore, at common law, to continue after an escape until the animal had resumed its wild natural state, but not thereafter.[73] However, the effect of section 6(3) is that liability is to continue until someone else becomes owner or possessor. This seems unduly wide in the case of the indigenous wild animal which, once it has returned to its wild state, is unlikely to be caught again. If a person owns a tamed fox with a known taste for chickens,[74] should he be liable for all the proven depredations of his fox, even after it has escaped back to its wild state, for the rest of the fox's life, except in the unlikely event of its becoming owned by someone else?[75]

2.23 The second type of animal is the non-indigenous wild animal such as a lion, tiger, puma, or cheetah. The risk of the escape of such animals has been increased by the proliferation of wildlife parks, and the apparent practice of releasing animals, such as pumas, into the wild when they become too big to manage as pets. In such a case, the original keeper, whether he be owner or possessor, remains liable until someone else becomes the keeper of the animal. Even if the escape of such an animal does terminate ownership or possession of it,[76] it is obviously desirable that liability under section 2 should be unaffected by the escape. By reason of section 6(3), liability continues until the animal acquires a new keeper.

2.24 The third class of case is that of the escape of an animal not belonging to a dangerous species, but which has known dangerous characteristics. If the original keeper is the owner he is most unlikely to cease to be the owner because of the escape; but even if he is merely the possessor and he loses possession because of the escape, the effect of section 6(3) is that he continues to be liable until the animal acquires a new 'keeper'. Therefore, liability will continue even after the escape[77] and it cannot be avoided by abandoning the animal, and certainly not by abandoning it *after* it has caused injury.[78] However, liability for any future conduct ceases once the animal has passed into the possession of a third party, even though that third party has not yet become aware of the animal's dangerous characteristics.[79]

2.25 A final problem relating to escapes is that of the liability of the former keeper of an animal not belonging to a dangerous species which has escaped and become wild, as perhaps with cattle in some jurisdictions[80] and which might occur in this country

[73] The distinction drawn in *Andrew v Kilgour* (1910) 13 WLR 608, 613, between escape in town and in the country could be justified on the grounds that in the latter case the fox has regained its wild state merely by escaping.

[74] Thereby avoiding any doubts as to whether the fox is a dangerous species.

[75] Perhaps some consolation may be derived from the Law Commission's view, Report, para 76, that this question 'arises in theory, although seldom in practice'.

[76] cf Law Commission Report, para 76, n 123.

[77] cf the deer in *Brady v Warren* [1900] 2 IR 632.

[78] *Deer Conservancy Board v McConnell* [1928] 2 KB 159, 163.

[79] cf Williams, pp 325–6.

[80] *Falkland Islands Co v R* (1863) 2 Moo PC NS 266, as discussed in *Reeve v Wardle, Ex parte Reeve* [1960] Qd R 143, 147–50; Williams, pp 148–9; although cf *Scott v Edington* (1888) 14 VLR 41.

with, for example, cats or tame deer,[81] or even mink or wallabies. Here again, section 6(3) seems unbending. Liability will continue until the unlikely eventuality of the animal acquiring a new keeper; but it will still be necessary for the animal to be of a species which satisfies the criterion of dangerousness under section 6(2)(b).[82]

There are two general points to be made as to the interpretation of section 6(3). The first is this. The keeper of an animal is, under section 6(3)(a), the owner or the person in possession of the animal and he, or they,[83] remain keepers, even if they lose ownership or possession, until another person becomes a keeper. Let us assume that a puma is owned by A and is in the possession of B. The puma escapes. Both A and B continue to be keepers until the puma comes into the possession of C. B then ceases to be keeper because he is no longer a possessor under section 6(3)(a) and his continued obligation for an escaped animal, under section 6(3), has now ceased. What about A? He is the owner throughout and the fact that the animal has changed possessors should not affect his status as a keeper under section 6(3)(a). It is not, in fact, affected by the general provisions of section 6(3) relating to escaping animals, for they merely state the circumstances in which the status of keeper continues notwithstanding apparent loss within the terms of section 6(3)(a). If A is still owner, he is still a keeper no matter what happens to the puma. **2.26**

The second point relates to the liability of the head of a household, under section 6(3)(b), if the animal escapes. Let us assume that A is the head of a household and that his 15-year-old son, B, has a dog known to be dangerous. Let us assume also that this dog is possessed, but not owned, by B. If that dog escapes so that B ceases to possess it, then A continues to be liable, until the dog acquires a new keeper. It does not matter that during that period B becomes 16. Although A would not now be responsible as head of the household for B's dog because of B's age, he was responsible for it when it left B's possession and section 6(3) states that 'any person who immediately before [it ceased to be owned or possessed] was a keeper thereof by virtue of the preceding provisions of [section 6(3)] continues to be a keeper until another person becomes a keeper'. The justification for holding A liable for an escaped dog, although not for one still in B's possession, must be that A is taken to bear some responsibility for the escape. Of course, in this type of case there is no doubt that B is liable throughout as the former possessor of the dog. **2.27**

Let us now assume the similar but more normal case of the facts being the same, except that B is the owner of the dog. If the dog escapes it does not cease to be owned by B, although it may cease to be possessed by him. A's liability for B's dog as head of the household would appear at first sight to end when B becomes 16 for, although the dog has escaped, B still remains its owner. However, section 6(3) appears to **2.28**

[81] cf *Brady v Warren*, above.
[82] In relation to deer, see below, paras 2.44, 2.51.
[83] The problems of their being joint tortfeasors are discussed, below, para 2.31.

continue A's liability notwithstanding that there is no loss of ownership by B. A's obligation as keeper, stemming from his headship of the household, continues, under section 6(3), 'if at any time an animal ceases to be owned by or to be in the possession of a person'. Although B has not ceased to own the dog, he has, in the above example, ceased to possess it and, because of that, A's liability will continue until the dog acquires a new keeper. But what if, in either of these cases, ie whether B owned or merely possessed the dog, no one else is known to have acquired the dog and eventually it is restored to B's possession? Can A now ever lose responsibility for it, even though B is well over the age of 16 and no longer a member of the household? Indeed, B has, by virtue of section 6(3), remained a keeper of it throughout, even though he lost possession, for no new person has become a keeper of it; and if B remained a keeper, so did and, apparently, does A.

2.29 The liability of the captor of an escaped animal is dealt with in section 6(4):

> Where an animal is taken into and kept in possession for the purpose of preventing it from causing damage or of restoring it to its owner, a person is not a keeper of it by virtue only of that possession.

Quite properly, such a captor of an escaped animal should not be held strictly liable for all injuries done by the animal. If, however, the captor is the owner, he will be liable under section 6(3) notwithstanding the fact that he merely has possession for the purposes of restoring it to its original possessor.

2.30 One point of detail in section 6(4) is that it refers to capture of the animal for the purpose 'of restoring it to its owner'. It does not include the case of restoration to its possessor. Assume that the captor takes the animal into his possession and while in his possession the animal causes injury; if the captor then restores it to a possessor other than the owner, he will have to rely on the argument that he captured it 'for the purpose of preventing it from causing damage'. Such minor difficulties might have been avoided if 'keeper' had been substituted for 'owner' in section 6(4).

2.31 Problems of joint liability will arise, under section 2, from the fact that more than one person may be a keeper of the same dangerous animal at the same time.[84] It is suggested that, where both the owner and the possessor of a dangerous animal are its keepers, they will be joint tortfeasors if the animal causes damage. That being so, they will be jointly and severally liable. The claimant may recover in full from either, but the keeper who is thus held responsible may seek apportionment from his fellow keeper under the Civil Liability (Contribution) Act 1978. The apportionment will be on the basis of that which the court finds to be 'just and equitable having regard to the extent of that person's responsibility for the damage in question'.[85] Although the court should look both to the relative blameworthiness of

[84] Joint liability for harm done by dogs, under s 3, is considered below, paras 7.19–7.20.
[85] Civil Liability (Contribution) Act 1978, s 2(1).

the defendants and to the extent to which each contributed to the cause of the damage, it may well be that in many cases of liability under section 2 apportionment will be equal. Of course, if there are two keepers and the animal does not belong to a dangerous species and thus falls under section 2(2), there will only be joint liability if the various conditions of liability laid down in section 2(2) are satisfied with regard to both keepers. If only one of them knows of the animal's abnormal characteristics,[86] and the other does not, then the keepers will not be joint tortfeasors. The one who has no knowledge will not be liable at all, and the other keeper will bear the full burden of damages.

This might be an appropriate point at which to examine the liability of the Crown under the Animals Act 1971, even though the provisions of the Act in that respect are general and are not confined to the case of liability under section 2. Section 12 states: **2.32**

> (1) This Act binds the Crown, but nothing in this section shall authorise proceedings to be brought against Her Majesty in her private capacity.
> (2) Section 38(3) of the Crown Proceedings Act 1947 (interpretation of references to Her Majesty in her private capacity) shall apply as if this section were contained in that Act.

The effect of section 12(1) is to make the Crown liable for injuries caused by animals to the extent provided by the Crown Proceedings Act 1947, section 2(2) of which states that:

> Where the Crown is bound by a statutory duty which is binding also upon persons other than the Crown and its officers, then, subject to the provisions of this Act, the Crown shall, in respect of a failure to comply with that duty, be subject to all those liabilities in tort (if any) to which it would be so subject if it were a private person of full age and capacity.

In other words, the Crown will be fully liable for injuries caused by animals.[87] The effect of section 12(2) of the Animals Act 1971 is that the phrase 'Her Majesty in her private capacity' has the extended meaning of including a reference to 'Her Majesty in right of her Duchy of Lancaster and to the Duke of Cornwall'.

5. Liability for Animals of a Dangerous Species

The general approach of section 2(1) is clear, as has been stated by Lord Nicholls:[88] **2.33**

> If you choose to keep a dangerous animal not commonly domesticated in this country, you are liable for damage done by the animal. It matters not that you take every

[86] Animals Act 1971, s 2(2)(c); see below, paras 2.97 et seq.
[87] See G Williams, *Crown Proceedings* (1948), ch 2.
[88] *Mirvahedy v Henley* [2003] UKHL 16, para 13; [2003] 2 AC 491.

> precaution to prevent the animal escaping.[89] You may not realise that the animal is dangerous. Liability is independent of fault. Liability is independent of knowledge of the animal's dangerous characteristics. You are liable, subject only to certain defences of general application set out in section 5.[90]

The scope of section 2(1) is inevitably very narrow, 'being almost entirely limited to incidents in (or following escapes from) zoos or circuses'.[91]

2.34 A number of special issues relating to liability, under section 2(1), for animals of a dangerous species must now be considered. The first problem is one, however, which also has necessary implications for section 2(2), namely that of defining an animal of a 'dangerous species'. This is the crucial factor which decides whether section 2(1) or section 2(2) is the relevant subsection applicable to the animal in question, and the most important difference between them is that there will only be liability under section 2(2) if the keeper has knowledge of the animal's dangerous characteristics, whereas such knowledge is not necessary under section 2(1).

(1) The meaning of 'dangerous species'

2.35 The general distinction under discussion here is that between domesticated animals which are not normally dangerous and those wild animals which are generally dangerous to mankind. The elements of the distinction were stated by the Law Commission thus:

> The question whether an animal belongs to a dangerous species should depend, as is at present the position with the category of animals *ferae naturae*, upon a test prescribed by law; and in determining this question a court should regard as the decisive consideration the risks to persons or property in the circumstances of this country. A species of animals which is generally domesticated in the British Isles should not be regarded in law as dangerous, but with regard to other species their domesticated or non-domesticated character abroad should be taken into account only to the extent that this factor may be relevant to the degree of risk which such species present in the circumstances of this country.[92]

2.36 The test for the determination of a 'dangerous species' is provided by section 6(2) of the Animals Act 1971, as follows:

> A dangerous species is a species—
>
> (a) which is not commonly domesticated in the British Islands; and
>
> (b) whose fully grown animals normally have such characteristics that they are likely, unless restrained, to cause severe damage or that any damage they may cause is likely to be severe.[93]

---

[89] An 'escape' is not in fact necessary; see below, paras 2.123–2.127.

[90] Defences are discussed below, paras 2.128 et seq.

[91] *Mirvahedy v Henley*, above, para 135.

[92] Law Commission Report, para 25(ii).

[93] And see the Animals (Northern Ireland) Order 1976, SI 1976/1040, Art 2(2 (a).

There are several general issues relevant to this subsection to be examined before considering the two specific conditions for classification as a 'dangerous species'. The question of whether a species of animal is dangerous or not is, as with the distinction between animals *ferae naturae* and *mansuetae naturae*, a question of law and a matter of judicial notice.[94] Subject to the operation of the doctrine of precedent, a classification once made on the basis of an interpretation and application of section 6(2) is binding, for 'it is not competent to the Courts to reconsider the classification of former times and to include domestic animals of blameless antecedents in the class of dangerous animals even when wandering on the roadsides'.[95] **2.37**

An animal is considered dangerous if it belongs to a species which is decided, in accordance with section 6(2), to be a dangerous species. It does not matter what the characteristics of the individual animal of that species may be. Thus, it has been held, at common law, that all elephants are *ferae naturae*[96] and indeed they are likely to be classed as a dangerous species under section 6(2),[97] even though the particular elephant in question is tame and causes damage from fright rather than viciousness. The peculiarity of this situation is well revealed by Devlin J in *Behrens v Bertram Mills Circus Ltd*:[98] **2.38**

> The particular rigidity in the *scienter* action which is involved in this case . . . is the rule that requires the harmfulness of the offending animal to be judged not by reference to its particular training and habits, but by reference to the general habits of the species to which it belongs. The law ignores the world of difference between the wild elephant in the jungle and the trained elephant in the circus. The elephant Bullu is in fact no more dangerous than a cow; she reacted in the same way as a cow would to the irritation of a small dog; if perhaps her bulk made her capable of doing more damage, her higher training enabled her to be more swiftly checked. But I am compelled to assess the defendants' liability in this case in just the same way as I would assess it if they had loosed a wild elephant into the funfair.

This rule and the problem just exemplified remain unaffected by the Animals Act 1971. Criticized though the rule has been, some justification for applying a fixed rule to all animals of one species, however tame, might be that: **2.39**

> a wild animal may become tame and kind. Its nature may sleep for a time, but it may also wake up, and, if the animal has lost its fear of mankind, it is undoubtedly more dangerous.[99]

---

[94] *Behrens v Bertram Mills Circus Ltd* [1957] 2 QB 1.

[95] *Heath's Garage Ltd v Hodges* [1916] 2 KB 370, 383; and see *Behrens v Bertram Mills Circus Ltd*, above, at p 30.

[96] *Filburn v People's Palace and Aquarium Co Ltd* (1890) 25 QBD 258; *Behrens v Bertram Mills Circus Ltd*, above.

[97] Below, para 2.46.

[98] [1957] 2 QB 1, 14–15.

[99] *Andrew v Kilgour* (1910) 13 WLR 608, 613; and see *Besozzi v Harris* (1858) 1 F & F 92, 93; *Temple v Elvery* [1926] 3 WWR 652, 655.

2.40 It is necessary now to consider the two specific conditions for classification as a dangerous species provided in section 6(2). The first condition is that the species 'is not commonly domesticated in the British Islands'.[100] This has the effect that all such commonly domesticated animals are excluded from classification as dangerous without proof of knowledge, despite the fact that they may commonly be regarded as dangerous as well as domesticated. Thus, not only cats[101] are excluded by this provision but so too are dogs,[102] horses,[103] and cattle,[104] including bulls.[105]

2.41 Under section 6(2)(a) the species must be one that is *commonly* domesticated in the British Isles. The original draft Bill referred to a species that was *generally* domesticated, but it was amended in the House of Lords. It may be difficult to envisage 'commonly' and 'generally' as other than synonyms, but the main difference is that 'commonly' is less wide in its ambit than 'generally'. The practical consequence of this is that, if an animal is a member of a species which is frequently domesticated in the British Islands, it will fall outside the class of dangerous animals, even though the species is not normally domesticated. As Lord Wilberforce has said:

> If one takes 'commonly' and applies it to rabbits, rabbits are 'commonly domesticated' one would say, even though the majority of them are not domesticated; and that is all right. As regards camels, elephants, cheetahs, snakes or crocodiles, they are not 'commonly domesticated' in this country, although there may be some that are.[106]

The consequence of this approach is that the tame rabbit, mouse, and pigeon, for example, may well remove their wild cousins from any possible category of dangerous animals,[107] unless one could say that wild rabbits and the like belong to a different species or sub-species from tame rabbits.

2.42 The species must also be 'domesticated'. If 'domesticated' meant merely 'tame',[108] then it would be true to say, contrary to the view of Lord Wilberforce, that the majority of elephants, and even camels, found in the British Islands are tame. However, the meaning of 'domesticated' is narrower than this, and would seem to relate only to those animals which are found in or near a household or farm.[109] This

[100] See s 6(2)(a).

[101] eg *Buckle v Holmes* [1926] 2 KB 125; and see *Mirvahedy v Henley* [2003] UKHL 16, para 153; [2003] 2 AC 491.

[102] eg *Curtis v Betts* [1990] 1 WLR 459, 462; *Smith v Ainger* (1990) CA, Unreported, 16 May; *Gloster v Chief Constable of Greater Manchester Police* [2000] PIQR 114; *Mirvahedy v Henley*, above, para 153.

[103] eg *Mirvahedy v Henley*, above, paras 12, 51, 129; *Freeman v Higher Park Farm* [2008] EWCA Civ 1185, para 20; [2009] PIQR 103; and see *Walsh v Connolly* [2006] NIQB 102, paras 13–14.

[104] eg *McKenny v Foster* [2008] EWCA Civ 173, para 22.

[105] eg *Hudson v Roberts* (1851) 6 Exch 697; *Dobbie v Henderson* 1970 SLT (Sh Ct) 27; *Mirvahedy v Henley*, above, at paras 129, 153.

[106] 305 HL Deb (1969) c 1433.

[107] 312 HL Deb (1970) c 869.

[108] 305 HL Deb (1969) c 1451.

[109] The definition in the *Shorter Oxford English Dictionary*, 5th edn (2002), is 'accustomed to being kept by or living with humans'.

would exclude those animals found in, but rarely outside, a zoo. Even then, it is not abundantly clear how to classify a pet monkey. Some are kept in private homes. These would seem to be domesticated. It is debateable whether enough are so kept to justify the conclusion that monkeys are 'commonly domesticated'.

The only domestication that is relevant under section 6(2)(a) is domestication in the British Islands.[110] So, 'species of animals which are commonly tamed and brought under control in this country cannot belong to a "dangerous species"'.[111] If, however, an animal is domesticated in those parts of the world where it is indigenous, as may be the case with the elephant and the camel, then this is a factor relevant, perhaps, under section 6(2)(b), as to whether the animals have such characteristics that they are likely to be dangerous.[112] However, such foreign domestication is irrelevant to liability under section 6(2)(a). Thus, if the facts of *McQuaker v Goddard*,[113] where the claimant was bitten by a camel at Chessington Zoo, were to recur, the fact that camels are usually domesticated in those countries where they are commonly found would not be conclusive as to the camel's character, as dangerous or non-dangerous, in England. This conclusion is supported by *Tutin v Mary Chipperfield Promotions Ltd*,[114] where the claimant was injured by falling off a camel at Olympia. Cantley J rejected the argument that camels, being commonly domesticated abroad, retain that character in this country unless and until 'turned out to become wild'. The judge made clear that his task was not just to determine whether camels were domesticated here, but rather whether they were 'commonly domesticated' in the British Islands. While it appeared that there were only about 100 camels in this country and that 'they were all in zoos, safari parks and circuses', nevertheless the judge said that: **2.43**

> Even though some of them may have become trained to the uses of man and accustomed to association with man, it does not seem to me that camels are commonly domesticated in this country.

The requirement that the species is one not commonly domesticated in the British Islands, quite properly, is not the sole test of a species' dangerous quality. The provisions of section 6(2)(b) must also be satisfied. It must be a species **2.44**

> whose fully grown animals normally have such characteristics that they are likely, unless restrained, to cause severe damage or that any damage they may cause is likely to be severe.

[110] 'British Islands' is defined by the Interpretation Act 1978, Sch 1, as 'the United Kingdom, the Channel Islands, and the Isle of Man'.

[111] *Mirvahedy v Henley* [2003] UKHL 16, para 87; [2003] 2 AC 491.

[112] See below, paras 2.44–2.52.

[113] [1940] 1 KB 687.

[114] (1980) Unreported, 23 May.

So, for example, it has been suggested that deer kept in a deer park, while not regarded as domesticated, would not be classed as a dangerous species because they do not satisfy section 6(2)(b).[115]

2.45 The characteristics relevant here are not those of the particular animal in question, but are those of the 'reasonable adult animal of the species'. If the young of the species do not normally evidence the tendency to cause severe damage although fully grown animals do then, if a young animal causes any damage, its keeper will be strictly liable. The relevant characteristics are those which fully grown animals of the species 'normally have'. If the tendency to cause severe damage is abnormal, the condition is not satisfied. However, the tendency may be subject to the further condition that it is normal in such animals, but only at particular times. It is well known that some females can be very fierce in protection of their young, even though generally docile. Their ferocious behaviour is only normal in the special circumstances. There is no indication in section 6(2)(b) whether such circumstances are relevant to a determination of normal behaviour.[116] The question of whether animals of the species under consideration have dangerous characteristics is likely to be treated by the courts as a matter of judicial notice, as is the whole question of classification.[117] Indeed, it has been said of the common law distinction:

> The doctrine has from its formulation proceeded upon the supposition that the knowledge of what kinds of animals are tame and what are savage is common knowledge. Evidence is receivable, if at all, only on the basis that the judge may wish to inform himself. This was clearly settled by the Court of Appeal in *McQuaker v Goddard*,[118] where Clauson LJ[119] said: 'The reason why the evidence was given was for the assistance of the judge in forming his view as to what the ordinary course of nature in this regard in fact is, a matter of which he is supposed to have complete knowledge.'[120]

2.46 The species envisaged by section 6(2)(b) fall into two categories. There are, first of all, those obviously fierce, wild animals which are likely to cause severe damage. This would include animals such as bears,[121] leopards,[122] lions,[123] tigers,[124]

[115] *Mirvahedy v Henley* [2003] UKHL 16, paras 87, 116–17; [2003] 2 AC 491.

[116] cf Animals Act 1971, s 2(2)(b). On the meaning of the term 'normally' in the context of this provision, see below, para 2.85.

[117] Above, paras 2.37–2.39.

[118] [1940] 1 KB 687.

[119] Ibid, at p 700.

[120] *Behrens v Bertram Mills Circus Ltd* [1957] 2 QB 1, 16.

[121] eg *Besozzi v Harris* (1858) 1 F & F 92; *Wyatt v Rosherville Gardens Co* (1886) 2 TLR 282, 283; *Shaw v McCreary* (1890) 19 OR 39.

[122] eg *Sylvester v Chapman* [1935] 1 LJCCA 261, 264.

[123] eg *Pearson v Coleman Bros* [1948] 2 KB 359; *Young v Green* [1958] OWN 426; and see *Besozzi v Harris* (1858) 1 F & F 92, 93; *Leniston v Phipps* (1988) CA, Unreported, 21 October; cf *Murphy v Zoological Society of London* [1962] CLY 68.

[124] eg *R v Huggins* (1730) 2 Ld Raym 1574, 1583; *Wyatt v Rosherville Gardens Co* (1886) 2 TLR 282, 283; *Buckle v Holmes* [1926] 2 KB 125, 128; *Behrens v Bertram Mills Circus Ltd* [1957] 2 QB 1, 17–18; *Mirvahedy v Henley* [2003] UKHL 16, paras 12, 67; [2003] 2 AC 491; cf *Canterbury City Council v Howletts and Port Lympne Estates Ltd* [1997] ICR 925; and see *Lewis v Oeming* (1983) 42 AR 58.

wolves,[125] gorillas,[126] and, possibly, zebras;[127] although it is, perhaps, debatable whether zebras are likely to cause *severe* damage unless restrained. The second category is that of more normally peaceful, but undomesticated, animals. They are included in the category of dangerous animals if they have a potential for causing severe damage. They are animals which are unlikely to cause damage in normal circumstances. If, however, they do cause any damage, it is likely to be severe damage. The best illustration of this type of animal is the elephant. It is normally quite docile and unlikely to cause any damage, severe or otherwise. If however, it does cause damage because, for example, it has been frightened, then there must be little doubt that it is likely to cause severe damage to person or property because of its great size.[128] One result of its classification as dangerous from its sheer size will be that its keeper will be strictly liable even though the damage it actually causes does not result from its size,[129] as where it takes and eats property using its trunk.

Both of these categories involve the requirement of likelihood of causing severe damage. Whether damage is likely to be severe is a judgment which must be left to the court. 'How severe is severe?' is a question which cannot be answered in the abstract. It may well be a factor which will vary from species to species. It is, however, crucial to the issue of whether the animal falls within the strict liability of section 2(1) or liability only on proof of knowledge of its dangerous characteristics under section 2(2). **2.47**

A further imprecise term in section 6(2)(b) is 'likely'. Lord Scott has suggested[130] that it should be given its natural meaning of 'to be reasonably expected',[131] explaining that: **2.48**

> It would not, in my opinion, be enough that the animal, unless restrained, could or might cause severe damage. Any animal could do that. You could trip over an escaped dormouse and break your neck falling downstairs. Nor would it be enough that damage, if caused by the animal, could or might be severe. The statutory language requires any damage caused by the animal to be likely to be severe. A mere possibility would not suffice. If a reasonable expectation, whether that the animal would, if free of restraint, cause severe damage or that any damage caused by the animal would be severe, were absent, the requirements of paragraph (b) of section 6(2) would not be satisfied. The animal would not belong to a 'dangerous species'. In short it would not be a dangerous animal.[132]

---

[125] eg Hale 1 PC 430; and see *Temple v Elvery* [1926] 3 WWR 652, esp at p 654: a cross between a dog and a wolf, classed as *ferae naturae*.

[126] eg *Buckle v Holmes* [1926] 2 KB 125, 128.

[127] *Marlor v Ball* (1900) 16 TLR 239.

[128] eg *Behrens v Bertram Mills Circus Ltd* [1957] 2 QB 1; *Mirvahedy v Henley* [2003] UKHL 16, at para 67; [2003] 2 AC 491.

[129] cf *Filburn v People's Palace and Aquarium Co Ltd* (1890) 25 QBD 258; and see the report of the facts in 6 TLR 402.

[130] *Mirvahedy v Henley*, above, at para 95.

[131] Quoting the *Concise Oxford Dictionary*, 9th edn, p 795.

[132] And see the discussion in the context of s 2(2)(a) and (b), below, para 2.66.

2.49 If 'severity' and 'likely' are incapable of precise definition, 'damage' creates less difficulty. At common law, the test for deciding whether an animal was *ferae naturae* was whether it was dangerous to mankind,[133] and the fact that an animal was naturally dangerous to property was not relevant.[134] It was, therefore, necessary to exclude from consideration, for example, the natural propensity of a cat to eat pigeons[135] or to fight dogs.[136] A corollary of this principle was that a number of species of 'wild animals' fell within the category of animals *mansuetae naturae*,[137] such as kangaroos,[138] rabbits,[139] and, probably, 'hares, pheasants and partridge',[140] as well as bees;[141] but not a raccoon in Canada,[142] nor a dingo in Australia.[143]

2.50 Undoubtedly, many 'harmless wild animals', ie animals not commonly domesticated in the British Islands, are very destructive of property, but the common law position was that there was no strict liability for damage to property by an animal likely only to damage property. However, as there seems little reason to doubt that the strict liability for animals *ferae naturae* extended to damage to property,[144] there was such strict liability for damage to property by an animal which was classed as 'wild' because of its tendency to injure mankind. This anomalous situation would appear to have been altered by the Animals Act 1971. The statutory test of the dangerous nature of an animal under section 6(2)(b) is based on the animal's likelihood to cause damage. There is no specific reference to the type of damage involved. The definition of 'damage' in section 11 does not resolve the matter either, for it merely states that '"damage" includes the death of, or injury to, any person (including any disease and any impairment of physical or mental condition)'. This states what is included, but it is neither an exhaustive definition of what is included, nor is there any indication that anything is excluded. That being so, 'damage' should be given its normal meaning which is broad enough to include 'damage to property'. Therefore, under section 6(2), the likelihood of animals of the species in question causing severe damage as a criterion of the dangerous nature of the species is not confined to cases of injury to persons, but extends to damage to property. An animal,

133 *Buckle v Holmes* [1926] 2 KB 125, 129; and see *Filburn v People's Palace and Aquarium Co* (1890) 25 QBD 258, 260; *Clinton v J Lyons & Co Ltd* [1912] 3 KB 198, 202, 207; *McQuaker v Goddard* [1940] 1 KB 687, 695; *Behrens v Bertram Mills Circus Ltd* [1957] 2 QB 1.

134 *Filburn v People's Palace and Aquarium Co Ltd*, above, at p 260.

135 *Buckle v Holmes* [1926] 2 KB 125, 129.

136 *Clinton v J Lyons & Co Ltd* [1912] 3 KB 198.

137 Thus, revealing the fallacy in equating 'domesticated animals' with 'animals *mansuetae naturae*'; cf *McQuaker v Goddard* [1940] 1 KB 687; although see Williams (1940) 56 LQR 354.

138 *Lake v Taggart* (1979) 1 SR (WA) 89.

139 *Behrens v Bertram Mills Circus Ltd* [1957] 2 QB 1, 14.

140 *Filburn v People's Palace and Aquarium Co Ltd*, as reported in (1890) 59 LJQB 471, 472.

141 *O'Gorman v O'Gorman* [1903] 2 IR 573, 581, 583, 588; *Stormer v Ingram* (1978) 21 SASR 93; and see *Robins v Kennedy and Columb* [1931] NZLR 1134, 1142.

142 *Andrews v Kilgour* (1910) 13 WLR 608.

143 *Fischer v Stuart* (1979) 25 ALR 336.

144 Williams, p 297.

not domesticated in the British Isles, which is likely to cause severe damage to property will be classed as dangerous. This will mean, also, that there will be strict liability where an animal, classed as dangerous because likely to cause one type of damage, in fact causes a different type.

The criterion of damage to property may raise some difficulties in that many English 'wild animals' are likely to cause damage to property, but not to persons. Obvious examples would be rabbits, squirrels, and pigeons. If one of these creatures was in captivity, then its keeper might be held strictly liable for any injury it caused because of the potential of such animals to cause damage to property, provided one can say that fully grown rabbits,[145] squirrels, and the like are likely to cause severe damage to crops.[146] If that is a correct assumption, then the keeper of a caged squirrel will be strictly liable if it bites the claimant. However, one might note that the view has been expressed, obiter, in the House of Lords[147] that deer cannot be regarded as dangerous animals; although no consideration was given to their capacity to cause considerable damage to crops and gardens. **2.51**

It might be mentioned finally that, while it has been suggested that 'there will seldom be any doubt whether a particular animal does or does not belong to a dangerous species as so defined',[148] provision is in fact made, elsewhere in the law, for the categorization of dangerous animals. Under the Dangerous Wild Animals Act 1976, it is an offence to keep a dangerous wild animal without a licence.[149] Such animals are specified in a Schedule to the Act.[150] All of the animals listed would satisfy the criterion of section 6(2)(a) of not being 'commonly domesticated' and most, if not all, would satisfy the risk of severe damage criterion in section 6(2)(b). It would, therefore, not be unreasonable for a court to have regard to the list of animals under the 1976 Act when addressing the issue of whether a particular species of animal is 'dangerous' within the meaning of the Animals Act 1971.[151] **2.52**

[145] Unless it can be said that the rabbit is 'commonly domesticated' so that there is no liability under s 2(1) for wild rabbits; see above, para 2.41.

[146] Likelihood of causing damage was amended to likelihood of causing *severe* damage in order to exclude rabbits and the like if they were not excluded already by 'commonly domesticated' in s 6(2)(a): 313 HL Deb (1970) cc 455–6.

[147] *Mirvahedy v Henley* [2003] UKHL 16, paras 87, 116–17; [2003] 2 AC 491.

[148] *Smith v Ainger* (1990) CA, Unreported, 16 May.

[149] See ss 1(1), 2(5), with exceptions for zoos and circuses: s 5.

[150] As amended by statutory instrument; see SI 1984/1111; SI 2007/2465.

[151] The Dangerous Dogs Act 1991 imposes criminal penalties on those who fail to comply with a variety of restrictions on keeping and breeding a range of fierce dogs, such as pit bull terriers and dogs bred for fighting; see s 1 and SI 1991/1743. However, the list of dangerous dogs under the 1991 Act is of no assistance in relation to s 2 (1) of the Animals Act 1971, as it is clear that, as dogs are regarded as domesticated, they cannot fall within the category of 'dangerous animals' for the purposes of the 1971 Act. For further consideration of liability for dogs, see below, ch 7.

(2) The scope of liability for animals of a dangerous species

2.53 It should be noted, at the outset, that, so far as the civil law is concerned, it is not unlawful to keep either an animal of a dangerous species or any other animal known to be dangerous; for 'the wrong is in allowing it to escape from the keeper's control[152] with the result that it does damage. Damage is thus the gist of the action.'[153] It was pointed out that to admit of a rule that it is unlawful to keep dangerous animals would mean that 'the proprietors of the Zoological Gardens would live in a perpetual state of law-breaking'.[154] These comments on liability under the *scienter* action are equally true of liability under section 2 of the Animals Act 1971. Liability arises thereunder on the causing of damage, not because a dangerous animal is being kept by the defendant.

2.54 Liability under section 2(1) is strict.[155] People who keep an animal of a dangerous species do so at their peril. It is no defence to an action for keeping such an animal which has injured the claimant that the defendant did not know of its ferocity. For it is still the law that 'it cannot be doubted that a person who keeps an animal [of a dangerous species] must prevent it from doing injury, and it is immaterial whether he knows it to be dangerous or not'.[156] The honest belief in the fact that a circus elephant,[157] a performing bear,[158] or a dingo in Australia kept as a family pet[159] is harmless is irrelevant if the animal in fact causes injury; for, as in the case of the bear,

> every one must know that such animals as lions and bears are of a savage nature. For though such nature may sleep for a time, this case shows that it may wake up at any time.[160]

2.55 A special problem, at common law, arising from strict liability for dangerous animals was whether their keeper was strictly liable for *any* injury caused by them or only for such injuries as could be attributed to their assumed dangerous characteristics. The problem might be illustrated by *Behrens v Bertram Mills Circus Ltd.*[161] The claimants were circus midgets occupying a booth in a funfair adjoining the

---

[152] Whether it is necessary for there to be an escape, or an escape from control, for liability under s 2 is discussed, below, paras 2.123–2.127.

[153] *Knott v LCC* [1934] 1 KB 126, 138–9; and see *Jackson v Smithson* (1846) 15 M &W 563; *Connor v The Princess Theatre* (1912) 27 OLR 466, 469–70; cf *May v Burdett* (1846) 9 QB 101, 111; *Card v Case* (1848) 5 CB 622, 632–4; *Baker v Snell* [1908] 2 KB 825, 833, although there are suggestions that this last dictum went too far; see Bray J in *Clinton v J Lyons & Co Ltd* [1912] 3 KB 198, 208.

[154] P Winfield, *Tort*, 8th edn (1967), p 474.

[155] Although it is strict, it is not absolute and the various defences are discussed below, paras 2.128–2.166.

[156] *Filburn v People's Palace and Aquarium Co Ltd* (1890) 25 QBD 258, 260; and see *Wyatt v Rosherville Gardens Co* (1886) 2 TLR 282, 283.

[157] eg *Filburn v People's Palace and Aquarium Co Ltd*, above; *Behrens v Bertram Mills Circus Ltd* [1957] 2 QB 1.

[158] *Besozzi v Harris* (1858) 1 F & F 92.

[159] *Fischer v Stuart* (1979) 25 ALR 336.

[160] *Besozzi v Harris*, above, p 93.

[161] [1957] 2 QB 1.

defendants' circus, and under licence from the defendants. The booth was in a passageway along which the defendants' elephants had to pass to get to the circus ring. One of the elephants, when frightened by a dog kept in the booth by the claimants' manager, against the defendants' rules, turned to follow the dog and, in so doing, knocked the booth down, killing the dog and seriously injuring the female claimant. In considering the claimants' claim for damages in the *scienter* action, Devlin J decided that an elephant was an animal *ferae naturae*. He then examined the problem raised by the fact that the injuries had been caused by the elephant acting out of fright, rather than acting viciously or savagely against human beings. Although the keeper of an animal *ferae naturae* was presumed to have knowledge of its vicious propensity, the strict liability for such animals applied to *all* harm done by them, even though not resulting from viciousness. Devlin J accepted that he who kept an animal *ferae naturae* kept it at his peril and was liable for all harm caused by it, whether as a result of viciousness or of fright or whether by its attacking, blundering, or its mere presence. He said:

> It does not seem to me that the logic of the matter necessarily requires that an animal that is savage by disposition should be put on exactly the same footing as one that is savage by nature. Certainly practical considerations would seem to demand that they should be treated differently. It may be unreasonable to hold the owner of a biting dog responsible thereafter for everything it does; but it may also be unreasonable to limit the liability for a tiger. If a person wakes up in the middle of the night and finds an escaping tiger on top of his bed and suffers a heart attack, it would be nothing to the point that the intentions of the tiger were quite amiable. If a tiger is let loose in a funfair, it seems to me to be irrelevant whether a person is injured as the result of a direct attack or because on seeing it he runs away and falls over.[162]

The effect of the Animals Act 1971 would appear to be to leave this position unchanged. Liability is imposed under section 2(1) for 'any damage' caused by an animal of a dangerous species; there is no need for the damage to be related to those characteristics which caused the animal to be classed as dangerous.[163] Of course, in the case of elephants the likelihood of damage caused by their sheer size is a factor which leads to their classification as dangerous. So if a horse is caused to bolt by the mere sight of an elephant and the horse is thereby injured, the keeper of the elephant will be strictly liable.[164] It is also the case that the damage does not need to be caused by an attack by the animal, as is illustrated by *Tutin v Mary Chipperfield Promotions Ltd*,[165] where the claimant's injury was caused by being thrown off a camel, rather than by, for example, being bitten by it. **2.56**

[162] Ibid, at pp 17–18.
[163] Under s 6(2).
[164] These are the facts of *Scribner v Kelly* 38 Barb 14 (NY 1862), although the decision there was against liability.
[165] (1980) Unreported, 23 May.

2.57 It will be apparent that the phrase 'any damage' is apt to cover both personal injuries to the claimant and damage to his property. Therefore, section 2(1) will apply to cases of personal injuries as a result of, for example, being mauled[166] or bitten by a bear,[167] mauled by a lion,[168] thrown off[169] or bitten by a camel,[170] bitten by a monkey[171] or a chimpanzee[172] or trampled on by an elephant.[173] Equally, if a marauding elephant merely damages property, an action for such damage will lie under section 2(1).

2.58 Damage is further defined by section 11 to include the death of any person and so, if the victim of a dangerous animal's attack is killed, his dependants will have a right of action under the Fatal Accidents Acts 1846–1959.[174] Furthermore, injury to a person extends, by reason of section 11, to cover 'any disease and any impairment of physical or mental condition'. If, therefore, an animal of a dangerous species is carrying a disease and the claimant is infected thereby, an action will lie under section 2(1). If the injury to the claimant takes the form of nervous shock or physical injury directly attributable to shock, such damage is actionable under section 2(1). A heart attack as a result of seeing a tiger at the end of the bed would clearly be actionable,[175] but mere 'fright' at seeing a rampaging elephant would not be actionable unless it led to physical or mental impairment.[176] If, however, the fright caused the claimant to fall and break his wrist,[177] such damage would be actionable.

2.59 There are two final factors to consider in relation to strict liability under section 2(1). First, the damage complained of must have been caused by the dangerous animal. This can be illustrated by the common law decision in *Brook v Cook*,[178] where the claimant fell when the defendant's monkey appeared on her garden wall. However, the County Court judge found that her fall was not caused by fright at the appearance of the monkey. Her action and her appeal to the Court of Appeal failed, as they would under section 2(1).

2.60 Second, the damage complained of must not be too remote. There is little or no direct authority on remoteness of damage in the case of animals which are *ferae naturae* or

166 *Besozzi v Harris* (1858) 1 F & F 92.

167 *Wyatt v Rosherville Gardens Co* (1886) 2 TLR 282; *Shaw v McCreary* (1890) 19 OR 39.

168 See *Leniston v Phipps* (1988) CA, Unreported, 21 October; cf *Young v Green* [1958] OWN 426.

169 *Tutin v Mary Chipperfield Promotions Ltd*, above.

170 *McQuaker v Goddard* [1940] 1 KB 687.

171 *Connor v The Princess Theatre* (1912) 27 OLR 466.

172 *James v Wellington City* [1972] NZLR 70, reversed on other grounds: [1972] NZLR 978.

173 *Behrens v Bertram Mills Circus Ltd* [1957] 2 QB 1.

174 Under s 10 of the Animals Act 1971, it is provided that 'For the purposes of the Fatal Accidents Acts 1846 to 1959 . . . any damage for which a person is liable under sections 2 to 4 of this Act shall be treated as due to his fault.'

175 *Behrens v Bertram Mills Circus Ltd* [1957] 2 QB 1, 17–18.

176 Ibid, at pp 27–8.

177 cf *Brook v Cook* (1961) 105 Sol Jo 684.

178 Ibid; cf *Scribner v Kelly* 38 Barb 14 (NY 1862).

belong to a dangerous species.[179] Some of the earlier common law cases contained dicta indicating very wide liability,[180] in that the keeper would be liable for 'any damage' caused by his animal. Later, this was modified[181] to indicate that there would be liability for any 'direct damage'.[182] More recently, it was suggested[183] that the remoteness test in the *scienter* action was 'a test of fore-seeability, but one which, in the case of such dangerous creatures as tigers, will encompass a very wide area of damage'.[184] It is a matter of conjecture which approach will be regarded as relevant to liability under section 2(1). However, although the House of Lords has held[185] that, despite liability under the rule in *Rylands v Fletcher*[186] being strict, the test of remoteness in that case is one of foreseeability, there seems little doubt that, under section 2(1) of the Animals Act 1971, the keeper of a dangerous animal will be liable for 'any damage' caused by it. This means that there is liability even for damage which does not stem from the animal's dangerous characteristics.[187] This would indicate liability for all direct consequences of the animal's conduct.[188]

6. Liability for Animals of a Non-dangerous Species

Strict liability for harm done by animals which do not belong to a dangerous species is governed by section 2(2) of the Animals Act 1971. All animals which do not fall into the category of dangerous animals, as defined by section 6(2) of the Act, fall into this category. Just as it has been noted that the scope of section 2(1) is, in reality, rather limited,[189] so that of section 2(2) is very wide, as has been made clear by Lord Walker: **2.61**

> Section 2(2) has to cover the whole range of incidents involving animals of species classified as non-dangerous . . . That range includes (i) physical injury to humans by biting (especially by dogs) or kicking or knocking down (especially by horses); (ii) injuries caused to livestock (such as a dog worrying a neighbour's sheep, or a cat killing a neighbour's chickens); (iii) road traffic accidents, especially those caused by animals straying on the highway; (iv) damage caused by livestock getting on to

[179] Williams, pp 320–21.

[180] *Cox v Burbidge* (1863) 13 CBNS 430, 439; *Filburn v Peoples Palace and Aquarium Co Ltd* (1890) 25 QBD 258, 260.

[181] *Hambrook v Stokes Bros* [1925] 1 KB 141, 156.

[182] *Re Polemis and Furness Withy & Co Ltd* [1921] 3 KB 560.

[183] Dias [1962] CLJ 178, 196.

[184] This would accord with *The Wagon Mound* [1961] AC 388; and see *The Wagon Mound* (*No 2*) [1967] 1 AC 617.

[185] *Cambridge Water Co Ltd v Eastern Counties Leather plc* [1994] AC 264; and see para 3.31, below.

[186] (1866) LR 1 Exch 265, affirmed (1868) LR 3 HL 330.

[187] eg falling off a camel, as in *Tutin v Mary Chipperfield Promotions Ltd* (1980) Unreported, 23 May; and see *Behrens v Bertram Mills Circus Ltd* [1957] 2 QB 1, 17–18.

[188] See M Jones and A Dugdale, *Clerk and Lindsell on Torts*, 20th edn (2010), para 2.137.

[189] See above, para 2.33.

> neighbouring land and destroying crops or gardens; and (v) injury or damage caused by the spread of animal infection or by the smell or noise of animals (a case which shades off into cases normally classified as nuisance). So section 2(2) has a lot of work to do. It is expressed in general, abstract terms and it has to be applied to a wide range of disparate problems.[190]

All animals within the class of non-dangerous species are presumed to be harmless unless the necessary statutory conditions of liability laid down by section 2(2) are satisfied. Once they have been satisfied, however, the keeper of the animal is liable even though he has not been proved to have been negligent.[191] Liability is strict, subject to the various defences provided in the Animals Act 1971.[192]

2.62 The keeper of an animal not belonging to a dangerous species will be liable for damage caused by it provided that the three general conditions laid down in section 2(2) are satisfied. It is provided by section 2(2) of the Animals Act 1971 that:

> Where damage is caused by an animal which does not belong to a dangerous species, a keeper of the animal is liable for the damage, except as otherwise provided by this Act, if—
>
> (a) the damage is of a kind which the animal, unless restrained, was likely to cause or which, if caused by the animal, was likely to be severe; and
>
> (b) the likelihood of the damage or of its being severe was due to characteristics of the animal which are not normally found in animals of the same species or are not normally so found except at particular times or in particular circumstances; and
>
> (c) those characteristics were known to that keeper or were at any time known to a person who at that time had charge of the animal as that keeper's servant or, where that keeper is the head of a household, were known to another keeper of the animal who is a member of that household and under the age of sixteen.

These conditions relate, basically, to the kind of damage likely to be caused, the abnormal characteristics of the animal which caused the damage, and the keeper's knowledge, actual, imputed, or inferred, of those characteristics.

2.63 The interrelation of these conditions and, especially, the meaning of section 2(2)(b) have proved to be challenging for the courts; and the drafting of section 2 has been the subject of widespread and strong criticism.[193] Hale LJ in the Court of Appeal in *Mirvahedy v Henley* has provided a catalogue of such comments:[194] 'very

---

[190] *Mirvahedy v Henley* [2003] UKHL 16, para 135; [2003] 2 AC 491.

[191] As in the *scienter* action, eg *Card v Case* (1848) 5 CB 622.

[192] Discussed below, paras 2.128–2.166.

[193] Robustly described as 'judicial excoriation': Lord Scott in *Mirvahedy v Henley* [2003] UKHL 16, para 88; [2003] AC 491.

[194] [2001] EWCA Civ 1749, para 18; [2002] QB 769; and see *Gloster v Chief Constable of Greater Manchester Police* [2000] PIQR 114, 116–17; *Freeman v Higher Park Farm* [2008] EWCA Civ 1185; [2009] PIQR 103, 107.

cumbrously worded',[195] 'remarkably opaque',[196] 'tortuous',[197] 'inept',[198] 'elusive meaning',[199] and the source of 'puzzlement'.[200] The House of Lords in the same case[201] felt no happier, describing the provision as 'opaque' and an instance where 'the parliamentary draftsman's zeal for brevity has led to obscurity',[202] 'tortuous language',[203] 'ambiguous',[204] and 'cumbersome'.[205]

(1) The kind of damage: section 2(2)(a)

2.64 The first requirement of section 2(2) is that the keeper of an animal which is not of a dangerous species will only be liable if the damage caused by his animal is of a kind which the animal, unless restrained, was likely to cause or if the animal, although unlikely to cause damage, would, nevertheless, be likely, if it caused any damage, to cause severe damage. These two elements will be considered separately, but it should be emphasized that this double-barrelled condition in section 2(2)(a) relates to the particular animal in question, rather than generally to animals of that species.[206]

2.65 It has been made clear by the Court of Appeal that, in determining the meaning of section 2(2)(a), the court should examine the wording of that provision without attempting to read words 'into requirement (a) itself through a process of implication effected by reference to the succeeding requirements'.[207] In other words, it is not appropriate to have regard to the issue of whether the animal has any abnormal characteristics in deciding whether the requirements of section 2(2)(a) have been met.[208] The correct approach is for judges to examine each of the requirements of section 2(2) in sequence, considering 'each part of the subsection in turn and satisfy themselves that the plaintiff has made out his case on one or other of the limbs of each part',[209] bearing in mind that, at the end of the day, the parts have to be considered in conjunction with each other. The consequence of this analysis is that

---

[195] *Cummings v Granger* [1977] QB 397, 404.
[196] Ibid, at p 407; and see *Bearfield v Culmer* (1981) Unreported, 17 July.
[197] *Curtis v Betts* [1990] 1 WLR 459, 462.
[198] Ibid, at p 468.
[199] *Breeden v Lampard* (1985) CA, Unreported, 21 March.
[200] Ibid.
[201] [2003] UKHL 16; [2003] AC 491.
[202] Ibid, at para 9.
[203] Ibid, at para 31.
[204] Ibid, at para 88.
[205] Ibid, at para 140.
[206] *Freeman v Higher Park Farm* [2008] EWCA Civ 1885; [2009] PIQR 103, 108; and see *Curtis v Betts* [1990] 1 WLR 459, 462.
[207] *Curtis v Betts*, above, at p 463; and see at p 469; and see *Cummings v Granger* [1977] QB 397, 404; *Smith v Ainger* (1990) CA, Unreported, 16 May.
[208] Disapproving the approach taken in P North, *The Modern Law of Animals* (1971), p 463 which has, however, been said to fit the wording of s 2(2)(a) better: WH Rogers, *Winfield and Jolowicz on Tort*, 18th edn (2010), p 806.
[209] *Curtis v Betts*, above, at p 471.

section 2(2)(a) has a much wider scope than would have been the case with the alternative approach.

2.66 Furthermore, both conditions depend on 'likelihood', ie that the animal is likely to cause the kind of damage in question or, if not, that any damage is likely to be severe.[210] It has been suggested that 'likely' is, in essence, concerned with foreseeability and there has been a willingness to give it a broad meaning.[211] That said, a mere possibility of the animal causing the kind of damage in question,[212] or of its being severe, does not satisfy the condition in section 2(2)(a).[213] In *Smith v Ainger*,[214] consideration was given by Neill LJ to just where the meaning of 'likely' should be pitched. While in many contexts 'likely' means 'probable' or 'more probable than not', he felt that, in the context of section 2(2)(a), it should be given a wider meaning so as to include an event 'such as might well happen' or 'where there is a material risk that it will happen'. His justification for this conclusion was that:

> Parliament cannot have intended that a keeper of a dog with a known propensity to bite strangers could escape liability by establishing that only 40 per cent of such persons had been bitten in the past.

This analysis was the subject of comment by Lord Scott in *Mirvahedy v Henley*,[215] where he agreed with Neill LJ's rejection of probability, but expressed concern over the term 'such as might well happen' as being too wide, in that it might include a mere possibility. He preferred the dictionary definition of 'reasonably to be expected', consistently with his view of the meaning of 'likely' in section 6(2)(b).[216]

(a) Likely kinds of damage

2.67 Under the first condition in section 2(2)(a), the keeper will be liable if the damage was of a kind that the animal, unless restrained, was likely to cause. Where the animal has not behaved in an abnormal way before, it is unlikely that this condition will be satisfied. So, where a horse bucked and injured the claimant, this condition was held not to have been satisfied because the horse had never bucked in this manner before,[217] a decision which might be compared with that where the defendant's horse was held to have been likely to cause damage to the claimant by crushing her

[210] 'Likelihood' is also a requirement of s 2(2)(b), below, paras 2.76 et seq, and of s 6(2)(b), above, para 2.48.

[211] *Hunt v Wallis* [1994] PIQR 128, 139.

[212] *Whippey v Jones* [2009] EWCA Civ 452, paras 20–21; and see *Elliott v Townfoot Stables* [2004] CLY 169.

[213] *Mirvahedy v Henley*, above, paras 95–7; and see *Freeman v Higher Park Farm* [2008] EWCA Civ 1185; [2009] PIQR 103, 109.

[214] (1990) CA, Unreported, 16 May.

[215] Above, para 96.

[216] See above, para 2.48. In Scotland, it has been indicated that, in considering the use of the term 'likely' in the Animals (Scotland) Act 1987, the court should not 'propose a definition of the word which the statutory draughtsman has not thought it necessary or appropriate to provide': *Welsh v Brady* [2009] CSIH 60; 2009 SLT 747, 749.

[217] *Freeman v Higher Park Farm* [2008] EWCA Civ 1185; [2009] PIQR 103, 108.

arm in a horse box, given that the horse had earlier misbehaved in a similar way.[218] Where a dog attacked a woman carrying a bag, the court held that section 2(2)(a) was satisfied because, given that the dog had previously attacked other people carrying bags, the damage was of a kind that this dog, unless restrained, was likely to cause.[219] On the other hand, where a large dog knocked into the claimant causing him to fall down a slope, breaking his ankle, it was held that such damage was not likely to be caused by the dog.[220]

(b) Likelihood of damage, if caused, being severe

The situation under consideration here is, logically, one where the animal is not likely to cause damage unless restrained, but where, if it did cause damage, that damage is likely to be severe. An early example under the 1971 Act is provided by *Cummings v Granger*,[221] where it was held that section 2(2)(a) was satisfied in the case of an attack by an Alsatian because, if such a dog did attack anyone, the damage was 'likely to be severe'.[222] It seems to have been assumed that the Alsatian was not likely generally to cause damage. Again, in *Curtis v Betts*,[223] a docile and lazy bull mastiff was held not to be likely to cause damage but that, when jumping up and biting a child, the damage it caused was likely to be severe.[224] If a horse bucks when beginning to canter, causing the claimant to fall off, it has been held that it is reasonable to expect that severe injury will result.[225] In the case of a very heavy horse, it has been held that any damage it causes is likely to be severe;[226] and the same has been said of a heavy cow.[227] It has also been held that damage caused by a bantam cockerel was likely to be severe.[228] **2.68**

---

[218] *Wallace v Newton* [1982] 1 WLR 375.

[219] *Kite v Napp* (1982) Unreported, 26 May; and see *Kane v McKenna* (1991) 1 BNIL 105; and see (1992) 2 BNIL 125, where the damages award was reduced: attack by a cockerel on a child, the cockerel having previously attacked and killed a goat.

[220] *Whippey v Jones*, above.

[221] [1977] QB 397.

[222] Ibid, at p 404; and see *Bearfield v Culmer* (1981) Unreported, 17 July; *Smith v Ainger* (1990) CA, Unreported, 16 May; *Dhesi v Chief Constable of West Midlands Police* [2000] Po LR 120; *Gloster v Chief Constable of Greater Manchester Police* [2000] PIQR 114, 117.

[223] [1990] 1 WLR 459, 462.

[224] And see *Burley v Gilbert* (1980) CA, Unreported, 25 April (Chow); *Kite v Napp* (1982) Unreported, 26 May (Irish Wolfhound); *Cockrill v Muff* (1987) CA, Unreported, 17 June (Labrador cross); *Hunt v Wallis* [1994] PIQR 128, 139 (Border Collie); *Chauhan v Paul* (1998) CA, Unreported, 19 February (Rotweiller).

[225] *Freeman v Higher Park Farm* [2008] EWCA Civ 1185; [2009] PIQR 103, 110; and see *Breedon v Lampard* (1985) CA, Unreported, 21 March; *Flack v Hudson* [2001] QB 698; *Walsh v Connolly* [2006] NIQB 102; cf *Elliott v Townfoot Stables* [2004] CLY 169; *Welsh v Stokes* [2007] EWCA Civ 796, paras 29, 33; [2008] 1 WLR 1224.

[226] *Jaundrill v Gillett* (1996) CA, Unreported, 16 January; *Clark v Bowlt* [2006] EWCA Civ 978; [2007] PIQR 143; and see *Mirvahedy v Henley* [2003] UKHL 16, paras 52, 68; [2003] 2 AC 491, where damage from a collision on the highway with an escaped horse was held to be likely to be severe; although see the doubts of Lord Scott, at paras 98–100.

[227] *Mirvahedy v Henley*, above, at para 46; and see *McKenny v Foster* [2008] EWCA Civ 173.

[228] *Kane v McKenna* (1991) 1 BNIL 105; (1992) 2 BNIL 125.

2.69 One should note that liability under this second head of section 2(2)(a) is based on the fact that the damage is likely to be severe. There is no requirement that in the actual eventuality it was severe, only that it was likely to be so.

(c) What kind of damage?

2.70 The alternative conditions in section 2(2)(a) refer to the 'kind of damage' which the animal is likely to cause or which, if caused, is likely to be severe. In most cases the nature of the damage caused will be of a kind which is likely, but what if the animal is likely to cause one kind of damage and then causes a different kind? This issue arose in *Smith v Ainger*,[229] where the claimant was injured when the defendant's dog—an Alsatian cross—attacked his dog but, in the process, knocked the claimant over, breaking his leg. The Court of Appeal was of the opinion that, while the defendant's dog was likely to attack other dogs, the damage in issue in this case was personal injury to the claimant, and the trial judge had held that the dog had no propensity to attack humans. However, on the evidence the dog had in the past attacked another dog and, in the process, had bitten its owner. In the light of that evidence, the Court of Appeal disagreed with the trial judge and concluded that the dog was likely to cause damage of the kind suffered by the claimant. Had there been no evidence of earlier bites, it is doubtful whether the first condition of section 2(2)(a) could have been satisfied.

2.71 The Court of Appeal also concluded that the second condition of section 2(2)(a) was satisfied, in that the damage was of a kind which was likely to be severe. It should be noted that the problem with the first condition does not arise in relation to the second condition. There is no requirement of likelihood of causing damage of the kind actually inflicted, only of a likelihood of the damage caused being severe. So even though there might have been no likelihood of this Alsatian cross causing damage to a person, if it did cause such damage there was a likelihood that, it being a large dog with sharp teeth, any damage would be severe.[230]

2.72 It is also necessary for the damage to be 'caused by' the animal of a non-dangerous species and the question has been raised as to how this might be determined. Wall J has suggested[231] that it must be a question of fact, giving the example of a claimant who, when barked at by an 'innocuous' dog, jumps into the path of an oncoming car. He suggested that, in such a case, the injuries were not caused by the dog but, rather, by the claimant's excessive reaction to the dog's bark. On the other hand, if the claimant was approached at speed by a large dog and chose to run away, then any injury resulting from falling over in the chase or 'having a heart attack' would have been caused by the dog.[232]

---

[229] (1990) CA, Unreported, 15 May.
[230] cf Lord Scott in *Mirvahedy v Henley*, above, at para 101.
[231] *Chauhan v Paul* (1998) CA, Unreported, 19 February.
[232] Ibid.

There are two final issues which are relevant to a discussion of the kind of damage for which liability is imposed under section 2(2). As has been seen,[233] a definition of 'damage' is provided by section 11 of the Animals Act 1971, as follows: '"Damage" includes the death of, or injury to, any person (including any disease and any impairment of physical or mental condition)' and the range of damage covered by section 2 has already been discussed in the context of section 2(1).[234] Similar issues arise in the context of liability under section 2(2). So, liability for non-dangerous animals has been held to cover personal injuries resulting from dog bites,[235] being knocked over by a dog,[236] being kicked[237] or squashed by,[238] or thrown from,[239] a horse, as a result of a highway collision with a horse,[240] and of an attack by a cockerel.[241] It will also include damage to property resulting from such incidents.[242] **2.73**

First, if the victim of an attack by an animal which is dangerous within the meaning of section 2(2) is killed by that animal, then his dependants[243] will have a right of action under the Fatal Accidents Acts 1846–1959.[244] If the claimant, or his animals, is infected by the disease carried by the defendant's animal and this abnormal state is known to the defendant, then again the defendant will be liable.[245] Whether a claimant could ever recover under section 2(2) for nervous shock is probably unlikely, for few animals of a non-dangerous species can have characteristics such that they are likely to cause nervous shock;[246] but there might well be liability for causing a heart attack.[247] **2.74**

Second, so far as remoteness of damage is concerned, it is suggested that the rule applicable under section 2(2) will be the same as that in relation to section 2(1),[248] namely a rule of direct consequences, rather than of reasonable foresight,[249] but restricted by the fact that liability will be limited to that which results from dangerous characteristics known to the keeper. **2.75**

---

233 See above, para 2.58.

234 Ibid.

235 *Cummings v Granger* [1977] QB 397; *Burley v Gilbert* (1980) CA, Unreported, 25 April; *Bearfield v Culmer* (1981) Unreported, 17 July; *Kite v Napp* (1982) Unreported, 26 May; *Cockrill v Muff* (1987) CA, Unreported, 17 June; *Curtis v Betts* [1990] 1 WLR 459.

236 *Smith v Ainger* (1990) CA, Unreported, 16 May.

237 *Walsh v Connolly* [2006] NIQB 102.

238 *Wallace v Newton* [1992] 1 WLR 375.

239 *Harrison v Gledstone* (1987) CA, Unreported, 30 June; *Flack v Hudson* [2001] QB 698; *Welsh v Stokes* [2007] EWCA Civ 797; [2008] 1 WLR 1224.

240 *Mirvahedy v Henley* [2003] UKHL 16; [2003] 2 AC 491.

241 *Kane v McKenna* (1990) Unreported, 30 November.

242 eg *Mirvahedy v Henley*, above.

243 eg *Flack v Hudson*, above.

244 See Animals Act 1971, s 10, above, para 2.58.

245 cf *Weller & Co v Foot and Mouth Disease Research Institute* [1966] 1 QB 569; *D Pride and Partners v Institute of Animal Health* [2009] EWHC 686.

246 cf *Gilligan v Robb* 1910 SC 856.

247 *Chauhan v Paul* (1998) CA, Unreported, 18 February.

248 Above, para 2.60.

249 And see Davis (1945) 18 ALJ 338.

(2) Abnormal characteristics: section 2(2)(b)

2.76 Section 2(2)(b) contains two alternative propositions, namely that the likelihood[250] of damage or of its being severe was either due to characteristics of the animal which, first, are not normally found in animals of the same species or, second, are not normally so found except at particular times or in particular circumstances. There is little doubt that the meaning of this provision has caused more difficulty of interpretation than any other provision of the 1971 Act.

2.77 The first of the propositions in section 2(2)(b) is much less problematic than the second. It is said that this proposition 'embraces a case where animals of the species are normally docile but the particular animal is not'.[251] What has to be shown is that one or other of the kinds of damage laid down in section 2(2)(a) was caused by the animal having characteristics which are abnormal for its species.[252] So, where injury was caused to the claimant as a result of the excitable characteristics of a Border Collie which were common to all such dogs, the defendant was not liable,[253] and the same has been said of a propensity to attack other dogs.[254] However, where an Alsatian attacked and bit a child who was patting it, the owner of the dog was held liable because the court concluded that it was not a natural characteristic of Alsatians to attack humans.[255] Turning to examples of problems with horses: where the claimant was injured because of the fact that the defendant's horse which she was riding was difficult to stop, this was held to be a characteristic which did not differentiate the horse from its species,[256] and nor have galloping,[257] kicking,[258] bucking,[259] biting,[260] inquisitiveness,[261] or a propensity occasionally to move other than as directed[262] been held to be characteristics not normally found in horses.[263] Where, however, a horse was inclined to bolt when in the vicinity of agricultural vehicles or machinery and did so, injuring the claimant, the defendant was held liable because the horse's bolting characteristic was not normally found in other horses,[264] nor was

[250] See discussion of 'likely', above, paras 2.48, 2.66.

[251] *Mirvahedy v Henley* [2003] UKHL 16, para 18; [2003] 2 AC 491.

[252] For the meaning of 'species', see, above, paras 2.05–2.10.

[253] *Hunt v Wallis* [1994] PIQR 128.

[254] *Smith v Ainger*, above.

[255] *Bearfield v Culmer* (1981) Unreported, 17 July; and see *Clinch v Sullivan* (1981) Unreported, 20 January; cf *Mirvahedy v Henley*, above, para 141.

[256] *Fox v Kohn* (1995) CA, Unreported, 2 November.

[257] *Jaundrill v Gillett* (1996) CA, Unreported, 16 January.

[258] *Walsh v Connolly* [2006] NIQB 102, para 18; and see *Breeden v Lampard* (1985) CA, Unreported, 21 March; *Doolan v EP Cornall & Sons* [2001] CLY 324; *Mirvahedy v Henley*, above, para 68.

[259] *Freeman v Higher Park Farm* [2008] EWCA Civ 1185; [2009] PIQR 103.

[260] *Whitehead v Alexander* [2000] CLY 205.

[261] *Fry v Morgan* [2006] CLY 192.

[262] *Clark v Bowlt* [2006] EWCA Civ 978, para 13; [2007] PIQR 143.

[263] Nor is the weight of the horse (or of a cow) a relevant characteristic because they are normal characteristics: *Mirvahedy v Henley*, above, paras 46, 48; *Clark v Bowlt*, above.

[264] *Flack v Hudson* [2001] QB 698; and see *Bennet v Bellm* [2005] CLY 189.

a horse's 'unpredictable and unreliable' behaviour characteristic of horses.[265] In the case of cattle, it has been held that the maternal instinct of a cow to seek out its calf is a normal characteristic.[266]

The second proposition in section 2(2)(b) has proved to be the troublesome one. **2.78**
The sub-section refers to characteristics of the animal which are not normally found in animals of the same species 'except at particular times[267] or in particular circumstances'.[268] Two strands of authority developed as to the meaning of this provision. The first might be described as the literal meaning approach and found support in two decisions of the Court of Appeal. The first was *Cummings v Granger*,[269] where the claimant was bitten by the defendant's Alsatian, which was used to guard his scrapyard. The dog was held to have the characteristic of 'barking and running around to guard his territory', characteristics which were not normally found in Alsatians except in circumstances, such as here, where they were used as guard dogs.[270] The court held that the requirement of section 2(2)(b) had been satisfied.[271] This decision was followed in *Curtis v Betts*,[272] a case concerned with an attack by a bull mastiff. Again, the issue was whether the dog had aggressive characteristics only found in particular circumstances, and it was decided that that requirement was satisfied when it attacked the claimant because the dog was held to be defending its territory and the trial judge had decided that 'bull mastiffs have a tendency to react fiercely at particular times and in particular circumstances, namely when defending the boundaries of what they regard as their own territory'.[273] In essence, this interpretation of section 2(2)(b) means that although, generally, there is no liability for harm done by an animal that behaves normally, even though aggressively, there will be liability for harm done by an animal which, while behaving normally but aggressively, is doing so in special circumstances where it is characteristic of the species so to behave.

The second strand of authority might be described as that of deciding what **2.79**
Parliament must have meant, rather than a literal reading of section 2(2)(b), ie that Parliament cannot have intended to hold the keeper liable for normal behaviour by his animal. This approach was also supported in two decisions of the Court of Appeal.

[265] *Wallace v Newton* [1982] 2 All ER 106.
[266] *McKenny v Foster* [2008] EWCA Civ 173.
[267] eg 'in the spring': *Kane v McKenna* (1991) 1 BNIL 105; (1992) 2 BNIL 125.
[268] eg when another dog 'offended [the defendant's dog] in some way'—*Smith v Ainger* (1990) CA, Unreported, 16 May; where a dog attacked people 'carrying shopping bags'—*Kite v Napp* (1982) Unreported, 26 May; or where a dog was in pain—*Collings v Home Office* [2006] CLY 160.
[269] [1977] QB 397.
[270] Ibid, pp 404, 407, 409.
[271] Although the claim failed because the claimant was held to have been a trespasser; see below, paras 2.149–2.150.
[272] [1990] 1 WLR 459; and see *Chauhan v Paul* (1998) CA, Unreported, 19 February.
[273] Ibid, at p 464.

The first was *Breeden v Lampard*,[274] where the claimant was injured during a hunt meeting when the defendant's horse kicked out and struck her leg. In considering section 2(2)(b), the Court of Appeal rejected the idea that the keeper should be held liable for what, as here, was considered to be normal behaviour by the defendant's horse, albeit only in the particular circumstances of the case, ie when approached too closely or too quickly from behind.[275] Lloyd LJ said:

> If liability is based on the possession of some abnormal characteristic known to the owner, then I cannot see any sense in imposing liability when the animal is behaving in a perfectly normal way for all animals of that species in those circumstances, even though it would not be normal for those animals to behave in that way in other circumstances, for example, a bitch with pups or a horse kicking out when approached too suddenly, or too closely, from behind.

This approach was summed up by Oliver LJ, saying: 'I cannot believe that Parliament intended to impose liability for what is essentially normal behaviour in all animals of that species.'

2.80 The same approach was also supported by Pill LJ in *Gloster v Chief Constable of Greater Manchester Police*,[276] a case concerning an Alsatian police dog biting a police officer. Although the Court of Appeal agreed that the claimant had failed to establish that the 'damage' element of section 2(2)(a) had been satisfied,[277] Pill LJ also took the view that the section 2(2)(b) requirement had not been satisfied either. Having quoted with approval the above comments of Lloyd LJ, he concluded that section 2(2)(b) 'is not concerned with animals behaving in a perfectly normal way for animals of the species or subspecies'.[278]

2.81 It fell to the House of Lords in *Mirvahedy v Henley*[279] to resolve the conflict between the two approaches. The claimant was injured when the car that he was driving collided with the defendant's horse, which, along with two other horses, had escaped from the defendant's field on to the road. It appeared that something had alarmed the horses and frightened them very badly so as to cause them to 'stampede' out of their field. It was held that such behaviour was usual in horses when alarmed by a threat: 'They attempt to flee, ignoring obstacles in their way, and are apt to continue in their flight for a considerable distance, even beyond the point where the perceived threat was detectable.'[280] The resolution of the conflict divided the House of

[274] (1985) CA, Unreported, 21 March.

[275] It should be noted, however, that the claim failed because the knowledge requirement of s 2(2)(c) was not satisfied; see, below, para 2.105.

[276] [2000] PIQR 114.

[277] See above, paras 2.64–2.75.

[278] [2000] PIQR 114, 118.

[279] [2003] UKHL 16; [2003] 2 AC 491; see Amirthalingam (2003) 119 LQR 563; Howarth [2003] CLJ 548.

[280] Ibid, at para 3; and see para 62. This might be compared with *Jaundrill v Gillett* (1966) CA, Unreported, 16 January, where the Court of Appeal did not think that escaped horses galloping in panic on a road were displaying a characteristic.

Lords 3–2. The majority[281] preferred the first approach, that adopted in *Cummings v Granger*,[282] while the minority[283] preferred that adopted in *Breeden v Lampard*.[284]

However, Lord Nicholls did not think that either approach provided a compellingly clear solution to the problem of identifying the dangerous characteristics which would exclude the keeper from strict liability because, in his view, 'a normal but dangerous characteristic of a species will usually be identifiable by reference to particular times or particular circumstances'.[285] Nevertheless, he concluded that the first approach should be adopted, not least because it 'accords more easily and naturally with the statutory language' and is more consistent with the legislative scheme recommended by the Law Commission.[286] A similar view was adopted by Lord Walker, who concluded that the first approach was both more consistent with the language of the 1971 Act and closer to 'the common experience of everyday life',[287] not least in circumstances such as those in this case, saying: **2.82**

> It is common knowledge (and was known to the defendants in this case) that horses, if exposed to a very frightening stimulus, will panic and stampede, knocking down obstacles in their path (in this case an electric fence, a post and barbed wire fence beyond that, and then high undergrowth) and may continue their flight for a considerable distance. Horses loose in that state, either by day or night, are an obvious danger on a road carrying fast-moving traffic. The defendants knew these facts; they could decide whether to run the unavoidable risks involved in keeping horses; they could decide whether or not to insure against those risks. Although I feel sympathy for the defendants, who were held not to have been negligent in the fencing of the field, I see nothing unjust or unreasonable in the appellants having to bear the loss from their horses' escape rather than the claimant (who suffered very serious and painful injuries in the accident, although he was wearing a seatbelt and slowed down as soon as he saw the first horse in his headlights).[288]

For the minority, Lord Scott took the view that the conditions in section 2(2)(b) should not be held to be met where damage 'is caused by an animal when responding to any external stimulus in a manner entirely normal for its species', giving the example of a horse which injures when shot by a catapult or jabbed in the rump with a sharp instrument.[289] He concluded that Parliament cannot have intended the subsection to have had this effect and that 'behaviour by the animal in a manner **2.83**

[281] Lords Nicholls, Hobhouse, and Walker.
[282] Above.
[283] Lords Slynn and Scott.
[284] Above.
[285] [2003] UKHL 16; [2003] 2 AC 491 at para 43; although in fact the courts have seemed well able to determine whether animals have characteristics which are or are not abnormal without having to refer to particular circumstances; see above, para 2.77.
[286] Ibid, at paras 44–5; and see Lord Hobhouse, at paras 70–73.
[287] Ibid, at para 156.
[288] Ibid, at para 157.
[289] Ibid, at paras 114–15.

normal for the species was not intended by Parliament to attract strict liability'.[290] Although he expressed the opinion that his approach is consistent with the language of the 1971 Act,[291] it is suggested that it is simply not possible to read section 2(2)(b) so as to reach that conclusion.

2.84 Since the decision in *Mirvahedy v Henley*, the courts have construed section 2(2)(b) in accordance with the views of the majority. For example, in *Freeman v Higher Park Farm*,[292] a case concerning injury caused to its rider by a bucking horse, the Court of Appeal, having decided that bucking was a normal characteristic of a horse, then went on to consider whether bucking was a characteristic normally to be found at particular times or in particular circumstances. They concluded that the defendant was not liable because there was no evidence that that was the case here in relation to a horse beginning to canter. This might be compared with *Welsh v Stokes*,[293] where the Court of Appeal concluded that, although rearing was a characteristic not normally found in horses, rearing, as in this case in the particular circumstances of the claimant trying to get the defendant's horse, which she was riding, to go forward, was a characteristic normally to be found in horses. As a consequence, the defendant was held liable for the claimant's injuries.

2.85 The courts have given attention to a number of detailed matters of interpretation of section 2(2)(b). Both propositions in the subsection use the term 'normally', ie as to whether the relevant characteristics of the animal are not 'normally' found. The meaning of this term was considered by the Court of Appeal in *Welsh v Stokes*.[294] Dyson LJ referred to the terminology used in *Mirvahedy v Henley*,[295] where there are passages suggesting, obiter, that the term means 'usually', rather than 'conforming to type' or 'naturally'. While 'usual' may include both of the other terms, he suggested that 'it does not necessarily follow that, if it is usual for horses to bolt when sufficiently alarmed, it is abnormal for them to bolt in such circumstances'.[296] Having considered the definition of 'normal' in the *Shorter Oxford Dictionary*,[297] he concluded that:

> The core meaning of 'normal' is 'conforming to type'. If a characteristic of an animal is usual, then it will certainly be normal. The best evidence that a characteristic conforms to the type of animals of a species is that the characteristic is usually found in those animals.[298]

[290] Ibid, at para 118.
[291] Ibid, at para 131; with which Lord Slynn concurred, at paras 57–60.
[292] [2008] EWCA Civ 1185; [2009] PIQR 103; and see *Walsh v Connolly* [2006] NIQB 102.
[293] [2007] EWCA Civ 796; [2008] 1 WLR 1224.
[294] Ibid; and see *Freeman v Higher Park Farm*, above.
[295] [2003] UKHL 16, at paras 3, 23; [2003] 2 AC 491.
[296] At para 43.
[297] As 'according to or squaring with a norm; constituting, conforming to, not deviating or differing from a type or standard, regular, usual'.
[298] At para 46.

Section 2(2)(b) requires the relevant 'characteristics' of the animal in question to be identified in order to determine whether such characteristics are not normally found in animals of that species or are only normally found at particular times or in particular circumstances. Consideration has been given in a number of cases to just what the term 'characteristics' means, although there is agreement that the determination of the existence of a characteristic is a question of fact in each case. In the House of Lords in *Mirvahedy v Henley*, Lord Walker[299] indicated that the expression cannot mean something 'buried in an animal's psyche' as it is inappropriate to introduce concepts of *mens rea* or malevolence in relation to animals.[300] It must, he said, 'refer to character or disposition as evidenced by overt behaviour', which he exemplified by the characteristic of a dog in attacking people carrying bags.[301] He suggested that any distinction between 'permanent' and 'temporary' characteristics[302] should be treated with some caution because: **2.86**

> All dangerous characteristics are likely to be more or less permanent but they may show themselves either frequently or randomly[303] . . . or under a stimulus peculiar to the particular animal[304] . . . or under some internal or external stimulus (such as the animal's hormones[305] or a perceived challenge to its territory[306]) which can be expected to produce similar behaviour in most animals of its species.[307]

In *Gloster v Chief Constable of Greater Manchester Police*,[308] the Court of Appeal was concerned with the issue of the liability of the police when an Alsatian police dog bit the claimant, a police officer. It had to be determined what was the relevant characteristic of this dog, and it was decided that it was not a propensity to bite, but, rather, the ability of the dog to respond to specific training and instruction, a characteristic normally found in Alsatians. In this context, Hale LJ made clear that characteristics may be innate or learnt, saying: **2.87**

> There are at least two good reasons for this. First, it would be impossible to know whether an animal's characteristics were a result of his character or of his early experiences. Secondly, some animals do not fall within the definition of a 'dangerous species' in section 6(2) because they are 'commonly domesticated in the British Isles' but

[299] [2003] UKHL 16, para 138; [2003] 2 AC 491.

[300] See *Behrens v Bertram Mills Circus Ltd* [1957] 2 QB 1, 18.

[301] *Kite v Napp* (1982) Unreported, 26 May.

[302] Drawn by Stuart-Smith LJ in *Curtis v Betts* [1990] 1 WLR 459, 469; and see *Smith v Ainger* (1990) CA, Unreported, 16 May.

[303] As with the unreliable horse in *Wallace v Newton* [1982] 1 WLR 375; or a horse being difficult to stop—*Fox v Kohn* (1995) CA, Unreported, 2 November.

[304] Such as bag carrying in *Kite v Napp*, above.

[305] eg a bitch defending its pups; *Cummings v Granger* [1977] QB 399, 407; and see *Barnes v Lucille Ltd* (1906) 96 LT 680.

[306] As in *Curtis v Betts*, above.

[307] In *Freeman v Higher Park Farm* [2008] EWCA Civ 1185; [2009] PIQR 103, the idea that the term 'particular' in the second limb of s 2(2)(b) somehow restricted characteristics to those which were not continuous, while those falling under the first limb would all have to be permanent, was rejected in the Court of Appeal.

[308] [2000] PIQR 114.

require early training in order to become so domesticated and thus not to have 'characteristics which are not normally found in animals of the same species.' Horses are an obvious example.[309]

2.88 Not all behaviour can readily be classed as a characteristic, as is illustrated by *McKenny v Foster*,[310] where a cow was held to have the normal characteristic of being agitated when separated from her calf, but the fact that the cow became so agitated that it climbed over a six-barred gate 'in the state of an excited wild animal' was regarded as 'scarcely a characteristic' and could not be described as a characteristic of either the cow or of its breed, even though the event actually occurred.[311]

(3) Interrelation of subsections 2(2)(a) and (b)

2.89 While the courts have made clear that it is important to consider each of the subsections in section 2(2) in order, and separately, it is also the case that they interrelate and this is clearly so in terms of the links between the damage requirement in section 2(2)(a) and the likelihood of the damage, or of its severity, being due to characteristics of the animal, under section 2(2)(b).[312] This can be illustrated by *Mirvahedy v Henley*,[313] where, it will be recalled, the claimant was injured by the defendant's horse which panicked and escaped on to the road, colliding with the claimant's car. The trial judge concluded that the claimant's damage was caused by the presence of the horse on the road, rather than by the characteristic of the horse in bolting when alarmed. However, the majority in the House of Lords[314] approved the rejection of such an approach by the Court of Appeal, where Hale LJ said:

> In this case, however, it is difficult to conclude that it was anything other than the particular characteristics of these horses once they had been terrified which led to their escape and to this accident taking place. They were still not behaving in the ordinary way in which they would behave when taken on the road. One witness referred to them bolting; another to them trotting across the road in front of the vehicles; they crashed into the vehicles rather than the other way about. It is precisely because they were behaving in the unusual way caused by their panic that the accident took place.[315]

2.90 The requirement for the causal link between the likelihood of damage and the characteristics of the animal may be illustrated by a number of decisions on the 1971 Act. So, the likelihood of damage to the claimant in *Curtis v Betts*[316] being severe was shown to have been due to the character of the defendant's dog in protecting

---

309 Ibid, at p 120; and see *Livesey v Chief Constable of Lancashire* (1994) Unreported, 10 November.
310 [2008] EWCA Civ 173.
311 Ibid, at para 39.
312 The interrelation of ss 2(2)(b) and (c) is considered, below, paras 2.99–2.107.
313 [2003] UKHL 16; [2003] 2 AC 491.
314 Ibid, at paras 48, 161–2.
315 [2001] EWCA Civ 1749, para 16; [2002] QB 769; and see *Welsh v Stokes* [2007] EWCA Civ 796, paras 39–40; [2008] 1 WLR 1225.
316 [1990] 1 WLR 459, 465–7; and see *Wallace v Newton* [1982] 1 WLR 375, 381.

its territory. Stuart-Smith LJ emphasized that, where the case falls under the second limb of section 2(2)(b), 'the time or circumstances in which the damage is caused must be those during which the particular characteristics are or were prone to be exhibited'.[317] This might be compared with *Dhesi v Chief Constable of the West Midlands Police*,[318] a case concerning a bite by an Alsatian police dog in the course of the arrest of the claimant. While it was found that the damage from a police Alsatian bite was likely to be severe, the injury was not due to the particular dog's characteristic of being inconsistent in tracking suspects because such a characteristic 'did not endanger the person being arrested so much as the handler'.[319] A similar view was reached in *Gloster v Chief Constable of Greater Manchester Police*,[320] where it was considered that the likelihood of damage being caused through the defendants' police dog biting the claimant police officer was not due to the characteristic of the dog having been trained as a police dog. Again, in *Clark v Bowlt*,[321] where the claimant was injured when his car was in collision with the defendant's horse, it was held that, although the weight of the horse meant that any damage was likely to be severe, the claim failed because the weight of the horse was a normal characteristic, even though causative of the damage.

The need for a causal link may also be illustrated by *Jaundrill v Gillett*,[322] where the claimant was injured when his car collided with the defendant's horses which had escaped from his field through a gate left open by intruders. The accident occurred when the horses were galloping along the road. Although the Court of Appeal had doubts as to whether galloping on the highway at night could be described as a characteristic, the court concluded that, even if it could be, that was not the cause of the claimant's injuries, because 'the real and effective cause . . . was the release of the animals onto the highway and their remaining there'. Similarly, in *McKenny v Foster*,[323] where, it will be recalled, a claim for injury resulting from a collision between a car and a cow which had escaped over a six-barred gate failed. The Court of Appeal concluded that the characteristic relied on by the claimant, namely agitation from the cow's normal maternal instinct in search of its calf, was neither dangerous nor causative, whereas the causative behaviour, namely 'exceptional and exaggerated agitation . . . so that the [cow] was in the state of an excited wild animal' was neither normal in the context of a cow separated from it calf nor known to the defendant.[324] **2.91**

---

[317] Ibid, at p 470.
[318] [2000] Po LR 120.
[319] Ibid, at p 124.
[320] [2000] PIQR 114.
[321] [2006] EWCA Civ 978; [2007] PIQR 143.
[322] (1996) CA, Unreported, 16 January.
[323] [2008] EWCA Civ 173.
[324] Ibid, at paras 39–40. This decision might be compared with that in *McKaskie v Cameron* (2009), Unreported, 1 July, where cows with calves attacked the claimant when walking her dog on the land

(4) Reform of section 2(2)(b)

2.92 In considering whether liability under section 2(2)(b) should extend to harm done by non-dangerous animals behaving in a normal way, there was clear realization in the House of Lords in *Mirvahedy v Henley*[325] that this involved a choice as to where the burden of responsibility, risk, and insurance should lie;[326] although it was perceived to be a choice for Parliament, rather than the courts. The role of the latter was to try to determine what Parliament had decided, through interpreting the provisions of section 2(2).[327] However, Lord Nicholls outlined the choice involved:

> Considered as a matter of social policy, there are arguments in favour of answering this question [whether the keeper should be liable for normal activity of an animal of the species in question] yes, and arguments in favour of answering no. It may be said that the loss should fall on the person who chooses to keep an animal which is known to be dangerous in some circumstances. He is aware of the risks involved, and he should bear the risk. On the other hand, it can be said that, negligence apart, everyone must take the risks associated with the ordinary characteristics of animals commonly kept in this country. These risks are part of the normal give and take of life in this country.[328]

The majority in the House of Lords interpreted section 2(2)(b) as placing the risk on the keeper of the animal.

2.93 That conclusion caused considerable concern because of the breadth of liability which flowed from it. Such concern was expressed by a variety of bodies, such as the National Farmers Union, the Country Land and Business Association, the Association of British Riding Schools, and the British Horse Society, with anxiety over the probable high cost of insurance for farmers and those who run riding schools or keep horses. This concern led to a series of attempts, all so far unsuccessful, to amend the 1971 Act. This process started with two Private Member's Bills introduced in the House of Commons under the 'Ten Minute Rule'. The first of these was the Accidents Involving Animals (Strict Liability) Bill 2006, the purpose of which was to create a new defence to liability under the 1971 Act of showing all reasonable care to avoid an accident.[329] This Bill made no progress and the following year a further Bill was introduced, namely the Animals Act (Amendment) Bill 2007, which adopted a different approach. Instead of introducing a new defence, it

---

where they were pastured, it being considered normal for cows with calves, when troubled by the presence of a dog, to attack walkers; see below, para 6.29.

[325] [2003] UKHL 16; [2003] 2 AC 491.

[326] Ibid, at paras 72, 157; and see *Welsh v Stokes* [2007] EWCA Civ 796, para 47; [2008] 1 WLR 1224.

[327] Paras 7, 130–31; and see para 120.

[328] Para 6.

[329] 448 HC Deb (2006), cc 1297–9.

sought to limit the scope of section 2(2)(b) itself;[330] but this Bill also failed to make progress.

It seems clear that the government was sympathetic to attempts to amend the 1971 Act[331] and, when a further Bill, the Animals Act (Amendment) Bill 2008,[332] was introduced, the Department for Environment, Food, and Rural Affairs (DEFRA) provided advice on the Bill and the government expressed support for it.[333] However, the Bill failed to proceed because an insufficient number of MPs were present for the vote on Second Reading.[334] **2.94**

The matter was not allowed to rest there, given the concerns expressed by various organizations representing animal owners and rural businesses. This led the government to explore the possibility of amending the 1971 Act by means of a Legislative Reform Order, under the Legislative and Regulatory Reform Act 2006; and DEFRA issued a consultation document[335] in 2009 seeking views on the need for any amendment, the appropriateness of that proposed and of the legislative process suggested. The amendment proposed would replace section 2(2)(b) with a new provision referring to damage caused by 'unusual or conditional' characteristics of the animal. Unusual characteristics were defined as those not shared by the species generally, and conditional characteristics were those shared generally by the species, but only in particular circumstances. In the case of unusual characteristics, liability would depend on the keeper having knowledge of the characteristic; and, in the case of conditional characteristics, there would be a defence if the keeper could show that, at the time of the incident, 'there was no particular reason to expect that the particular circumstances that provoked the conditional characteristic would arise at that time'.[336] The DEFRA proposal was intended to have the same effect as the unsuccessful Private Member's Bill in 2008. **2.95**

Some thirty-five organizations responded to the consultation and, although a large majority supported clarification of the 1971 Act, only about a third agreed with the proposed amendment. When the Consultation Response was published by DEFRA in March 2010, the government did not accept the minority of comments opposed to any amendment of the 1971 Act and indicated that, having regard to the detailed **2.96**

[330] 462 HC Deb (2007), cc 335–8.

[331] See 445 HC Deb (2006), c 971; 462 HC Deb (2007), c 337.

[332] See 468 HC Deb (2007), c 854; 473 HC Deb (2008), cc 514–88. This Bill was introduced by Stephen Crabb MP, who had introduced the previous Bill with the same title; but this time he introduced the Bill on the basis of his success in the ballot for Private Member's Bills.

[333] 473 HC Deb (2008), cc 536, 547.

[334] Ibid, c 588.

[335] Consultation on changes to the Animals Act 1971 to clarify the application of strict liability to the keepers of animals: March 2009.

[336] The proposal would also simplify section 2(2)(b) by substituting the term 'the damage' for 'the likelihood of the damage or of its being severe', as suggested in *Curtis v Betts* [1990] 1 WLR 459, 463, 468, 470.

comments made, it would 'press ahead' with preparing further proposals to amend section 2(2)(b). However, it accepted that further work was needed on the drafting and to meet a number of concerns. No new proposals have come forward, as yet; but it would appear that the use of a Legislative Reform Order is not regarded as an appropriate legislative procedure for such a reform, with the result that reform may have to await another opportunity via a Private Member's Bill.

(5) **Knowledge: section 2(2)(c)**

2.97 The final condition of liability under section 2(2) is that provided by section 2(2)(c). The keeper of an animal will be liable if the abnormal characteristics of the animal in question, whether those not normally found in such animals or not normally found at particular times or in particular circumstances:

> were known to that keeper or were at any time known to a person who at that time had charge of the animal as that keeper's servant or, where that keeper is the head of a household, were known to another keeper of the animal who is a member of that household and under the age of sixteen.

There are, therefore, three situations envisaged here: the knowledge of the keeper himself or his 'vicarious knowledge' through either an employee or a member of his household under the age of 16. There seems little doubt that what constitutes knowledge of the abnormal characteristics will be the same in each case. Furthermore, there is no definition of knowledge in the Animals Act 1971. That being so, one may assume that it is an issue left to be resolved by the common law and that the meaning of knowledge for the purposes of liability under section 2(2) will be similar to that for liability under the *scienter* action for animals *mansuetae naturae*. So the issue of knowledge will be considered in the light of both the common law decisions and those under the 1971 Act.

2.98 There are two aspects to the issue of knowledge, namely what has to be known, and by whom; these aspects will be considered separately.

(a) What has to be known

2.99 The requirement of knowledge is one of actual knowledge. It is not enough to claim that the keeper 'ought to have known';[337] although there are common law decisions where very slight evidence of knowledge was accepted.[338] What is it, however, in relation to section 2(2)(b), that has to be known by the defendant? The requirement of knowledge necessary for liability under section 2(2)(b) will vary depending on that part of the subsection on which the claim is based. If the basis is that the animal

[337] *Hunt v Wallis* [1994] PIQR 128, 140; and see *Chauhan v Paul* (1998) CA, Unreported, 19 February. If the defendant ought to have known of the animal's dangerous characteristics, then he may well be liable in negligence: *White v Steadman* [1913] 3 KB 340; and see ch 6.

[338] eg *Judge v Cox* (1816) 1 Stark 285; cf *Sneddon v Baxter* 1967 SLT (Notes) 67.

displayed characteristics not normally found in animals of that species, the required knowledge must be of those abnormal characteristics. If, however, the defendant's animal displays a common characteristic which would not normally make such an animal dangerous, then the defendant will only be liable if he actually knew of the propensity of his animal to display this characteristic in an abnormal and dangerous way. This might be illustrated by *McKenny v Foster*.[339] As may be recalled, the claimant's car collided with the defendants' cow which had strayed onto the road, and the passenger in the car was killed. The cow had escaped from the defendants' land by climbing or jumping over a six-barred gate, apparently in a state of extreme agitation in search of its calf. The general behavioural characteristic here was that of agitation from the normal maternal instinct of a cow with a calf, of which the defendants were aware. However, the dangerous behaviour which was causative of the accident was 'exceptional and exaggerated' agitation of which the defendants had no knowledge, and for which, as a consequence, they were held not liable.

2.100 The requirement of knowledge may be satisfied in a variety of ways. It is, obviously, enough to prove that the animal has, to the knowledge of its keeper, actually caused this kind of damage before. Thus, if the keeper knows that his dog has previously bitten a human being, that is adequate knowledge that it has characteristics such that it is likely to do so again.[340] Perhaps the most striking example of this is the common law decision in *Parsons v King*.[341] The claimant was a potman in a public house visited by the defendant and his terrier. The dog bit the claimant slightly and half an hour later in the street the dog bit the claimant more seriously and the claimant sought damages under the *scienter* action. During the half hour the defendant had taken no steps to secure the dog, and the claimant succeeded for

> the action was not for the first bite, but for the second. Half an hour had intervened between them, and during that time it was the duty of the defendant, who knew his dog had just bitten a man, to secure him in some way so as to prevent him from biting again. This he might very easily have done, but had not done.[342]

In *Kite v Napp*,[343] the defendant was held liable because she knew that her 'dog goes for people that hold bags', which was exactly what happened to the claimant as she was carrying a hold-all home.

2.101 It will also be enough to prove that the keeper knows that the animal has attempted to do the harm in question even though it has not yet succeeded in so doing. Thus, in the common law decision in *Worth v Gilling*,[344] the defendants kept a dog chained

---

[339] [2008] EWCA Civ 173.

[340] *Charlwood v Greig* (1851) 3 Car & Kir 46; *Pacy v Field* (1937) 81 Sol Jo 160; *Gladman v Johnson* (1867) 36 LJCP 153.

[341] (1891) 8 TLR 114.

[342] Ibid, at p 115.

[343] (1982) Unreported, 26 May; and see *Burley v Gilbert* (1980) Unreported, 25 April; *Bearfield v Culmer* (1981) Unreported, 17 July.

[344] (1866) LR 2 CP 1; and see *Wood v Vaughan* (1888) 28 NBR 472.

to its kennel on a seven-foot chain, and they knew that, whenever anyone passed, it ran out to the limit of its chain, barking and trying to bite. When it succeeded in biting the claimant in the arm the defendants were considered to have knowledge of its ferocity, as they knew of its attempts to bite. The 1971 Act applies in a similar way, as illustrated by *Cummings v Granger*,[345] where it was found that the characteristics of the defendant's Alsatian of barking and running around to guard its territory were not normally found in such dogs except, as here, 'where they were used as guard dogs',[346] and these particular characteristics were known to the defendant. If, however, the animal unexpectedly causes injury in quite different conditions, then the defendant will not have had the requisite knowledge and will not be liable.

2.102 If it can be proved that the keeper knows that the animal has a vicious characteristic which make it aggressive in certain conditions, that will be sufficient even though the animal has not yet attempted to cause any injury. In such a case, the defendant will be liable when the animal attacks and injures the clamant when these conditions are present. At common law, this can be illustrated by *Barnes v Lucille Ltd*,[347] where the defendant's chow bitch with pups bit the claimant, an employee of the defendants, but it was not clear that the defendants knew that the dog had bitten or attempted to bite anyone before, although they did know that it had a propensity to do so and was dangerous unless guarded. It was sufficient to know that the dog would be likely to bite without provocation.[348] Thus, if an owner knows that 'his bull would run at anything red', this has been held to be evidence that he is aware that it is a dangerous animal.[349] Again, the fact that the defendant had warned people to take care lest her dog bite them was considered evidence of *scienter*.[350]

2.103 In relation to the second limb of section 2(2)(b) of the 1971 Act, it has to be shown that the defendant had the requisite knowledge of the dangerous characteristics in the particular circumstances. This may be illustrated by *Curtis v Betts*,[351] where the claimant was bitten by the defendants' large bull mastiff when being loaded on to a Land Rover at the roadside. The dog was held to have the characteristic of acting fiercely when defending its territory, a school playground. Evidence of the fact that the defendants exercised the strictest control over their dogs, in 'almost a military operation', when they were taken out, and the fact that the dog growled and snarled at passers-by, was held to satisfy the requirement of knowledge of the dog's dangerous characteristics. However, a central issue for the Court of Appeal was whether the exceptional characteristic of defending its territory extended to the Land Rover at the roadside, because the defendants would not be liable if it could not be said to

345 [1977] QB 397.
346 Ibid, at p 404.
347 (1907) 96 LT 680.
348 Ibid, at p 681; and see *Duggan v Armstrong* [1992] IR 161.
349 *Hudson v Roberts* (1851) 6 Exch 697.
350 *Judge v Cox* (1816) 1 Stark 285.
351 [1990] 1 WLR 459.

extend to the roadside. The court concluded that the defendants were liable because it was reasonable to infer that the dog regarded the vehicle as part of his territory.

If, for example, the defendant is aware that his dog has characteristics which render it likely to attack other dogs, such knowledge may be sufficient to render him liable when, in such an attack, his dog also injures the owner of another dog, as in *Smith v Ainger*.[352] In this case, both the defendant and the claimant were walking their dogs. The defendant's large dog lunged at the claimant's dog and, in the course of doing so, knocked the claimant over, breaking his leg. The trial judge described the event as 'an attack by dog on dog to which the plaintiff's accident was incidental'. It was held, by the Court of Appeal, that the defendant's dog had a propensity to attack other dogs of which the defendant was aware. Furthermore, 'there was a material risk that the owner of the other dog would intervene to defend his own animal and would be bitten or buffetted as a result of his intervention'. Given that the damage to the claimant was of a kind that a dog which attacked other dogs was likely to cause and that it was likely to be severe, the defendant was held liable even though there was no known propensity of his dog to attack people. **2.104**

This decision might be compared with *Breeden v Lampard*,[353] where the defendant was riding a young horse in a hunt and had put a red ribbon on its tail, that being the usual sign to other riders not to come too close. The defendant had done this because of the youth and inexperience of the horse; but she was not held liable under section 2 of the 1971 Act when the horse kicked out at the claimant because the defendant's knowledge of the youth of her horse did not amount to knowledge of a propensity to kick out. At common law, the mere placing of a notice saying 'Beware of the dogs' on a front gate was held not to imply knowledge of a dog's viciousness;[354] and the fact that a dog was kept on a running lead did not of itself prove that the keeper knew of its vicious characteristic.[355] **2.105**

If the claim is based either on the abnormal characteristics of the defendant's animal or on dangerous characteristics which are found at particular times or in particular circumstances, then the required knowledge is that his animal had those characteristics. The defendant does not have to know whether such characteristics were abnormal or only found in special circumstances. **2.106**

Furthermore, the requirement of knowledge is satisfied if the keeper knows that animals of the same species normally display characteristics such as those displayed by the animal in question. This issue was examined by the Court of Appeal in *Welsh* **2.107**

---

352 (1993) CA, Unreported, 16 May; and see the decision, under the Animals (Scotland) Act 1987, in *Flynn v Lothian and Borders Police* (2010) Unreported, 12 August.

353 (1985) CA, Unreported, 21 March.

354 *Dolan v Bright* [1962] CLY 72; and see *Cruttendon v Brenock* [1949] VLR 366; *Simpson v Bannerman* (1932) 32 SR (NSW) 126, 133.

355 *Beck v Dyson* (1815) 4 Camp 198; *Hogan v Sharpe* (1837) 7 C & P 755; *McNeill v Frankenfeld* (1963) 44 DLR (2d) 132, 146.

v Stokes.[356] Here the claimant was injured when she fell off a horse, owned by the defendants, which had reared up and then fallen on her after she had tried to get it to move on. The court found that, although the horse had no previous history of misbehaviour, it was, like other horses, capable of rearing up in the particular circumstances that were encountered in this incident; but the court did not conclude that it had to be shown that the defendant knew that this particular animal had behaved in this way before. Dyson LJ said that the requirement as to the keeper's knowledge, under section 2(2)(c), can be satisfied if it can be established that he knew that horses, as a species, normally behave in the particular circumstances in the way in which this horse behaved, saying: 'It makes no sense to require a keeper, if aware of the general characteristic, to have some additional and more particular knowledge.'[357]

(b) Whose knowledge is relevant?

2.108 It will be recalled that the keeper of an animal is considered to have knowledge of his animal's abnormal characteristics in three circumstances, as laid down by section 2(2)(c). These must now be examined.

(a) The knowledge of the keeper himself

2.109 This is obvious. Whoever is the keeper will be liable if he, himself, knows of the animal's dangerous characteristics. Provided that the keeper has knowledge himself, or through third parties,[358] it does not matter that it was acquired from some other person's statement as to the dangerous nature of the animal.[359] There is, however, no general rule that the knowledge of one keeper is attributed to another keeper.[360] So the fact that the possessor of the animal has sufficient knowledge, and is liable as a keeper, does not mean that the owner, who is also a keeper,[361] is liable in the absence of knowledge.

(b) The knowledge of the keeper's servant

2.110 The keeper will be deemed to have knowledge of the animal's abnormal characteristics if they 'were at any time known to a person who at that time had charge of the animal as that keeper's servant'. There are a number of elements to examine here. The first is that the person who has the knowledge must be the servant of the keeper.

[356] [2008] EWCA Civ 796; [2008] 1 WLR 1224.

[357] Ibid, at para 71.

[358] This can be the knowledge of a servant or member of the keeper's household which is deemed to be that of the keeper, under s 2(2)(c), (see (b) and (c) below); or it may be that, because a third party has knowledge, it is assumed that this has been communicated to the keeper, below paras 2.119–2.122.

[359] *Soames v Barnardiston* (1689) Freem KB 430, 431–432; and see *McIntyre v Carmichael* (1870) 8 Macph (Ct of Sess) 570, 574; *Arnold v Diggdon* (1887) 20 NSR 303.

[360] This only applies in the case of a 'household' animal, below, paras 2.116–2.117.

[361] See s 6(3)(a).

This might be illustrated by *Baldwin v Casella*.[362] The defendant's dog was under the care and control of the defendant's coachman and was kept in the stables. The coachman knew of the dog's propensity to attack people and this knowledge was considered at common law, as it would be under the Animals Act 1971, to be attributable to the master, the keeper, whether it had been communicated to him or not. Again, knowledge by the defendant's servants that cattle, entrusted to their control to be driven along a highway, were dangerous, has been held, at common law, to be the knowledge of the defendant.[363]

The requirement that the person envisaged by section 2(2)(c) must be the servant of the keeper will both incorporate into the interpretation of this subsection all the learning on how to determine whether a person is a servant[364] and exclude anyone who does not fall into that category. It has been held, in Australia, that if the custody and control of an animal is delegated by the keeper to any third party, such as a friend as well as a servant, then the knowledge of the third party is, as a matter of law, that of the keeper.[365] This is not the position under the Animals Act 1971. The knowledge of a mere friend is not to be attributed to the owner as keeper. **2.111**

The second element relating to the knowledge of a servant is that the servant must have 'had charge of the animal as that keeper's servant'. He must both be in charge of the animal and be so in his capacity as a servant. It is not, therefore, enough that the person who has the knowledge of the characteristics of the keeper's animal is the keeper's servant unless he has some close relationship of control with the animal. The situation was the same at common law. Lord Coleridge CJ has said: 'It may be taken to be quite clear that a mere notice to any servant of the owner of the [animal] will not do.'[366] This might be exemplified by *Colget v Norris*,[367] where the defendant's dog bit the claimant, a postman, as he was delivering letters to the defendant's house. There was evidence that complaints about the dog had been made to the defendant's domestic servants, but that they had not been communicated to the defendant. The action failed because 'notice to the domestic servant could not be said to be notice to the master',[368] and the fact that the servant 'had taken the dog **2.112**

[362] (1872) LR 7 Exch 325; and see *Nadeau v City of Cobalt Mining Co* (1912) 3 DLR 495; cf *Shelfontuck v Le Page* [1937] 2 WWR 16, 19; affirmed [1938] 1 DLR 513.

[363] *Scott v Edington* (1888) 14 VLR 41, 50. It has since been doubted whether this is a true master/servant relationship in the case of drovers: *Queensland Stations Ply Ltd v Federal Commissioner of Taxation* (1945) 70 CLR 539.

[364] P Atiyah, *Vicarious Liability in the Law of Torts* (1967), Pt II; M Jones and A Dugdale, *Clerk and Lindsell on Torts*, 20th edn (2010), paras 6.04–6.27.

[365] *Cruttendon v Brenock* [1949] VLR 366, 370.

[366] *Applebee v Percy* (1874) LR 9 CP 647, 655; and see *Stiles v Cardiff Steam Navigation Co* (1864) 33 LJQB 310, 312.

[367] (1886) 2 TLR 414, and 471 (CA).

[368] (1886) 2 TLR 471, 472; and see *Stiles v Cardiff Steam Navigation Co*, above, where knowledge of porters or carters, employed by the defendant company, of the dangerous characteristics of a dog was insufficient to render the company liable, as the employees had no control over the business,

to the door and had occasionally washed it'[369] was insufficient to place the dog in the control of the servant. Equally, such an employee would not be considered to 'have charge' of the dog within the meaning of section 2(2)(c) of the Animals Act 1971. The same might well be said where the servant's only contact with the animal is that he has merely taken it for a walk,[370] or fed it occasionally.[371] An example of where the animal was in the charge of one servant but another servant had knowledge of its dangerous characteristics is provided by the Scottish decision in *Maclean v The Forestry Commission*.[372] The pursuer, an employee of the defenders, was injured by a horse belonging to them. Another of the defenders' employees knew that the horse was dangerous, but he was held not to have charge or control of the horse.[373] The employee who did have charge of it did not know of its dangerous characteristics. The court was not prepared to combine the knowledge of one employee with the control of the other. Lord Wheatley went so far as to say 'if each is to be regarded in his own way as the alter ego of the employers it seems to produce a schizophrenic legal persona, and I cannot imagine that the law leads to such a result'.[374]

2.113 Not only must the person in charge be a servant, but he must be in charge of the animal in that capacity in order for the keeper to be fixed with the employee's knowledge under section 2(2)(c). This may be illustrated by *Wallace v Newton*.[375] The claimant was employed by the defendant to look after a number of horses at the defendant's stables. She was injured by one of the horses becoming violent when loading it into a trailer. There had been a previous similar incident with the same horse, which the claimant had reported to the defendant's employee, who was employed as 'the head man in charge of the defendant's horses' and who had already warned the claimant to be careful with the horse in question. The knowledge of the employee was considered sufficient to satisfy section 2(2)(c).

2.114 The mere fact of a master/servant relationship does not necessarily lead to the conclusion that the former is fixed with the latter's knowledge of the animal's dangerous characteristics. An example where knowledge would not be attributed might be the case where an animal is kept by the employee for his own purposes as a pet

the premises, or the dog in question, even though the dog was kept for guarding and protecting the defendant company's premises.

369 (1886) 2 TLR 414, 415.

370 cf *Cleverton v Uffernel* (1887) 3 TLR 509.

371 cf *Cruttendon v Brenock* [1949] VLR 366, 374.

372 1970 SLT 265. The Animals Act 1971 does not apply to Scotland: see s 13(4); but see now the Animals (Scotland) Act 1987, where strict liability, under s 1, is not dependent on knowledge by the pursuer of the animal's dangerous attributes or habits.

373 There was some evidence that, at one stage, although not at the time of the accident, the employee who knew of the viciousness was in charge of the horse: 1970 SLT 265, 266–7. That would be enough, in an English case under s 2(2)(c) of the Animals Act 1971, for the defendants to have imputed knowledge: see below, para 2.115.

374 1970 SLT 265, 271.

375 [1982] 1 WLR 375.

and not on behalf of his employer, as in *Knott v LCC.*[376] Here, a school caretaker who lived on the school premises kept a large dog there which he knew to be vicious. The dog bit the claimant, a cleaner at the school, who alleged *scienter*, at common law, on the part of the defendants, the school authority. They had no knowledge of the existence, let alone the propensities, of the dog. It was held that the caretaker did not keep the dog as a servant, but for his own private purposes and so his knowledge was not to be attributed to the defendants. In such cases there would be no liability placed on the employer by section 2(2) of the Animals Act 1971 for the two reasons that the employer is not a keeper of the animal where he is neither owner nor possessor, and the employee is not in charge of the animal as an employee. There would still be no liability if, although the employer owned the animal and was, therefore, a keeper, the animal was kept by the employee as a pet or was being looked after by the employee during the employer's absence, unless this was done in his capacity as a servant.

The third, and final, element relating to the knowledge of a servant is that of time. **2.115** Section 2(2)(c) speaks of characteristics which 'were *at any time* known to a person who *at that time* had charge of the animal as that keeper's servant'.[377] The italicized phrases indicate that, for the knowledge of the servant to be deemed that of the master, the servant must have had his knowledge at a time when he was a servant, but that need not have been the time of the claimant's injury. Thus, if a servant has charge of an animal which he knows to be dangerous, that knowledge will be attributed to the master even though the injury occurs several years later[378] or at a time when the servant is no longer in charge of the animal,[379] nor employed by the master, or even when the servant is dead.[380]

(c) The knowledge of another keeper who is a member of the keeper's household under the age of sixteen

The keeper will be deemed to have knowledge of the dangerous characteristics of his **2.116** animal if, 'where that keeper is the head of a household, [the dangerous characteristics] were known to another keeper of the animal who is a member of that household and under the age of sixteen'. A number of the factors relevant to this provision in section 2(2)(c) were considered earlier when the definition of a keeper was examined. For example, it is necessary that the keeper to whom knowledge is to be attributed should be a head of a household and that the keeper under 16 should be

[376] [1934] 1 KB 126.

[377] Italics added.

[378] There was a time lag of a year in *Baldwin v Casella* (1872) LR 7 Exch 325; of two years in *Cruttendon v Brenock* [1949] VLR 366; and there was a four-year time lag in *Gladman v Johnson* (1867) 36 LJCP 153, below, para 2.121; a case of a wife's knowledge being evidence of her husband's.

[379] cf *Maclean v The Forestry Commission* 1970 SLT 265.

[380] 306 HL Deb (1969) cc 691–3; 312 HL Deb (1970) cc 846–9; 313 HL Deb (1970) cc 446–7.

a member of that household.[381] It is, however, also necessary that the member of the household must either own or possess the animal. A father will not be fixed with the knowledge of his children under 16 unless they are keepers of the animal also. This situation might be illustrated by the common law decision in *Elliott v Longden*,[382] where the owner of a dog was held liable for damage it caused by biting or frightening a horse and causing it to bolt, thereby injuring the horse and damaging the carriage it was pulling. The owner of the dog had no knowledge of its dangerous propensities, but his 11-year-old son did. That knowledge was considered to be enough for the defendant to be held liable in the *scienter* action. However, such knowledge was not held to be enough for the High Court of Australia,[383] and nor is it enough under section 2(2)(c) unless the child was also a keeper of the dog. Such a keeper must also be under the age of 16; there will be no knowledge attributable to the head of a household from the knowledge of a child who is a member of the household over 16.[384]

2.117 It has been argued that, in the case of a family household pet which 'is freely taken out in public by different members of a household, the knowledge of the propensity should as a matter of equity and general rule be attributed to all'.[385] This argument is not accepted in the Animals Act 1971 and, unless the provisions of section 2(2)(c) are satisfied, the knowledge of a child is not attributed to a parent as a matter of law, nor is the knowledge of a spouse or partner ever to be deemed to be that of the other spouse or partner.

2.118 There is also a 'time problem' in relation to the knowledge of a keeper under the age of 16 being attributed to a keeper who is the head of a household of which the child is a member. It will be recalled that the knowledge of a servant was attributed to his master whether or not the servant was still employed at the date of the accident, so long as he was in charge of the animal as a servant at the time when he acquired the knowledge.[386] The position in the present context is different. Section 2(2)(c) stipulates that the keeper who is the head of a household will be liable if the characteristics of the animal '*were* known to another keeper of the animal who *is* a member of that household and under the age of sixteen'.[387] Here the characteristics may be known to the young keeper at any time in the past, but he must still be a keeper and a member of the household and under the age of 16 at the time when the damage is caused to the claimant by the animal. If any of these requisites are not satisfied at the time of the injury, the head of the household will not be fixed with his knowledge.

381 Above, para 2.19.
382 (1901) 17 TLR 648; see also *Duggan v Armstrong* [1992] IR 161 and see below, para 7.06.
383 *Eather v Jones* (1974) 2 NSWLR 19; affirmed (1975) ALJR 254.
384 cf *McIntyre v Carmichael* (1870) 8 Macph (Ct of Sess) 570, 574; *Stanford v Robertson* [1946] 3 DLR 313.
385 *Flockhart v Ferrier* 1959 SLT (Sh Ct) 2, 4.
386 Above, para 2.115.
387 Italics added.

The obviously likely case is that where a child who knew of the characteristics when under 16 has now reached that age. When he does, his knowledge ceases to be imputed to the head of the household.

Finally, it should be mentioned that knowledge is imputed to the head of the household as keeper under section 2(2)(c) whether he is a keeper both by reason of his ownership or possession of the animal[388] and by reason of his headship of a household in which someone under 16 is also a keeper,[389] or whether he is a keeper merely by reason of the latter. This does not necessarily mean that a keeper will not have the knowledge of a third party attributed to him outside the provisions of section 2(2). There were a variety of circumstances at common law where the fact that a servant, child, or spouse had knowledge of an animal's dangerous characteristics led to a presumption that the master, parent, or other spouse had such knowledge. There is nothing in section 2(2) to indicate that such decisions will not be relevant to a determination of whether the keeper himself has knowledge; this being an issue quite separate from the issue of whether he is fixed with knowledge, which he may manifestly not have, through his servant or young member of his household. It could well be that 'the relationship of the defendant to the third party may be such that it is open to the jury[390] to infer, as a matter of probability, that the knowledge would be and was communicated'.[391] **2.119**

In the case of servants, there may be those who do not 'have charge' of the animal, but nevertheless know of its dangerous characteristics. In such cases, it has been held that 'notice to them of the vicious and ferocious nature of a dog kept about the premises . . . was, upon principle and upon authority, evidence fit to be submitted to the jury of a notice to their employer'.[392] Thus, where complaints of the viciousness of the defendant's dog were made to barmen serving in the defendant's public house, the knowledge of the barmen, although not considered as a matter of law to be that of their employer because the barmen were not in control of the dog, was evidence of the employer's *scienter* to be submitted to a jury.[393] Under section 2(2), the barmen's knowledge would not be deemed to be that of their employer, for they did not 'have charge' of the dog, but it is suggested that it could still be evidence of the keeper's own knowledge. **2.120**

The position has been held to be similar in the case of husband and wife. In *Gladman v Johnson*,[394] the knowledge by a wife of her husband's dog's vicious propensity **2.121**

388 Section 6(3)(a).
389 Section 6(3)(b).
390 Today, of course, the judge as trier of fact.
391 *Cruttendon v Brenock* [1949] VLR 366, 370. It was the view of the Law Commission, Report, para 79, that such inferred knowledge should remain.
392 *Applebee v Percy* (1874) LR 9 CP 647, 656.
393 Ibid.
394 (1867) 36 LJCP 153; and see *Norton v Fitzgerald* [1928] 3 DLR 474; *Flockhart v Ferrier* 1959 SLT (Sh Ct) 2.

acquired 4 years prior to the incident was attributed to her husband, not as a matter of law, but on the grounds that the jury could infer that the wife had told her husband of this. There is no reason why such knowledge of a spouse or partner should not be relevant under section 2(2) as evidence of the knowledge of the keeper. Furthermore, a similar approach should be adopted to one spouse or partner's knowledge raising an inference of communication to the other spouse or partner.[395] It should not be forgotten that, where a servant, spouse, partner, or member of a household is the keeper of an animal jointly with the master, other spouse, partner, or head of the household, then his knowledge of the animal's dangerous characteristics will be relevant to his own liability as keeper.[396]

2.122 Finally, it should be borne in mind that, as with the keeper, it is necessary to prove actual knowledge on the part of the third party whose knowledge under section 2(2)(c) is deemed to be that of the keeper. Where the knowledge of a spouse, partner, or child is attributed to the keeper, it is as evidence of the keeper's own knowledge.

7. Escape of a Dangerous Animal

2.123 Nothing in the Animals Act 1971 altered the general common law rule applicable to the *scienter* action that, in the case both of dangerous and non-dangerous animals, it was not necessary to prove that the animal escaped from the land on which it was kept. There could have been liability irrespective of where the animal caused the damage. The law was the same whether the claimant was injured or suffered loss on his own land,[397] on the defendant's land,[398] on a third party's land,[399] on the highway,[400] or, even, in a car.[401] The duty of the keeper of the animal both at common law and, now, under section 2 of the Animals Act 1971 is 'to keep that beast so confined as to be incapable of doing damage'.[402] So, similarly, there has been held to be liability under section 2 of the Animals Act 1971 where the claimant

[395] *Miller v Kimbray* (1867) 16 LT 360; Williams, pp 307–8.

[396] eg *Stanford v Robertson* [1946] 3 DLR 313 (child); *Duncan v Carleton* (1895) 11 TLR 524 (wife).

[397] eg *Read v Edwards* (1864) 17 CBNS 245; *Behrens v Bertram Mills Circus Ltd* [1957] 2 QB 1.

[398] eg *Besozzi v Harris* (1858) 1 F & F 92; *Wyatt v Rosherville Gardens Co* (1886) 2 TLR 282. There is also the possibility in such cases of an action based on occupiers' liability: eg *Gould v McAuliffe* [1941] 2 All ER 527; *Pearson v Coleman Bros* [1948] 2 KB 359; *McNeill v Frankenfeld* (1963) 44 DLR (2d) 132, 139–40; below, paras 6.26–6.33.

[399] eg *Parsons v King* (1891) 8 TLR 114: injury on the employer's premises.

[400] eg *Hudson v Roberts* (1851) 6 Exch 697; in these circumstances there may be liability in the absence of negligence, although negligence has for a long time been a usual requirement in other actions for injuries on the highway: see J Fleming, *Torts*, 9th edn (1998), p 404, n 91.

[401] *Sycamore v Ley* (1932) 147 LT 342.

[402] *Pearson v Coleman Bros* [1948] 2 KB 359, 380; and see *Read v J Lyons & Co Ltd* [1947] AC 156, 171; *Behrens v Bertram Mills Circus Ltd* [1957] 2 QB 1, 19.

was injured on the defendant's land,[403] the highway,[404] or a third party's land.[405] A corollary of the proposition that there need be no actual escape by the defendant's animal is that it is irrelevant to liability whether or not the defendant's animal is trespassing.[406]

A vexed issue at common law was whether the animal must have escaped from the defendant's control, even though it did not have to escape from the defendant's land. It was said by Lord Wright that: **2.124**

> It is not unlawful or wrongful to keep such an animal; the wrong is in allowing it to escape from the keeper's control with the result that it does damage.[407]

Nevertheless, it was quite sufficient for liability at common law for a lion to maul a child through its cage[408] or for a bear kept on a six-foot chain to seize someone walking past its house.[409] Such liability was justified by Crowder J in that: **2.125**

> A person who keeps such an animal is bound so to keep it that it shall do no damage. If it be insufficiently kept, or so kept that a person passing is not sufficiently protected, the owner is liable.[410]

However, in *Rands v McNeil*,[411] it would appear that the fact that there was no escape was considered significant in denying liability in the *scienter* action. The defendant kept a bull, known by him to be dangerous, for stud purposes. The bull was dehorned and kept untethered in a loose box. The claimant, the defendant's employee, entered the loose box without tethering the bull and he was injured when the bull charged at him. His action based on *scienter* failed and one of the reasons given in the Court of Appeal was that the bull had not escaped from the loose box.[412] Despite its obvious disadvantages, the requirement that the defendant **2.126**

---

[403] *Cummings v Granger* [1977] QB 397; *Bearfield v Culmer* (1981) Unreported, 17 July; *Wallace v Newton* [1982] 1 WLR 375; *Elliott v Townfoot Stables* [2004] CLY 169; *Walsh v Connolly* [2006] NIQB 102.

[404] *Curtis v Betts* [1990] 1 WLR 459; *Smith v Ainger* (1990) CA, Unreported, 16 May; *Kane v McKenna* (1991) 1 BNIL 105; (1992) 2 BNIL 125; *Fox v Kohn* (1995) CA, Unreported, 2 November; *Flack v Hudson* [2001] QB 698; *Mirvahedy v Henley* [2003] UKHL 16; [2003] 2 AC 491; *Clark v Bowlt* [2006] EWCA Civ 978; [2007] PIQR 143; *Welsh v Stokes* [2007] EWCA Civ 796; [2008] 1 WLR 1224; *McKenny v Foster* [2008] EWCA Civ 173.

[405] *Tutin v Mary Chipperfield Promotions Ltd* (1980) Unreported, 23 May; *Burley v Gilbert* (1980) CA, Unreported, 25 April; *Clinch v Sullivan* (1981) Unreported, 20 January; *Kite v Napp* (1982) Unreported, 26 May; *Breeden v Lampard* (1985) CA, Unreported, 21 March; *Freeman v Higher Park Farm* [2008] EWCA Civ 1185; [2009] PIQR 103; *Whippey v Jones* [2009] EWCA Civ 452.

[406] eg *Manton v Brocklebank* [1923] 2 KB 212, 231.

[407] *Knott v LCC* [1934] 1 KB 126, 138; and see *Maynes v Galicz* [1976] 1 WWR 557.

[408] *Pearson v Coleman Bros* [1948] 2 KB 359.

[409] *Besozzi v Harris* (1858) 1 F & F 92; *Wyatt v Rosherville Gardens Co* (1886) 2 TLR 282.

[410] Ibid, at p 93.

[411] [1955] 1 QB 253; noted by Payne (1955) 18 MLR 295; and see *Henderson v John Stuart (Farms) Ltd* 1963 SC 245.

[412] Ibid, at pp 257, 267, 269–71.

should only be liable if there was an escape or at least an escape from control was emphasized by Devlin J in *Behrens v Bertram Mills Circus Ltd*,[413] for he stated that:

> It does not follow . . . that if an elephant slips or stumbles, its keeper is responsible for the consequences. There must be a failure of control.[414]

2.127 The requirement of escape from control was not accepted by the Law Commission,[415] and there is no such requirement in the Animals Act 1971. It was abolished along with the abolition of the *scienter* action[416] and was not resuscitated for the purposes of statutory liability under section 2. If the defendant fails to restrain a dangerous animal or an animal with known dangerous characteristics, he will be liable if it causes injury. The animal need neither escape nor escape from control, nor, indeed, is there any need for an attack by it. It merely needs to injure. Therefore, there is now liability if an elephant 'slips or stumbles' and thereby causes injury, or if someone is injured by a dangerous horse or bull in its stall,[417] or simply by colliding with a cow[418] or a horse[419] in the middle of the road.

8. Defences

2.128 There are four defences to liability under section 2 for harm caused by dangerous animals which are provided by the Animals Act 1971. Two are peculiar to liability under section 2, while the other two are more general defences to liability under the 1971 Act. The two special defences will be examined first.

(1) Voluntary acceptance of risk

2.129 This is really the defence of consent and assumption of risk,[420] and it is provided by section 5(2) of the Animals Act 1971 that:

> A person is not liable under section 2 of this Act for any damage suffered by a person who has voluntarily accepted the risk thereof.

---

[413] [1957] 2 QB 1.

[414] Ibid, at p 19.

[415] Law Commission Report, para 19.

[416] Animals Act 1971, s 1.

[417] Subject to any defence of assumption of risk, the fault of the claimant or contributory negligence.

[418] eg *McKenny v Foster* [2008] EWCA Civ 173—although on the facts the defendant had no knowledge of the cow's relevant characteristics.

[419] eg *Jaundrill v Gillett* (1996) CA, Unreported, 16 January; *Mirvahedy v Henley* [2003] UKHL 16; [2003] 2 AC 491.

[420] For a discussion of the general principles of this defence, see M Jones and A Dugdale, *Clerk and Lindsell on Torts*, 20th edn (2010), paras 3.97–3.116; WH Rogers, *Winfield and Jolowicz on Tort*, 18th edn (2010), paras 25.2–25.17.

This defence is closely related to those of contributory negligence[421] and the default of the claimant.[422] If the claimant not only knows of the danger from the defendant's dangerous animal but also agrees, expressly or impliedly, to run the risk of that danger, he could not later complain of his injuries in the *scienter* action,[423] nor can he under section 2.[424]

While common law decisions on the defence of consent in the context of the *scienter* action are of illustrative interest, they have to be treated with some caution because Ormrod LJ has made clear that the words of section 5(2) should be read 'in their ordinary English meaning', without complicating 'the question too much with the old long history of volenti'. He added: **2.130**

> That doctrine was developed in quite different conditions. It has nothing to do with strict liability; and I would not, for my part, like to see that defence whittled down by too fine distinctions as to what 'voluntarily accepted the risk' means. They are, to my mind, fairly simple words and should in this context be treated as such.[425]

This general approach has since been approved and applied on a number of occasions.[426]

Knowledge alone of the dangerous characteristics will not suffice[427] and so the exercise of a right by the claimant cannot be prevented simply because the claimant knows that the defendant's dangerous animal may be in the vicinity.[428] On the other hand, the claimant must not be reckless, for: **2.131**

> The pursuit of one's own rights may sometimes be so foolhardy that the reasonable man should desist and seek another remedy. If a man is on the highway and he sees elephants approaching in procession, the law does not require him to elect between turning down a side street or accepting the risk of their misbehaviour if he goes on; but if he sees them stampeding and remains where he is because he considers that he has as much right to the highway as they have, he might fail to recover.[429]

Although it has been suggested that to intervene in a fight between your own and the defendant's dog may amount to consent or assumption of risk if you are bitten,[430] yet such a claimant acting in defence of his property ought to be in no worse position **2.132**

---

[421] Animals Act 1971, s 10, below, paras 2.159–2.164.

[422] Ibid, s 5(1), below, paras 2.154–2.158.

[423] *Rands v McNeil* [1955] 1 QB 253, 266; *Behrens v Bertram Mills Circus Ltd* [1957] 2 QB 1, 20–21; and see *Carroll v Kehoe* (1927) 61 ILTR 192; *Stanford v Robertson* [1946] 3 DLR 313, 316–17; affirmed [1947] 1 DLR 493.

[424] *Leniston v Phipps* (1988) CA, Unreported, 21 October; *Dhesi v Chief Constable of the West Midlands Police* [2000] Po LR 120.

[425] *Cummings v Granger* [1977] QB 397, 408.

[426] *Tutin v Mary Chipperfield Promotions Ltd* (1980) Unreported, May 23; *Flack v Hudson* [2001] 1 QB 698, 706–7; *Freeman v Higher Park Farm* [2008] EWCA Civ 1185, para 48; [2009] PIQR 103.

[427] *Shelfontuck v Le Page* [1938] 1 DLR 513.

[428] *Tarasoff v Zielinsky* [1921] 2 WWR 135, 140–41.

[429] *Behrens v Bertram Mills Circus Ltd* [1957] 2 QB 1, 20.

[430] *Smith v Shields* (1964) 108 Sol Jo 501.

than a third party who is injured when attempting to prevent harm being done. The latter is not taken to consent to his injuries if there is some 'serious exigency pressing upon him to incur the risk which he did'.[431] However, someone who climbs a barrier beside a leopard's cage to extinguish a smouldering cigarette-end clearly assumes the risk of being mauled,[432] as does someone who climbs up a lion's cage to reach a notice on top of it,[433] or goes into a Siberian tiger's cage to retrieve a cap.[434]

2.133 Section 5(2) has been held to have provided a defence when a trespasser entered premises where she was bitten by a guard dog in circumstances where there was a huge notice saying 'Beware of the Dog' and she knew of the dog's presence.[435] She was held to have known of the risk and had exposed herself to it.[436] Similarly, where the claimant was aware of the propensity of the horse that she was riding to buck, both from having been told of this by the defendant's employee and from having experienced this when first riding the horse, and having said that, nevertheless, she wanted to continue the ride, she was held to have assumed the risk of the horse doing it again and injuring her, which it did.[437] In the case of a claimant who fell off a camel during a celebrity camel race at Olympia, it was held that, although, applying an objective test, she knew of and accepted the risk of falling off a camel during the race, she did not contemplate or accept the risk of the defendant's employee starting off her camel before the race was intended to start, which was 'the real cause of her fall'.[438] If someone claims in negligence, rather than under section 2 of the Animals Act 1971, for the injuries caused by the defendant's animal, the defence of assumption of risk is equally applicable.[439]

2.134 There was some opposition to the inclusion of section 5(2) in the Animals Act 1971[440] and there is, undoubtedly, a danger that those who keep dangerous animals in zoos and parks will exculpate themselves by notices stating that the members of the public enter at their own risk.

2.135 There is a special provision in the Animals Act 1971 to deal with the issue of assumption of risk in the employment context. It is provided by section 6(5) that:

> Where a person employed as a servant by a keeper of an animal incurs a risk incidental to his employment he shall not be treated as accepting it voluntarily.

---

[431] *Sylvester v G B Chapman Ltd* [1935] LJCCA 261, 265. Compare *Cutler v United Dairies (London) Ltd* [1933] 2 KB 297, with *Haynes v Harwood* [1935] 1 KB 146.

[432] *Sylvester v G B Chapman Ltd*, above.

[433] *Young v Green* [1958] OWN 426.

[434] *Lewis v Oeming* (1983) 42 AR 58.

[435] *Cummings v Granger* [1977] QB 397, discussed further below, para 2.149.

[436] Ibid, at pp 410–11; cf *Flack v Hudson* [2001] QB 698, discussed above, para 2.16.

[437] *Freeman v Higher Park Farm* [2008] EWCA Civ 1185; [2009] PIQR 103.

[438] *Tutin v Mary Chipperfield Promotions Ltd* (1980) Unreported, May 23.

[439] See below, para 6.25 and see *Breen v Slotin* [1948] 4 DLR 46; *Collins v Richmond Rodeo Riding Ltd* (1966) 56 DLR (2d) 428.

[440] 305 HL Deb (1969) cc 1415–21.

The purpose of this provision would appear to be to alter an anomalous rule of the common law that an employer would only be liable to his employees for *negligently* subjecting them to risk or for providing an unsafe system of work. An employer was not held strictly liable to his employees under the *scienter* action. The leading authority for this rule was *Rands v McNeil*,[441] where the claimant, the defendant's employee, was injured by a bull kept in a loose box. His claim against his employer based on the *scienter* action failed, inter alia, because, as Jenkins LJ said:

> I do not think that this doctrine of absolute liability can reasonably be applied as between a farmer and the persons employed by him on his farm in relation to the handling by those persons of an animal such as a bull kept by the farmer for breeding purposes.[442]

This really amounted to an irrebuttable presumption of assumption of risk by the employee.[443]

If, of course, there was evidence of negligence on the part of the employer in his provision of safe working conditions for his employee he would, and still will, be liable, as where he keeps a bull in a loose box without providing any means of tethering it before the box is cleaned out. There will be liability for negligence in such cases even though the employer is unaware of the dangerous nature of the bull, so long as he ought to have known of the dangers.[444] **2.136**

The denial of any action to an employee in *scienter* in these types of cases really amounted to confusion of strict liability under that action with the employer's obligations to provide a safe system of work, a confusion which may well have been avoided in Scotland.[445] It would appear to be the purpose of section 6(5) of the Animals Act 1971 to reverse the effect of *Rands v McNeil*, so that an employee will not always be deemed to have assumed risks incidental to his employment.[446] When one examines section 6(5), however, it may be that it achieved too much. In providing **2.137**

[441] [1955] 1 QB 253, above, para 2.126; and see *Henderson v John Stuart (Farms) Ltd* 1963 SC 245, 253; *James v Wellington City* [1972] NZLR 70, 77; reversed on appeal: [1972] NZLR 978; cf *Brock v Copeland* (1794) 1 Esp 203 discussed in *Bird v Holbrook* (1828) 4 Bing 628, 642. *Barnes v Lucille Ltd* (1907) 96 LT 680, another employment case, is confusing as to whether the action therein was based on *scienter* or negligence.

[442] [1955] 1 QB 253, 266; and see at p 257.

[443] It did not serve to protect the employer against a claim by a third party: *Henderson v John Stuart (Farms) Ltd* 1963 SC 245, 253.

[444] Ibid; cf *Beer v Wheeler* (1965) 109 Sol Jo 457, another case concerning a bull in a pen where, on the evidence, the claimant's employer was not negligent.

[445] There seems to have been an assumption in *Clark v Armstrong* (1862) 24 D 1315 that an action would lie; and see *Henderson v John Stuart (Farms) Ltd* 1963 SC 245, 251, 253; *Sneddon v Baxter* 1967 SLT (Notes) 67; cf *Daly v Arrol Bros* (1886) 14 R 154. See now the Animals (Scotland) Act 1987, s 2(1)(b).

[446] Law Commission Report, para 20. However, in *Canterbury CC v Howletts and Port Lympne Estates Ltd* [1997] ICR 925, it was held to be reasonable, under health and safety legislation, for keepers to enter tigers' cages in order to pursue a zoo's policy of establishing 'bonding' between keepers and tigers, even though a keeper had been killed by one of the tigers after entering its cage.

that, when an employee incurs a risk incidental to his employment, he shall not be treated as accepting it voluntarily, it undoubtedly altered the law in the situation where the employee did not, in fact, assume the risk. *Rands v McNeil* has been reversed, and in such a case the employee could succeed under section 2. No longer is he to be deemed to have accepted the risk. There is also, however, another situation to consider. There could be situations where an employee both knows of risks from his employer's dangerous animals and agrees to run them, ie cases of actual, rather than presumed, assumption of risk. It has, for instance, been suggested that the custodian of a bull with dangerous propensities may be taken to assume the normal risks of his employment.[447] Similarly, it has been said that a man employed as a horse-breaker 'must take the risk of being thrown or injured by a restive or unbroken horse'.[448] It is debateable whether this type of case was not also affected by section 6(5). Undoubtedly, the employee has incurred a risk incidental to his employment. If he has accepted it voluntarily, can he fall within a provision that 'he shall not be treated as accepting it voluntarily'? The better interpretation of section 6(5) is that it covers both the case where, at common law, assumption of risk was presumed, and the case where it was actual. If that is so, then section 6(5) has placed employees in a privileged position in relation to their employers' liability under section 2, so that an employee may sue for damage from a risk which he has actually assumed. The only way to avoid such a conclusion would be to interpret section 6(5) as applicable only to cases where there is no actual assumption of risk, by emphasizing that the phrase 'he shall not be *treated* as accepting it voluntarily'[449] refers only to situations where, but for section 6(5), assumption of risk might have been presumed. It is suggested that, although such an interpretation can be thought to have considerable merit in terms of justice, it hardly accords with the words of the subsection. One is left, therefore, with the conclusion that the defence of assumption of risk is not open to an employer whose employee claims under section 2 of the Animals Act 1971,[450] provided that the risk in question was one incidental to his employment.

2.138 If, although the parties are employer and employee, the risk in question is not incidental to the claimant's employment, then section 6(5) is inapplicable. In *Mansfield v Baddeley*,[451] the claimant was employed by the defendant as a dressmaker. At the request of the defendant she visited the defendant's kitchen, where she was bitten by the defendant's dog. The court decided that the claimant could not recover for risks incidental to her employment. Was the visit to the kitchen and the risk from the dog incidental to her employment? The court thought it was not. Grove J said:

> No doubt she cannot recover for risks incidental to the service. I think that this risk is not incidental to the service . . . If the plaintiff when she entered her employment

[447] *Rands v McNeil* [1955] 1 QB 253, 272.
[448] *Bowater v Rowley Regis Corp* [1944] KB 476, 481; cf *Yarmouth v France* (1887) 19 QBD 647.
[449] Italics added.
[450] Because the employer should insure against such liability: Law Commission Report, para 20.
[451] (1876) 34 LT 696.

> knew the character of the dog, and that in the ordinary course of her employment she would have to go by the place where it was tied up, it might perhaps be said she took the risk. But here she was asked to do something which was no part of her service, in fact a mere good-natured act, it being something *ultra* her service to go to the kitchen. The dog then rushes out and bites her. Such a risk was not incidental to the service, nor one which by her conduct she has undertaken to bear.[452]

Although this case starts from the opposite position from the present law, ie that all risks incidental to employment are assumed, whereas the present law is that none are, it does provide some indication of what risks might be considered incidental to employment. Under section 5(2), those which are not incidental to an employee's employment are ones which he may assume, so as to relieve his employer from liability.

Finally, it should be mentioned that, even if an employee has actually assumed risks **2.139** incidental to his employment, although he is protected by section 6(5) from any defence of assumption of risk raised by his employer, under section 5(2) he is not protected from any claim that his injury is due to his own fault,[453] or from a claim of contributory negligence.[454] This is of some importance in a case where an employee is injured by an animal which he knows to be dangerous. His knowledge is deemed to be that of his employer, the keeper.[455] If the employee has not informed his employer of the danger, the employer will nevertheless be liable under section 2 and cannot rely on the employee's assumption of risk, but can only rely on the employee's own fault or contributory negligence.

(2) Injuries to trespassers

While there was substantial authority, at common law, for the view that an occupier **2.140** of premises was not liable in negligence to a trespasser[456] injured on the premises by a dangerous animal unless the occupier intended the injury or acted with reckless disregard of the presence of the trespasser,[457] there was very little direct authority[458] at common law on the question of whether the fact that the claimant was a trespasser

452 Ibid, at p 697.

453 Section 5(1), below, paras 2.154–2.158.

454 Section 10, below, paras 2.159–2.164.

455 Section 2(2)(c).

456 The general liability of an occupier to trespassers is now governed by the Occupiers' Liability Act 1984; see below, paras 6.30–6.33.

457 Williams, pp 349–52. A number of the 'animals' cases concerned with occupiers' liability at common law were concerned primarily with the issue of whether the claimant was a trespasser or a lawful visitor; eg *Lowery v Walker* [1910] 1 KB 173, reversed [1911] AC 10; *Gould v McAuliffe* [1941] 1 All ER 515; [1941] 2 All ER 527; *Pearson v Coleman Bros* [1948] 2 KB 359; cf *Murphy v Zoological Society of London* [1962] CLY 68.

458 See *Pearson v Coleman Bros*, above, at pp 370–71, 377; *Murphy v Zoological Society of London*, above. *Sarch v Blackburn* (1830) 4 C & P 297 might be such a case, for Tindal CJ, at p 300, refers to the requirement of the defendant's knowledge of the dog's propensity to bite; but, later, at p 301, he discusses the requirement that the defendant be shown to be negligent.

afforded a defence to the *scienter* action.[459] However, it was stated by Lord Greene MR that 'if facts established by the plaintiff herself show her to be a trespasser, then the obligations of the defendants must be treated on that footing, and it is impossible to put on them a greater obligation than the law imposes with regard to trespassers on their land'.[460]

2.141 Under the Animals Act 1971, the issue of liability for injuries to trespassers by dangerous animals is dealt with specifically by section 5(3), which provides:

> A person is not liable under section 2 of this Act for any damage caused by an animal kept on any premises or structure to a person trespassing there, if it is proved either—
> (a) that the animal was not kept there for the protection of persons or property; or
> (b) (if the animal was kept there for the protection of persons or property) that keeping it there for that purpose was not unreasonable.

2.142 Before examining the two specific provisions of section 5(3), a number of general issues must be considered. The first is that the subsection applies to the keeping of an animal 'on any premises or structure'. These terms are not defined in the Animals Act 1971, but they are very reminiscent of the phraseology used in the Occupiers' Liability Act 1957 and the Occupiers' Liability Act 1984.[461] Those Acts apply, respectively, to liability for injuries to visitors to, and trespassers on, 'premises', which term covers 'any fixed or moveable structure, including any vessel, vehicle or aircraft'.[462] If that analogy may be applied to the Animals Act 1971, then the scope of section 5(3) is quite wide. It would apply to dangerous animals kept not only in a house, a farm building, or a field,[463] but also in a zoo[464] or a wildlife park. Furthermore, 'structure' would encompass the keeping of such an animal in temporary circus premises,[465] on board a ship or aircraft, or in a car.[466]

2.143 Second, the claimant envisaged by section 5(3) is 'a person trespassing' on the premises or structure; and it is necessary for an actual trespass to be proved.[467] Just walking up the path to the defendant's house has been held not to amount to

---

[459] Although contrast the position under the Dogs Acts 1906–28; and see now the position under the Animals Act 1971, ss 3, 5(4), below, paras 7.13–7.17.

[460] *Pearson v Coleman Bros*, above, at p 371.

[461] As amended by the Countryside and Rights of Way Act 2000, s 13(2), and the Marine and Coastal Access Act 2009, s 306.

[462] Occupiers' Liability Act 1957, s 1(3); Occupiers' Liability Act 1984, s 1(2), (9). Under the latter Act, premises have been broadly interpreted to include, eg, a tidal harbour owned and occupied by the defendants—*Donoghue v Folkestone Properties Ltd* [2003] EWCA Civ 231; [2003] QB 1008; and a lake in a country park—*Tomlinson v Congleton Borough Council* [2003] UKHL 47; [2004] 1 AC 46.

[463] 305 HL Deb (1959), c 1424; cf 795 HC Deb (1970), c 557.

[464] cf *Murphy v Zoological Society of London* [1962] CLY 68.

[465] cf *Pearson v Coleman Bros* [1948] 2 KB 359.

[466] cf *Sycamore v Ley* (1932) 147 LT 342.

[467] cf *Beattie v McConnell* [2005] NIQB 47.

trespass under section 5(3).[468] One assumes that 'trespass' has its normal meaning of someone on the premises without permission or lawful authority and against whom an action of trespass to land could lie at the suit of a person with an adequate interest in the land.[469] Thus, the position of the car thief who is bitten by a dog in the car he steals would fall within section 5(3). However, section 5(3) does not require that the claimant be a trespasser *vis à vis* the keeper of the animal against whom his action under section 2 is being brought. There may be varied instances where the statutory liability under section 2 is placed on a keeper who has no interest in the land where the animal is kept and *vis à vis* whom the claimant will not be a trespasser. An obvious example would be that where an animal is owned by one person but is in the possession of another person who is the occupier of the premises where it is kept. Both are keepers within the meaning of section 6(3)(a), but the claimant would only be a trespasser as against the possessor and not as against the owner. Nevertheless, both keepers can rely on the fact that the claimant was a trespasser as against one of them. Indeed, where premises are protected by guard dogs supplied with a handler each evening by a security firm, then the security firm will be the keeper of the dogs, and the occupier of the premises where they roam at night has no responsibility under section 2, for he is neither owner nor possessor of them.[470] If a trespasser is injured by the dogs, the owner may rely, under section 5(3), on the fact that the dogs are kept[471] by him on premises on which the claimant was trespassing even though no trespass is committed against the owner, and the occupier of the premises is not a keeper.

Third, section 5(3) provides a defence and so it is for the defendant to satisfy the court that the various elements of the defence laid down in that subsection are satisfied. No doubt this is right, for the purpose for which the animal is kept[472] is peculiarly within the knowledge of the defendant. **2.144**

To turn now to the two specific provisions of section 5(3), the first states that the defence applies if 'the animal was not kept [on the premises] for the protection of persons or property'.[473] The vast majority of animals will fall into this category; although there may, of course, be some which fulfil the function of protection, even though it is claimed that they are not kept for that purpose. A dog may be kept for companionship, but it is very convenient that it will bark when burglars appear. **2.145**

---

468 *Cockhill v Muff* CA (1987) Unreported, 17 June.

469 P North, *Occupiers' Liability* (1971), pp 162–70.

470 He may be liable for any injuries caused through his negligence, or he may be liable to a trespasser if he acted recklessly in allowing the dogs to roam his premises at night.

471 Despite doubts expressed in the House of Lords: 305 HL Deb (1969), c 1426; 306 HL Deb (1969), cc 687, 690; 312 HL Deb (1970), cc 224, 231; there would seem little likelihood that a court would conclude that such dogs were not 'kept' on the premises trespassed upon, even though they were only there for a relatively short time. While they are there, they are 'kept' there.

472 Discussed below.

473 Section 5(3)(a).

No doubt the courts will have to decide which is the predominant purpose. It has been said by Nourse LJ

> that it is not inherently inconsistent to say, on the one hand, that a dog is not a guard dog but that it is a pet and, on the other, that it is there for the protection of (the defendant) herself. Many dogs do protect their owners simply by barking at anyone who comes on to the premises.[474]

The consequence of the general provision in section 5(3)(a) is that, if the claimant is injured by a bull grazing in a field, no action will lie under section 2 if the claimant is a trespasser, for the bull is not kept for the protection of persons or property.[475] Again, any trespasser in a zoo[476] or a wildlife park will be unable to succeed under section 2, for there will be little doubt that the animals kept in such places are kept to entertain the public and not for the protection of persons or property.[477]

2.146 The second specific provision in section 5(3) is that there will be no liability to a trespasser injured by an animal kept on the premises for the protection of persons or property if keeping it there for that purpose was not unreasonable.[478] There are three factors relevant here. Was the animal kept on the premises, on which the claimant trespassed, for the purpose of the protection of persons or property? Was it reasonable to keep that animal for that purpose? And was it reasonable to keep it on the premises in question for that purpose?

2.147 The obvious type of case envisaged is the keeping of guard dogs. There may be other, albeit rare, instances of other dangerous animals, such as snakes, being kept to guard property. There seems little doubt that, at common law, it was considered wholly reasonable to keep fierce dogs for the purposes of guarding property,[479] and it would be surprising if the law were otherwise under the Animals Act 1971. On the other hand, it is very likely that a court would conclude that the keeping of poisonous snakes for the guarding of property was quite unreasonable.[480] This will, however, mean that, if you keep snakes merely for entertainment, there will be no liability under section 2 to a trespasser injured by them, but that if they are kept to protect property, liability to a trespasser may ensue. If the keeper of the snakes is the

---

474 *Cockhill v Muff* CA (1987) Unreported, 17 June.

475 The same was true at common law: *Deane v Clayton* (1817) Taunt 489, 532–3; *Blackman v Simmons* (1827) 3 C & P 138, 140; *Hudson v Roberts* (1851) 6 Exch 697, 699.

476 *Murphy v Zoological Society of London* [1962] CLY 68; and see *Marlor v Ball* (1900) 16 TLR 239.

477 An unsuccessful attempt to apply s 5(3) only to animals not belonging to a dangerous species and to make the keeper of the latter liable to trespassers was made in the House of Lords: 312 HL Deb (1970), cc 852–7.

478 Section 5(3)(b). The burden of proof of reasonableness would appear to rest on the defendant.

479 *Brock v Copeland* (1794) 1 Esp 203; *Sarch v Blackburn* (1830) 4 C & P 297, 300; *Sycamore v Ley* (1932) 147 LT 342, 344; and see *Wilkins v Manning* (1897) 13 WN (NSW) 220; *Trethowan v Capron* [1961] VR 460.

480 Lord Gardiner LC considered that any other conclusion was 'unthinkable': 306 HL Deb (1969), c 685; and see ibid, c 689.

occupier of the premises trespassed upon, then, under the statutory provisions[481] relating to an occupier's liability to trespassers, he will only be liable if his conduct in keeping the dangerous animals amounted to a failure to take reasonable care for a trespasser whom he knew or had reasonable grounds to believe would be in the vicinity.[482] If, on the other hand, the keeper is not the occupier of the premises trespassed upon, he cannot rely on the fact that the claimant was a trespasser and he will be liable if he has been negligent in the way in which he kept the animals.[483]

It must also be reasonable to keep the dangerous animal on the premises in question **2.148** for the purpose of protection. It may be reasonable to keep guard dogs in some places but not in others; it might be reasonable for them to guard enclosed buildings, but not open fields.[484] What is, perhaps, a very significant factor in assessing reasonableness, and one not dealt with directly in section 5(3), is that of a warning of the presence of the dangerous animal. It may be reasonable to keep a fierce guard dog to protect premises, but only if due warning of its presence is given.[485] Otherwise, it appears as though it is being kept to injure as well as to protect, and that would be unreasonable.

The leading decision on this issue is *Cummings v Granger*.[486] The claimant was a **2.149** barmaid who worked in a pub next door to the defendant's scrapyard. The defendant kept an Alsatian in the scrapyard as a guard dog and let it run loose in the locked yard. There was a large notice on the main scrapyard gate saying 'Beware of the Dog'. One night, the claimant left the pub with a friend who was allowed by the defendant to park his car in the yard. He opened a small wicket gate into the yard to get some tools from his car. The claimant followed him into the yard and was attacked by the defendant's dog, which was running loose. Having decided that, in principle, the defendant was strictly liable under section 2(2) of the 1971 Act, the Court of Appeal had to consider whether the defence under section 5(3) was applicable, and decided that the defendant was a trespasser. She had no authority to follow her friend into the yard.[487] The issue then to be addressed was whether the keeping of the Alsatian in the yard by the defendant was 'not unreasonable' for the protection of his property. Lord Denning MR was clear that this requirement was satisfied:

> This was a yard in the East End of London where persons of the roughest type come and go. It was a scrap-yard, true, but scrap-yards, like building sites, often contain much valuable property. It was deserted at night and at weekends. If there was no protection, thieves would drive up in a lorry and remove the scrap with no one to see

[481] Occupiers' Liability Act 1984.
[482] See below, paras 6.30–6.33.
[483] cf *Creed v McGeoch & Sons Ltd* [1955] 3 All ER 123; P North, *Occupiers' Liability* (1971), pp 28–31.
[484] 306 HL Deb (1969), c 685.
[485] This passage was approved in *Cummings v Granger* [1977] QB 397, 410.
[486] [1977] QB 397.
[487] Ibid, at 403, 407–8.

> them or stop them. The only reasonable way of protecting the place was to have a guard dog. True it was a fierce dog. But why not? A gentle dog would be no good. The thieves would soon make friends with him. It seems to me that it was very reasonable—or, at any rate not unreasonable—for the defendant to keep this dog there.[488]

2.150 This case was decided after the passage of the Guard Dogs Act 1975, but in relation to events occurring earlier. However, the Court of Appeal considered whether the 1975 Act might in future affect similar cases. That Act in itself does not create civil liability;[489] rather, it makes it a criminal offence to use a guard dog unless a handler is present on the premises and the dog is under the control of the handler while the dog is being used, unless it is secured so that it cannot go freely about the premises.[490] It is also necessary to display a notice at the entrance to the premises warning of the presence of the guard dog.[491] On the facts of *Cummings v Granger*, while a large warning notice was displayed, the Alsatian in that case was allowed to roam freely, which would now constitute an offence under the 1975 Act. Lord Denning MR indicated[492] that the 1975 Act may have the effect in civil proceedings of making it unreasonable for the defendant to let a dog free at night in the yard (as the defendant did) and it may thus deprive the defendant of a defence under section 5(3)(b).[493]

2.151 Finally, it should be borne in mind that section 5(3) is not the only provision of the Animals Act which may be relevant to liability under section 2 for injuries caused to trespassers by dangerous animals. If a trespasser is injured by an animal unreasonably kept for the protection of persons or property, then, although no protection is afforded to the keeper by reason of section 5(3), it could be that there is no liability by reason of section 5(2).[494]

2.152 Furthermore, section 5(1) provides that a person is not liable under section 2 for 'any damage which is due wholly to the fault of the person suffering it',[495] and there is common law authority suggesting that, if a trespasser is injured by an animal on the premises trespassed against, such injury is the result of his own fault. Tindal CJ has said:

> If a man puts a dog in a garden, walled all round, and a wrongdoer goes into that garden, and is bitten, he cannot complain in a Court of Justice of that which was brought upon him by his own act.[496]

---

[488] Ibid, at 405; and see at 408, 409–10.

[489] Section 5(2).

[490] Section 1(1). Although, if the dog is secured, the handler does not need to be on the premises; and a dog on a 13-foot chain has been held to be 'secured': *Hobson v Gledhill* [1978] 1 WLR 215.

[491] Section 1(3).

[492] [1977] QB 397, 406; and see Bridge LJ, at 409–10.

[493] But not the defence of voluntary acceptance of risk, under s 5(2): [1977] QB 397, 406.

[494] Discussed in more detail, above, paras 2.129–2.139; and see *Cummings v Granger* [1977] QB 397, 406.

[495] Discussed in more detail, below, paras 2.154–2.158.

[496] *Sarch v Blackburn* (1830) 4 C & P 297, 300; and see *Brock v Copeland* (1794) 1 Esp 203, 203–4; *Marlor v Ball* (1900) 16 TLR 239, 240.

This principle could apply where a trespasser is injured by a dangerous animal unreasonably kept for the guarding of premises, at least where the trespasser is warned of its presence. There is also no reason why the defences under section 5(1) and section 5(2) should not operate in the case of a trespassing claimant, claiming under section 2, whether or not the defendant, the keeper of the animal in question, was occupier of the premises trespassed upon.

It should be reiterated, in conclusion, that the strict liability of a keeper of a dangerous animal to a trespasser based on section 2 of the Animals Act 1971 is based on principles different from other heads of liability to trespassers. What may be a defence to liability under section 2 is not, necessarily, relevant to a claim based on the negligence of a keeper who is not an occupier of the premises trespassed upon or to a claim based on the liability of an occupier, as such, to a trespasser injured on his premises by a dangerous animal.[497] **2.153**

(3) Damage due wholly to the fault of the claimant

At common law, if the claimant's own conduct was the cause of his injury, then he could not claim damages for it.[498] This is equally true under the Animals Act 1971, for section 5(1) provides that: **2.154**

> A person is not liable under sections 2 to 4 of this Act for any damage which is due wholly to the fault of the person suffering it.

This defence is applicable not only to claims for injuries caused by dangerous animals, under section 2, but also to claims for damage caused by a dog injuring or killing livestock, under section 3,[499] and to claims for damage done by straying livestock, under section 4.[500]

One general problem is that it is not always easy to determine in what circumstances the claimant is to be considered to have brought his injury upon himself. If the claimant goes up to zebras in a stall to stroke them, then probably he cannot complain if one kicks him and the other bites him,[501] or, indeed, if he so shouted at a horse that it kicked him.[502] On the other hand, a claimant could claim in *scienter*[503] and can claim under section 2(2) of the Animals Act 1971[504] when bitten **2.155**

---

497 General liability at common law for injuries caused by animals is examined in ch 6.

498 eg *Filburn v People's Palace and Aquarium Co Ltd* (1890) 25 QBD 258, 260.

499 Below, para 7.12.

500 Below, paras 3.36–3.38.

501 *Marlor v Ball* (1900) 16 TLR 239; see also *Young v Green* [1958] OWN 426. Nor could a claimant complain if he foolishly tried to take some smouldering straw out of a leopard's cage and was mauled by the leopard: *Sylvester v G B Chapman Ltd* [1935] LJCCA 261 (also briefly reported in (1935) 79 Sol Jo 777) for 'he was bringing the trouble upon himself', (at p 264).

502 *Bowler v Bravender* (1968) 67 DLR (2d) 734.

503 *Gordon v Mackenzie* 1913 SC 109.

504 *Bearfield v Culmer* (1981) Unreported, 17 July.

by a dog which he had patted on the head. A small boy who put his arm round a dog and kissed it to induce it to play was considered to be the cause of his own injury when the dog bit him;[505] but another small boy who lay down beside a dog and put his arms round its neck was able to recover.[506] Both were cases involving the *scienter* action, but both seem relevant to liability under section 2(2). Again, when a child, a lawful visitor, chose to relieve herself near a lion's cage, the defendants, the proprietors of a circus, were held liable when the child was mauled by the lion. The child, who was only 5 years old, was not considered to be the cause of her own injury.[507]

2.156 Other common law authorities held it not to be default on the part of the claimant merely to walk near where a dangerous animal was kept,[508] at least if the claimant was unaware of the existence of the animal. If the claimant was aware of the existence of an animal of a dangerous species, then he might also be taken to know that it was dangerous. Indeed, in *Besozzi v Harris*,[509] where the claimant was injured by a bear, it was suggested that 'if the plaintiff, with knowledge that the bear was there, put herself in a position to receive the injury, she could not recover'. In such a case the injury was due to the fault of the claimant because the animal was of a dangerous species. Probably, however, in the case of animals which do not belong to a dangerous species, the claimant must have been aware both of the existence of the animal and of its dangerous characteristics[510] before it could be said that his injury was due to his own fault. Indeed, one can argue that that should always be the case where the claimant is injured by such an animal,[511] unless he provokes it. If the claimant actually provoked or teased the animal, he would have had no claim in *scienter*[512] if injured,[513] and his injury would appear to be due wholly to his own fault within the meaning of section 5(1) of the Animals Act 1971. On the other hand, an earlier teasing of an animal will not justify its later attack.[514]

2.157 The main circumstance where the defence under section 5(1) of the Animals Act 1971 has been directly addressed by the courts is that of the behaviour of police dogs. In *Dhesi v Chief Constable of West Midlands Police*,[515] the claimant was one of

505 *Lee v Walkers* (1939) 162 LT 89.

506 *Charlwood v Greig* (1851) 3 Car & Kir 46; and see *Smith v Pelah* (1747) 2 Stra 1264.

507 *Pearson v Coleman Bros* [1948] 2 KB 359.

508 *Besozzi v Harris* (1858) 1 F & F 92.

509 (1858) 1 F & F 92, 93; and see *Young v Green* [1958] OWN 426; cf *Wyatt v Rosherville Gardens Co* (1886) 2 TLR 282, where the claimant recovered in *scienter*, although he had gone into an inner gallery close to a bear's den. That case might be distinguished, today, as one of contributory negligence and not of the claimant's default.

510 eg *Sycamore v Ley* (1932) 147 LT 342.

511 cf *Lee v Walkers* (1939) 162 LT 89.

512 Or under the Dogs Acts 1906–28; see *Elliott v Longden* (1901) 17 TLR 648, 649, below, para 7.12.

513 *Behrens v Bertram Mills Circus Ltd* [1957] 2 QB 1, 19; and see *Simpson v Bannerman* (1932) 47 CLR 378, 384.

514 *Brown v Stewart* (1824) 3 S 127; and see *Smith v Pelah* (1747) 2 Stra 1264.

515 [2000] Po LR 120.

a number of youths who had been fighting. Police officers were called to the incident. The claimant had threatened the police with a hockey stick and had then run away and hidden. A police dog was used to try to find him, with the result that the claimant was discovered 'sitting on the ground fighting with [the dog] in an attempt to get him away'. During this struggle, the claimant was bitten several times. The claimant then attacked the police with his hockey stick and the police dog then took hold of his trouser leg, causing a puncture wound. The Court of Appeal, having decided that the claimant's arrest was lawful, considered whether the police were liable under section 2(2) of the Animals Act 1971. Although the court concluded that there was no liability under that subsection, it was also held that the claimant's injuries were wholly due to his own fault, under section 5(1). Stuart-Smith LJ said that:

> A suspect who ignores clear warnings to come out or a dog will be sent to find him has only himself to blame if he suffers injury as a result.[516]

Section 5(1) of the Animals Act 1971 refers to damage which is due 'wholly to the fault of the person suffering it'. 'Fault' is defined[517] as having the same meaning as in the Law Reform (Contributory Negligence) Act 1945. Under section 4 of the 1945 Act, fault is defined as 'negligence, breach of statutory duty or other act or omission which gives rise to a liability in tort or would, apart from this Act, give rise to the defence of contributory negligence'.[518] In order for the defence under section 5(1) to benefit the defendant, the claimant's injuries must be due *wholly* to his fault.[519] This requirement must be read subject to some limitations. The injury must have been caused by an animal, but the fact that the animal caused it must have been wholly attributable to the fault of the claimant and in no way to the fault, ie the negligence, breach of statutory duty, or the like, of the defendant. If a visitor to a wildlife park ignores the many notices warning him not to get out of his car or open its windows in an enclosure full of lions, his mauling by the lions would be due wholly to his own fault. **2.158**

(4) Contributory negligence

The connection between contributory negligence and the previous defence of the default of the claimant is obvious. However, the differentiation between the two defences is made here[520] because if the claimant is the cause of his own injury he cannot recover at all, but if he is contributorily negligent his damages will be apportioned under the Law Reform (Contributory Negligence) Act 1945 according to **2.159**

---

[516] Ibid, at para 39. A similar approach was adopted by Russell LJ in *Nelmes v Chief Constable of Avon and Somerset Constabulary* (1993) CA, Unreported, 9 February.

[517] Animals Act 1971, s 11.

[518] eg breach of contract: *Quinn v Burch Bros* [1966] 1 QB 370.

[519] See *Cummings v Granger* [1977] QB 397, 404.

[520] cf *Chittenden v Hale* [1933] NZLR 836, 847; *Rands v McNeil* [1955] 1 QB 253, 266.

his degree of responsibility for his own injuries; although, of course, the claimant may still be held fully responsible.[521]

2.160 The defence of contributory negligence was applied to *scienter* actions at common law,[522] and it was the view of the Law Commission[523] that contributory negligence should be available as a defence to liability under section 2 of the Animals Act 1971.[524] Section 10 of the Animals Act 1971 provides that:

> For the purposes of . . . the Law Reform (Contributory Negligence) Act 1945 . . . any damage for which a person is liable under sections 2 to 4 of this Act shall be treated as due to his fault.[525]

This provision has then to be read against the provisions of the Law Reform (Contributory Negligence) Act 1945, section 1(1) of which states:

> Where any person suffers damage as the result partly of his own fault and partly of the fault of any other person or persons, a claim in respect of that damage shall not be defeated by reason of the fault of the person suffering the damage, but the damages recoverable in respect thereof shall be reduced to such extent as the court thinks just and equitable having regard to the claimant's share in the responsibility for the damage.[526]

The effect of all this in the context of liability under section 2 of the Animals Act 1971 is that, although liability under section 2 is strict, if a claimant is injured partly as the result of his own negligence or breach of statutory duty and partly as the result of the defendant's breach of his statutory obligations under section 2, the defence of contributory negligence is open to the defendant.

2.161 Decisions under the *scienter* action ought to be regarded as relevant in indicating what type of conduct by a claimant amounts to contributory negligence. At common law, it was considered that the issue of contributory negligence was raised when the claimant went into an inner gallery close to a bear's den[527] and again when the claimant patted a strange dog on the head in the street.[528] The defence has been allowed where two cats were killed by the defender's dog in or near the pursuer's shop, for 'to allow an animal liable within common knowledge to be attacked by other domestic animals to be at large in a public place where these other animals

---

[521] *Beer v Wheeler* (1965) 109 Sol Jo 457.

[522] Just as it had been applied to ordinary actions of negligence based on injury by animals, eg *Flett v Coulter* (1903) 5 OLR 375; and see, below, para 6.25.

[523] Law Commission Report, para 21. The Law Commission doubted whether public opinion would accept the stricter rule that a defendant should be wholly liable irrespective of the negligence of the claimant.

[524] As it is also a defence to a claim both under s 3 of the 1971 Act, see below, para 7.12, and under s 4, see below, paras 3.34–3.35; and see *Matthews v Wicks* (1987) CA, Unreported, 22 May.

[525] 'Fault' is defined by the Animals Act 1971, s 11; see above, para 2.158.

[526] See G Williams, *Joint Torts and Contributory Negligence* (1951), Pt II.

[527] *Wyatt v Rosherville Gardens Co* (1886) 2 TLR 282, 283.

[528] *Gordon v Mackenzie* 1913 SC 109; cf *Simpson v Bannerman* (1932) 47 CLR 378.

may legitimately be is contributory negligence'.[529] Again, in *Rands v McNeil*,[530] the case of injury by a bull in a loose box, the issue raised by the fact that the claimant actually went into the box was considered by Denning LJ:

> I realise, of course, that [a third party] and the plaintiff were both at fault. They ought not to have gone into the box at all, because they must have known it was a dangerous thing to do and that they ought not to do it; but their fault does not excuse the farmer from his share of the responsibility, if he also was at fault. It is only a ground for reducing the damages.[531]

Very common situations where the issue of contributory negligence has arisen are those where the claimant is driving a dangerous animal off his land. If the animal is known by its keeper to be dangerous, the claimant's action for injuries caused to him by the animal will only be defeated if he acts unreasonably and negligently in the way in which he drives the beast off.[532] If the claimant hits the animal to drive it off, this will not amount to contributory negligence, provided that it was reasonable in the circumstances to do so.[533] The mere fact that one knows that the defendant's dangerous animal is on one's land does not require one either to remain indoors until it has gone or face the defence of contributory negligence if one is injured while working the land.[534] Mere knowledge alone of the fierce or dangerous nature of the defendant's animal does not, of itself, amount to contributory negligence, as where a postman was bitten by the defendant's dog, which the postman knew to be dangerous, when delivering a telegram to the defendant.[535] **2.162**

In cases where there is a warning or notice of the dangerous characteristics of the animal, this does not automatically indicate contributory negligence on the part of a claimant who goes near the animal, especially if the defendant's conduct leads the claimant to believe that the animal is safe.[536] All the more is this true if the notice in question is inadequate to convey awareness of the danger to the claimant. A painted notice has been considered to be an inadequate warning to a claimant who could **2.163**

---

[529] *Brown v Soutar* 1914 2 SLT 399, 400; and see Williams, pp 317–18. This should not prevent a cat, in such circumstances, from being allowed to act in self-defence; Williams, p 333.

[530] [1955] 1 QB 253, above, para 2.126; and see *McNeill v Frankenfeld* (1963) 39 DLR (2d) 332; varied on appeal: (1963) 44 DLR (2d) 132—a decision on the British Columbia Contributory Negligence Act 1960.

[531] [1955] 1 QB 253, 259; and see ibid, at pp 266, 269. See also *Behrens v Bertram Mills Circus Ltd* [1957] 2 QB 1, 19–20.

[532] eg *Jacobson v Schneider* [1927] 2 WWR 257, 259; and see *Dawson v Warren* (1884) 2 NZLR 255.

[533] *Blackman v Simmons* (1827) 3 C & P 138; *Shelfontuck v Le Page* [1937] 2 WWR 16, 19; affirmed (1938) 1 DLR (2d) 513, 519.

[534] *Tarasoff v Zielinsky* [1921] 2 WWR 135, 140.

[535] *Carbury v Measures* (1904) 4 SRNSW 569.

[536] *Curtis v Mills* (1833) 5 C & P 489; cf *Dolan v Bright* [1962] CLY 72; and see *Forbes v M'Donald* (1874) 7 ALT 62; *O'Dolan v Burke* (1962) 96 ILTR 285.

not read.[537] The warning, to be effective, must be such as to warn against the danger which actually occurred.[538]

2.164 Where contributory negligence is a defence, the court must apportion damages as between the claimant and the defendant on such basis 'as the court thinks just and equitable having regard to the claimant's share in the responsibility for the damage'.[539] Where liability is strict, as under section 2 and especially under section 2(1), there may be little or no blameworthiness on the part of the defendant, but the court must nevertheless attempt to apportion the damage, rather than impose responsibility for it all on the negligent claimant. The two main factors of causative potency and relative blameworthiness have to be considered by the court in a flexible manner in cases of strict liability.[540]

(5) Inapplicable defences

2.165 Two possible defences to liability under the *scienter* action do not apply to liability under section 2 of the Animals Act 1971. The first is Act of God. The more acceptable view was that this defence was applicable to common law liability.[541] There is no provision for such a defence in the Animals Act 1971. To take an example given by Bramwell B,[542] the law now is that 'if a man kept a tiger, and lightning broke his chain, and he got loose and did mischief' the keeper of the tiger would be liable under section 2(1).

2.166 The second inapplicable defence is that of act of a third party. It was debatable whether such a defence to an action of *scienter* existed. While there was Scottish authority favouring such a defence,[543] the preponderance of English authority indicated that no such defence existed.[544] The Law Commission was of the opinion that there should be no such defence to liability under section 2 of the Animals Act 1971, for 'the act of a third party is one of the circumstances against which the person creating the risk should take precautions'.[545] If the claimant is injured by the defendant's dangerous animal, it will be no defence that the injury was caused by

---

[537] *Sarch v Blackburn* (1830) 4 C & P 297, 300–301; *Pearson v Coleman Bros* [1948] 2 KB 359, 370.

[538] *Pearson v Coleman Bros*, above, at pp 369–70.

[539] Law Reform (Contributory Negligence) Act 1945, s 1(1).

[540] *Sahib Foods Ltd v Paskin Kyriakides Sands (A Firm)* [2003] EWCA Civ 1832; [2004] PNLR 22; *St George v Home Office* [2008] EWCA Civ 1068; [2009] 1 WLR 1670; and see G Williams, *Joint Torts and Contributory Negligence* (1951), pp 326–8.

[541] *Baker v Snell* [1908] 2 KB 825, 834, 836; *Rands v McNeil* [1955] 1 QB 253, 266; Williams, p 336; Law Commission Report, para 24.

[542] *Nichols v Marsland* (1875) LR 10 Exch 255, 260. See also *Barker v Herbert* [1911] 2 KB 633, 647.

[543] *Fleming v Orr* (1857) 2 Macq 14.

[544] *Baker v Snell* [1908] 2 KB 825, 833, 834; *Behrens v Bertram Mills Circus Ltd* [1957] 2 QB 1, 21–5; and see *Kavanagh v Centreline Ltd* (1987) 7 ILRM 306.

[545] Law Commission Report, para 24.

the negligence or the wilful misconduct of a third party. In *Baker v Snell*,[546] the claimant, who was the defendant's housemaid, was injured when the defendant's dog, known to be dangerous, was brought by the defendant's potman into the kitchen and was incited to attack her by the potman, saying: 'Go it Bob.' Such conduct would, today, impose liability on the defendant under section 2(2) of the Animals Act 1971.

546 [1908] 2 KB 825.

3

STATUTORY LIABILITY FOR STRAYING LIVESTOCK

The common law action of cattle trespass[1] provided that if animals, within the description of cattle, strayed from A's land on to B's, then A was strictly liable per se. He would be held responsible for any damage done to the land,[2] to chattels thereon or to the occupier.[3] **3.01**

In its examination of this head of liability, the Law Commission took the view: **3.02**

> that the retention of strict liability for cases of cattle trespass can only be justified if it provides a clear rule as to liability for trespassing cattle, enabling disputes to be settled normally without recourse to litigation.[4]

Rather than recommend piecemeal alterations to the existing law, the Law Commission proposed a restatement of the principles of strict liability for straying

[1] G Williams, *Liability for Animals* (1939), Pt 2; Delany (1952) 10 NILQ 135, 137–45; Davis (1964) 1 NZULR 206, 213–22.

[2] *Sutcliffe v Holmes* [1947] KB 147.

[3] *Wormald v Cole* [1954] 1 QB 614.

[4] Law Commission Report, para 63.

animals to replace the law of cattle trespass. The essential provisions of this restatement, as now embodied in the Animals Act 1971,[5] are:

(1) the statutory abolition of liability for cattle trespass;[6] and
(2) its replacement by a new head of liability for damage caused by straying livestock.

3.03 It is provided by section 4 of the Animals Act 1971 that:

> (1) Where livestock belonging to any person strays on to land in the ownership or occupation of another and—
>
> (a) damage is done by the livestock to the land or to any property on it which is in the ownership or possession of the other person; or
>
> (b) any expenses are reasonably incurred by that other person in keeping the livestock while it cannot be restored to the person to whom it belongs, or while it is detained in pursuance of section 7 of this Act[7] or in ascertaining to whom it belongs;
>
> the person to whom the livestock belongs is liable for the damage or expenses, except as otherwise provided by this Act.
>
> (2) For the purposes of this section any livestock belongs to the person in whose possession it is.

There are a number of elements in this statutory tort which should be considered separately.

1. The Animals in Question Must Fall within the Definition of 'Livestock'

3.04 The action of cattle trespass, a mediaeval cause of action, was based on liability for animals falling within the term 'avers'. This included most, if not all, domestic productive farm animals, namely, oxen, cows, sheep, goats, pigs, horses, asses, hens, geese, ducks, and, probably, turkeys.[8] It was extended to include deer;[9] but it

---

[5] In Northern Ireland, provision is made to similar effect in terms which, substantially, follow those of the 1971 Act; see the Animals (Northern Ireland) Order 1976, SI 1076/1040, Arts 3(b), 5. Cattle trespass has been replaced by statutory provisions in some of the jurisdictions in Australia: see F Trindade, P Cane, and M Lunney, *The Law of Torts in Australia*, 4th edn (2007), para 12.2; H Luntz et al, *Torts*, 6th edn (2009), para 15.2.1. There have also been varied forms of statutory changes across Canada: G Fridman, *The Law of Torts in Canada*, 2nd edn (2002), pp 251–3; L Klar, *Tort Law*, 4th edn (2008), p 644.

[6] See s 1(1)(c).

[7] Discussed below, paras 3.47–3.60.

[8] cf *Fettiplace v Bates* (1624) Benl 143.

[9] *Brady v Warren* [1900] 2 IR 632; Williams, pp 147–8.

excluded dogs,[10] cats,[11] bees,[12] and, probably, domestic pigeons.[13] All wild animals were excluded from the law of cattle trespass and therefore there was no such liability for rats,[14] rabbits,[15] or pheasants[16] which bred on A's land and then strayed and caused damage to B's land or crops, although there might have been liability for nuisance[17] or negligence[18] in such cases.

Liability under the statutory action is for the straying of 'livestock', rather than 'cattle'. The former is defined, for the purposes of section 4, as: 'cattle,[19] horses, asses, mules, hinnies,[20] sheep,[21] pigs, goats and poultry, and also deer not in the wild state'.[22] There is a further sub-definition of poultry as: 'the domestic varieties of the following, that is to say, fowls, turkeys, geese, ducks, guinea-fowls, pigeons, peacocks and quails'. This would seem to be little different from the common law definition of 'cattle'. Dogs and cats, as well as wild animals, are still excluded, as are bees. However, the general law of negligence, nuisance, and trespass to land may provide some protection.[23] **3.05**

The one possible change in the law made by the Animals Act 1971 is that domestic pigeons are included in the definition of poultry. The definition of poultry appears to make the owner of pigeons liable if they stray and cause damage.[24] As pigeons are very capable of both straying and of causing damage by eating crops,[25] this provision may strike terror into the hearts of pigeon fanciers. The addition of peacocks and quails to the categories of creatures for whose straying their owner will be liable takes account of the growing number of farms for the commercial breeding of such creatures. Nevertheless, as pheasants, partridges, and grouse are excluded from the definition of livestock for the purposes of section 4, the domestic breeder or, for **3.06**

---

[10] *Beckwith v Shordyke* (1767) 4 Burr 2092; *Brown v Giles* (1823) 1 C & P 118; *Sanders v Teape and Swan* (1884) 51 LT 263; *Buckle v Holmes* [1926] 2 KB 125, 128–9, 130; *Tallents v Bell & Goddard* [1944] 2 All ER 474; cf *Doyle v Vance* (1880) 6 VLR (L) 87.

[11] *Buckle v Holmes* [1926] 2 KB 125; *Toogood v Wright* [1940] 2 All ER 306, 308.

[12] *O'Gorman v O'Gorman* [1903] 2 IR 573; cf *McStay v Morrissey* (1949) 83 ILTR 28 on liability for the negligent keeping of bees. On the whole question of liability for bees, see Paton (1939) 2 *Res Judicatae* 22; J Frimston, *Bee-Keeping and the Law* (1966); K Swan, *A Receiver of Stolen Property* (1956).

[13] Williams, p 148; cf *Brady v Warren* [1900] 2 IR 632, 645.

[14] *Stearn v Prentice Bros* [1919] 1 KB 394.

[15] *Boulston's Case* (1597) 5 Co Rep 104b; *Brady v Warren* [1900] 2 IR 632.

[16] *Seligman v Docker* [1949] 1 Ch 53; cf *Robson v Marquis of Londonderry* (1900) 34 ILTR 88; *Foley v Berthoud* (1903) 37 ILTR 123.

[17] See, eg *Farrer v Nelson* (1885) 15 QBD 258; *Bland v Yates* (1914) 58 Sol Jo 612; *Pratt v Young* (1952) 69 WN (NSW) 214.

[18] cf *McStay v Morrissey* (1949) 83 ILTR 28.

[19] *McLoughlin v Cooper* [1999] NIJB 90.

[20] The converse of mules.

[21] *ACV Telling Ltd v Sheppey* (1982) CA, Unreported, 5 February.

[22] See s 11.

[23] See below, ch 6.

[24] Thus affirming the view of Johnson J in *Brady v Warren* (1900) 2 IR 632, 645.

[25] Discussed, below, para 3.21.

example, a shooting estate can still let them stray on to neighbouring land without liability under that section.[26] The common law of nuisance will, however, still provide some protection to the neighbour.[27]

2. Parties to the Claim

(1) Claimant

3.07 Under the law of cattle trespass,[28] the claimant had, as in all cases of trespass to land, to be in possession of the land trespassed against at the time of the trespass.[29] This excluded a person who had merely a right of common,[30] a passer-by on the highway,[31] the employee of the occupier or possessor,[32] or any other person such as a relative[33] or guest who was not in occupation. Included, however, in the categories of persons able to sue in cattle trespass were a licensee[34] and the buyer of a growing crop damaged by the trespassing animals.[35] Possibly the agent of the occupier could have been able to sue, if injured while driving off a trespassing animal on the occupier's behalf.[36]

3.08 The statutory liability under section 4 is no longer based on a technical trespass, for it would *seem* to depend upon the fact that livestock have *strayed.* The reason for the qualification of that statement is that, although section 1 abolishes liability for cattle trespass, the marginal note to section 4 states 'Liability for damage and expenses due to trespassing livestock'.[37] There is some indication from that that 'straying' means 'trespassing'. On the other hand, it is, perhaps, proper to assume that, had it been intended that section 4 should apply to 'trespassing' livestock, that phrase would have been used in the actual section.[38] That is why it is suggested, therefore, that

---

[26] They are only included as livestock, under s 11, for the purposes of ss 3 and 9, ie the liability of the keeper of a dog for killing or injuring livestock and the right to kill or injure such a dog; see ch 7.

[27] Discussed, below, paras 6.07–6.09.

[28] Williams, pp 175–8.

[29] Except perhaps in cases of 'depasturing of chattels': Williams, pp 152–6.

[30] *Cox v Burbidge* (1863) 13 CBNS 430, 435–6.

[31] See below, paras 5.37–5.38.

[32] *Wormald v Cole* [1954] 1 QB 614, 623, 627, 631; and see *Child v Hearn* (1874) LR 9 Exch 176; cf *Bradley v Wallaces Ltd* [1913] 3 KB 629.

[33] cf *Waugh v Montgomery* (1882) 8 VLR 290; *Whalley v Vandergrand* (1919) 44 DLR 319, where the successful claimant was both the son of, and an employee of, the occupier; and see *Street v Craig* (1920) 56 DLR 105.

[34] *Rutherford v Hayward* (1877) 3 VLR (L) 19. It is hard to see how such a licensee has an adequate interest to maintain an action of trespass to land when, eg, a person whose livestock are on the land trespassed upon by the defendant's bull, under a contract of agistment, does not have such an interest: *Edwards v Rawlins* [1924] NZLR 333.

[35] *Wellaway v Courtier* [1918] 1 KB 200; cf *Wiseman v Booker* (1878) 3 CPD 184.

[36] *Waugh v Montgomery* (1882) 8 VLR 290; cf *Winters v Owens* [1950] IR 225, 230.

[37] Similarly, the heading and marginal note to s 7 refer to 'trespassing livestock': see below, para 3.50. The equivalent provisions in the Animals (Northern Ireland) Order 1976, SI 1976/1040 are Arts 5 and 9, the headings of which refer to 'straying livestock'.

[38] It should be pointed out that 'the kind of heading used in Acts nowadays neither is nor should be treated as part of the text of an Act': D Greenberg, *Craies on Legislation*, 9th edn (2008), para 26.1.8.

liability under section 4 is based on 'straying' rather than on 'trespassing'. This being so, then the class of possible claimants does not need to be limited to those in possession of the land strayed upon. There is Northern Ireland authority[39] that 'stray' is to be given its dictionary meaning of 'wander free from confinement or control'.

The Law Commission proposed[40] that the owner out of occupation of the land strayed upon should also be able to sue, in so far as the 'trespass' had injured his interest in the land or chattels thereon, ie strict liability for injury to his reversionary interest. The example was given of damage to a cottage and garden leased by a farmer, for a short term, to a holidaymaker.[41] However, section 4 is drafted in wider terms than this, for it talks of livestock straying on to land 'in the ownership or occupation of another'. By inference, this allows an action to be brought by the owner out of occupation for damage done to the land or property owned by him, irrespective of whether this constitutes an injury to his reversionary interest. This would seem, therefore, to include the long lease as well as the short lease; for section 4(1)(a) refers to damage to the land and not to the owner's interest in the land. **3.09**

The term 'straying onto the land in the ownership or occupation of another' is not to be interpreted as meaning straying 'directly' onto the other's land. So it is no defence that cattle strayed first onto a road and then into a garden from which they were chased out and eventually strayed onto the claimant's land.[42] **3.10**

One question of interpretation is whether both owner and occupier can sue for actual damage. While section 4 indicates clearly who may be liable,[43] the section is not explicit on the question of the circumstances in which the owner or the occupier may sue. It appears clear from section 4(1)(a) that an action will lie if damage is done to any property on the land which is in the ownership or possession of the claimant. Thus, if straying horses damage the landlord's car when parked in the drive of a house he has leased to a third party, a claim can be brought by the landlord; but if the landlord has not only leased his house to a tenant, but has allowed the latter to use a bicycle owned by the landlord, then if the bicycle is damaged by straying livestock, a claim can be brought by both the landlord, as the owner of the bicycle, and the tenant as the possessor of it. There is still, however, no liability for injuries done to someone, or his property, who has no interest in the land arising from ownership or occupation, for example the employee or spouse of the owner or occupier. **3.11**

[39] *McLoughlin v Cooper* [1999] NIJB 90. This is a decision under the Animals (Northern Ireland) Order 1976, SI 1976/1040, Arts 5 and 6 of which are in substantially the same terms as ss 4 and 5 of the 1971 Act.

[40] Law Commission Report, para 66.

[41] Ibid, para 66, n 96.

[42] *McLoughlin v Cooper* [1999] NIJB 90, 92.

[43] Section 4(2), below, paras 3.12–3.15.

(2) Defendant[44]

3.12 Liability is imposed on the person to whom the livestock belongs. Such a person is defined by section 4(2): 'For the purposes of this section any livestock belongs to the person in whose possession it is.' This means that the only possible defendant under section 4 will be the same person who was the normal defendant in an action of cattle trespass, namely the possessor of the livestock which have strayed.[45] He will also, normally, be the occupier of the land from which they have strayed;[46] but the possessor of ponies has been held liable when they strayed from common land where he had pastured them.[47] The possessor of the animals is liable even though he is not their owner, as where he has possession under a contract of agistment[48] or even from his wife.[49] In such circumstances, the owner out of possession is not liable;[50] nor will he be liable if he is a bailor, for he has no possession of the animal.[51] Similarly, when livestock is acquired under a hire purchase arrangement, the technical owner of the livestock during the running of the arrangement will not be liable, but the hirer, the farmer, will be, for he is the possessor of the livestock.

3.13 The requirement that the proper defendant should be the possessor of the livestock will exclude from liability those who have an interest less than possession. If livestock are in the possession of a farmer, then his cowman, as an employee, will merely have custody of the livestock in his charge and the cowman will not be held liable under section 4 if the livestock stray.

3.14 At common law, it was a debatable issue whether the occupier or owner of the *land* could be liable in cattle trespass for cattle straying from his land, although he was not in possession or control of the animals. In the Irish case of *Noonan v Hartnett*,[52] the defendant was the owner and occupier of land which he let to a third party for grazing, and the latter undertook to maintain the fences and herd the cattle. Some of the cattle which were on the land pursuant to the grazing contracts strayed on to the claimant's land and damaged his crops. The claimant's action in cattle trespass succeeded against the defendant, the owner of the land, although the cattle in

---

[44] Liability may be imposed on the Crown: Animals Act 1971, s 12, discussed, above, para 2.32.

[45] *Dawtry v Huggins* (1635) Clay 32; and see *Winters v Owens* [1950] IR 225.

[46] As in *ACV Telling Ltd v Sheppey* (1982) CA, Unreported, 5 February. On the common law liability for cattle straying from common land, see B Harris and G Ryan, *The Law Relating to Common Land* (1967), p 63.

[47] *Morris v Blaenau Gwent District Council* (1982) 80 LGR 793.

[48] *Hammond v Mallinson* [1939] LJCCR 357; and see *Dawtry v Huggins* (1635) Clay 32, 33.

[49] *Broderick v Forbes* (1912) 5 DLR 508.

[50] Williams, pp 177–8; *Hickey v Cosgrave* (1854) 6 Ir Jur NS 251; *Hammond v Mallinson* [1939] LJCCR 357; *Dalton v O'Sullivan* [1947] Ir Jur Rep 25.

[51] If the owner of cattle under a grazing letting does retain some control over them, then he is still liable provided the control is enough to amount to possession; cf *Winters v Owens* [1950] IR 225. A contract of sale may pass possession, and thus liability, to the buyer even before actual delivery: *Alsop v Lidgerwood* (1916) 22 Argus LR (N) 13.

[52] (1950) 84 ILTR 41.

question were neither owned by him nor under his occupation or control: for they were on his land in pursuance of a contract made with him.[53] Notwithstanding this decision, it was generally thought that liability in cattle trespass ought to depend on control of the animal, rather than occupation of the land from which it strayed.[54]

When one turns to the statutory liability under section 4, it is clear that there is no liability on either the owner out of possession of the livestock in question nor on the owner or occupier of the land from which the animals strayed. Liability is placed only on the person in possession of the livestock. Is this wholly desirable? We are told that liability is to be imposed solely on the possessor of the straying livestock on the ground that the object of a simple rule of strict liability is to ensure speedy settlement of disputes between neighbours.[55] One can see that such a justification explains the exclusion of the liability of the owner out of possession or control of the animals in question, as did the law of cattle trespass;[56] but if the speedy settlement of disputes between neighbours justifies strict liability, then is not the relevant issue that the parties are neighbours, and not that one is the possessor of the livestock in question? Naturally, most possessors of animals occupy the land on which the animals are pastured or kept; but section 4 excludes the liability, as such, of the occupier of the land (the neighbour) from which the cattle have strayed.[57] **3.15**

3. Scope of the Claim

(1) Place on to or from which the livestock strays

(a) General rule

Any owner or occupier of land may sue under section 4 if livestock stray on to land owned or occupied by him. **3.16**

(b) Exceptions[58]

(a) If livestock stray on to the highway, only the owner or occupier thereof may sue, and not a passer-by.[59] **3.17**

(b) If livestock lawfully using a highway stray from the highway on to adjoining property, then it is provided by section 5(5) of the Animals Act 1971 that there is

---

[53] It is difficult to accept the reliance on the principles of *Rylands v Fletcher* here, for pasturing cattle would seem to be a natural use of land; see below, paras 6.10–6.11.

[54] Williams, pp 176–8; 198–9; *Manton v Brocklebank* [1923] 2 KB 212; cf *Hammond v Mallinson* [1939] LJNCCR 357, 360–61; *Dalton v Sullivan* [1947] Ir Jur Rep 25, 27; *Winters v Owens* [1950] IR 225, 229.

[55] Law Commission Report, para 63.

[56] Above, para 3.12.

[57] cf *Noonan v Hartnett* (1950) 84 ILTR 41, above, para 3.14.

[58] More apparent than real.

[59] See the discussion of liability for animals straying on to the highway, below, paras 5.37–5.38.

no statutory liability under section 4. The only liability that will exist will be that which, at common law, emanates from negligence on the part of the person in control of the livestock.[60] If livestock are not lawfully on the highway, then there will be liability under section 4 if they stray from the highway on to land owned or occupied by the claimant.[61]

(c) There was, at common law, normally no obligation to prevent cattle from straying from common land.[62] Indeed, there was, and presumably still is, often an obligation on the adjoining occupier to 'fence against the common'. Thus, in *Barber v Whiteley*,[63] this is justified by Cockburn CJ, who said:

> The purpose of enclosing lands is that they may be used as cultivated land, and since such a use of them, beneficial to the person to whom it is permitted, makes it the more necessary that the land should not be open indifferently to grazing animals, it is more likely that the obligation of preventing such a trespass was imposed on the occupier than on the tenants of the manor, who had rights of common on the waste, formerly exercisable without such risks of distress, and who were a varying and uncertain body. Therefore, granting it to be a principle of law that where no obligation to fence is shown upon either of two adjoining landowners, each must take care his cattle do not stray; yet a different legal relation arises where . . . there is, on the one hand, a person inclosing from common land, and, on the other a body of persons entitled by law to exercise commonable rights on the land adjacent.[64]

3.18 No express provision is made in the Animals Act 1971 to deal with animals straying from common land. If, however, there was an obligation on the adjoining occupier to fence against the common, failure to fence constituted a defence to an action of cattle trespass and this defence is continued in the 1971 Act.[65] In the absence of such a fencing obligation, section 4 would appear to cover the situation and thus impose liability where animals which belong to a commoner stray on to a neighbour's land. It is suggested, however, that there should be no liability in such circumstances, as it is unlawful for the commoner to erect fences to contain his animals unless he has obtained the consent of the appropriate national authority.[66]

---

[60] *Tillett v Ward* (1882) 10 QBD 17; *Gayler and Pope Ltd v B Davies & Son Ltd* [1924] 2 KB 75; *Goldston v Bradshaw* [1934] LJNCCR 355; Williams, p 369; cf *Timothy White Ltd v Byng* [1934] LJNCCR 47, which would seem to be incorrectly decided.

[61] See below, paras 3.40–3.45.

[62] cf G Gadsden, *The Law of Commons* (1988), para 10.10.

[63] (1865) 13 WR 774, 775.

[64] cf *Coaker v Willcocks* [1911] 2 KB 124; C Sara, *Boundaries and Easements* (2008), para 22.03; B Harris and G Ryan, *The Law Relating to Common Land* (1967), p 63.

[65] Animals Act 1971, s 5(6), below, paras 4.16–4.41; cf *Crow v Wood* [1971] 1 QB 77.

[66] Commons Act 2006, s 38.

(2) Kinds of damage recoverable

There was little doubt that damages in an action of cattle trespass[67] could be recovered for damage to the claimant's land and crops.[68] Damages could also be recovered for injury to the claimant's animals on the land trespassed against. Thus, if the trespassing animals kicked[69] or bit[70] the claimant's horse or killed his cow,[71] damages were recoverable. Again, where the claimant's animals became infected by disease carried by the defendant's animals, the defendant would be liable.[72] Special problems arose when animals of different sexes were put in proximity through a trespass. If a bull trespassed into a field containing cows, the owner of the cows could recover damages for the fact that his cows were served by the bull[73] or even that there was no guarantee that they had not been.[74] If cows strayed into land containing a bull, then the owner of the latter could recover damages for injuries to the bull in trying to serve the cows.[75] If the trespassing animals ate all of the grass on the land so that the claimant's sheep died of starvation, such loss was actionable.[76] An action in cattle trespass would also lie where the defendant's animals injured inanimate chattels on the claimant's land, such as machinery[77] or vehicles.[78] A dramatic example of such recovery is provided by *Cooper v Railway Executive*.[79] The claimant's cattle strayed on to the defendants' railway line and a claim for injury to the cows failed as the defendants were not in breach of their duty to fence.[80] However, the cows caused a train to be derailed by the impact of hitting them and the defendants' counterclaim for damages for repair to the train and the track was successful. **3.19**

Finally, despite arguments to the contrary,[81] it appeared that, in England at least, damages could be recovered in cattle trespass for personal injuries. In *Wormald v Cole*,[82] **3.20**

---

[67] Williams, pp 157–73; on the measure of damages, see Williams, p 164.

[68] *Park v J Jobson & Son* [1945] 1 All ER 222; *Sutcliffe v Holmes* [1947] KB 147; *Wormald v Cole* [1954] 1 QB 614; and see *Brady v Warren* [1900] 2 IR 632; *Noonan v Hartnett* (1950) 84 ILTR 41.

[69] *Lee v Riley* (1865) 18 CBNS 722; *Holgate v Bleazard* [1917] 1 KB 443; *Whalley v Vandergrand* (1919) 44 DLR 319.

[70] *Ellis v Loftus Iron Co* (1874) LR 10 CP 10.

[71] *Messenger v Stevens* (1910) 9 ELR 91.

[72] *Anderson v Buckton* (1719) 11 Mod 304; *Earp v Faulkner* (1875) 34 LT 284, 286; *Theyer v Purnell* [1918] 2 KB 333.

[73] *McLean v Brett* (1919) 49 DLR 162, and cases cited in Williams, p 166, n 8; and see *Daniel Logan & Son v Roger* 1952 SLT (Sh Ct) 99; *Dobbie v Henderson* 1970 SLT (Sh Ct) 27; 305 HL Deb (1969) cc 1394–5.

[74] *Halstead v Mathieson* [1919] VLR 362.

[75] *Eustace v Eyre* [1947] LJNCCR 106.

[76] *Challoner v McPhail* (1877) Knox 157 (NSW).

[77] *Moon v Stephens* (1915) 23 DLR 223.

[78] *Welch v Dominion Transport Co* (1922) 69 DLR 588.

[79] [1953] 1 All ER 477.

[80] Discussed below, para 4.09.

[81] Williams, pp 168–73.

[82] [1954] 1 QB 614.

the defendant's cattle strayed into the claimant's garden. The claimant was knocked down and injured by a heifer and the Court of Appeal allowed recovery of damages for her personal injuries. It was, however, essential that there should have been a trespass, however technical,[83] to the claimant's land.[84]

3.21 Under the Animals Act 1971, liability for straying livestock applies, under section 4(1)(a), to the case where '[d]amage is done by the livestock to the land or to any property on it which is in the ownership or possession of the other person'. This is, in many respects, a statutory enactment of the heads of damage for cattle trespass. Thus, the damage which is actionable under this subsection will extend, as at common law, to damage to the land, including domestic gardens,[85] crops, and buildings thereon, and chattels on the land, which will include, presumably, animals[86] and other chattels such as trains[87] and other vehicles.[88] The Law Commission rejected[89] as impractical any attempts to limit the property in question to agricultural property, and there is no such limitation in the Act. There is, however, no liability for personal injuries under this head of statutory liability; so the decision in *Wormald v Cole*[90] has been abrogated.[91] Of course, there can still be liability for such personal injuries on proof of negligence.[92]

3.22 It is, perhaps, relevant to note that section 4(1)(a) deals with the situation where straying livestock cause *damage*, rather than cause *loss*. This may be illustrated by the case of the straying of diseased or potentially diseased animals. If a diseased cow strays from the defendant's land on to the claimant's and there infects the claimant's cows with the disease in question, there is no doubt that damage has been caused to the claimant's property, in that his cow has become diseased and an action will lie under section 4.[93] If, however, the defendant has a cow found to be suffering from foot and mouth disease and that cow strays on to the claimant's land, then even though no cow of the claimant's can be proved to have been infected it may well be that an order restricting the movement of the claimant's cattle could be imposed on

---

83 *Ellis v Loftus Iron Co* (1874) LR 10 CP 10.

84 *Cox v Burbidge* (1863) 13 CBNS 430; *Bradley v Wallaces Ltd* [1913] 3 KB 629; and see *Theyer v Purnell* [1918] 2 KB 333, 338; *Manton v Brocklebank* [1923] 2 KB 212. See also Williams, pp 152–7.

85 eg *McLoughlin v Cooper* [1999] NIJB 90.

86 As in, eg, *Lee v Riley* (1865) 18 CBNS 722; and see 305 HL Deb (1969) cc 1392–3.

87 *Cooper v Railway Executive* [1953] 1 All ER 477.

88 eg *Welch v Dominion Transport Co* (1922) 69 DLR 588.

89 Law Commission Report, para 65.

90 [1954] 1 QB 614.

91 This is so even though 'damage' is defined in the Animals Act 1971, s 11, so as to include the death of or injury to a person. The wording of s 4(1)(a) would appear to confine liability thereunder to damage to land or property. That being so, it is rather strange to find that, by reason of s 10 of the Animals Act 1971, the Fatal Accidents Acts 1846–1959 (and see the Fatal Accidents Act 1976, s 6(1), Sch 1, para 1(1); Sch 2) are held to be applicable to claims under s 4.

92 See ch 6, below.

93 cf *Theyer v Purnell* [1918] 2 KB 333.

the claimant. The consequence would be that the claimant would suffer financial loss in being unable to take his cattle to market at the proper time, even though none had been infected or damaged. Such loss is not actionable under section 4, although it might be actionable on proof of negligence on the part of the defendant.[94] A similar situation would arise if a cow from the defendant's herd, not being brucillosis-free, strayed on to the claimant's land, the latter having a brucillosis-free herd.[95] Even though none of the claimant's cattle were proved to be infected, he would cease to be an accredited brucillosis-free farmer and thereby suffer consequential financial loss. As with the foot and mouth example, he could only recover under section 4 if his cows became infected or, possibly, under the common law if the straying was due to the negligence of the defendant.[96]

Some instances of financial loss were, however, recoverable at common law in cattle trespass. A claimant could claim not only for actual damage to his land or property caused by trespassing cattle, but also for the cost of maintaining animals which had strayed on to his land,[97] and for the extra cost of feeding his own animals; in short for 'any loss naturally following from the trespass'.[98] Similar provision is made under the Animals Act 1971, section 4(1)(b). Even though no damage is done to the claimant's land or to the property on it, the claimant may claim for any expenses which are reasonably incurred by him in keeping the defendant's livestock while it cannot be restored to him or while it is being detained in pursuance of section 7 of the Act,[99] or for expenses reasonably incurred in ascertaining to whom it belongs. The Court of Appeal has held[100] that, where the problem of livestock straying off common land was so great that the local authority had to establish a pound and employ animal catchers, it was entitled to a reasonable standard charge for the cost of impounding each pony in question and for its daily maintenance. A merit of using a reasonable standard charge was that it would enable the owner to calculate the amount to be paid, under section 7(3)(b), to secure the release of the animals. **3.23**

At common law, in order for an action of cattle trespass to lie, the damage done by the animal had to be 'natural to the species of the animal'. While there was no doubt that there was liability, for example, for damage caused by the spread of disease, this **3.24**

[94] cf *Weller & Co v Foot and Mouth Disease Research Institute* [1966] 1 QB 569; *D Pride and Partners v Institute of Animal Health* [2009] EWHC 685; and see ch 6.

[95] This was a problem that led to much debate during the passage of the Animals Act: 305 HL Deb (1969), cc 559, 1393–1400, 1409–14; 306 HL Deb (1969), cc 659–65, 677–84; 815 HC Deb (1971), c 611.

[96] cf *Weller & Co*, above; *D Pride and Partners*, above; and see ch 6.

[97] *Theyer v Purnell* [1918] 2 KB 333, 336–7.

[98] Ibid, at p 341; *Buckle v Holmes* [1926] 2 KB 125, 130; *Wormald v Cole* [1954] 1 QB 614, 627.

[99] Which replaces the law of distress of animals damage feasant; see Law Commission Report, paras 69–72; and below, paras 3.47–3.60.

[100] *Morris v Blaenau Gwent District Council* (1982) 80 LGR 793; and see *Matthews v Wicks* (1987) CA, Unreported, 22 May.

being regarded as a natural consequence of diseased animals straying,[101] damage which did not result from the natural behaviour of the animal would appear to have been irrecoverable.[102] Thus, it was suggested that it was not natural for a horse to kick human beings;[103] although in *Wormald v Cole*[104] doubt was cast on the assumption that there would be no liability if a horse *attacked* a human being,[105] for Lord Goddard stated:

> I leave open the question whether it follows that if a trespassing animal attacks the occupier he can recover, though I incline to the opinion that he can.[106]

3.25 There is no indication in section 4 of the Animals Act 1971 that the damage in question must be natural to the species of the animal. Liability will exist whether or not this is so, provided that the damage is to land or property thereon.[107] The exclusion of liability for personal injuries[108] will, in fact, greatly minimize the circumstances where straying livestock cause 'non-natural' damage, for the area at common law where difficulty arose was that of personal injuries. Nevertheless, an action will lie under section 4 for any damage caused to land or property thereon by straying livestock, even though of a kind unusual for the animal in question.

4. Strict Liability

3.26 There was no doubt that cattle trespass[109] was a tort of strict liability and was independent of proof of negligence.[110] It has been held

> again and again, that there is a duty on a man to keep his cattle in, and if they get on another's land it is a trespass; and that is irrespective of any question of negligence whether great or small.[111]

It is equally true that liability under section 4 is strict. No proof is required of fault on the part of the possessor of livestock who allows them to stray on to land owned

---

[101] *Theyer v Purnell* [1918] 2 KB 333; and see the explanation at pp 339–40; cf *Cooke v Waring* (1863) 2 H & C 332.

[102] The burden of proof of abnormality of behaviour appeared to rest on he who alleged it: *McCabe v Delany* [1951] Ir Jur Rep 10.

[103] *Cox v Burbidge* (1863) 13 CBNS 430, 437; *Bradley v Wallaces Ltd* [1913] 3 KB 629.

[104] [1954] 1 QB 614.

[105] Rather than another horse, as in *Lee v Riley* (1865) 18 CBNS 722; *Ellis v Loftus Iron Co* (1874) LR 10 CP 10.

[106] [1954] 1 QB 614, 625; cf ibid at pp 632–3; and see *Hennigan v M'Vey* (1882) 9 R 411—trespassing boar; cf *Mark v Barkla* [1935] NZLR 347.

[107] Although see the discussion of remoteness of damage, below, paras 3.31–3.32.

[108] However, the Court of Appeal has upheld an award of general damages for 'distress, inconvenience and loss of enjoyment' as a result of damage done to a garden: *Matthews v Wicks* (1987) CA, Unreported, 22 May.

[109] Williams, pp 185–94.

[110] eg *Cox v Burbidge* (1863) 13 CBNS 430, 438; *Fletcher v Rylands* (1868) LR 1 Exch 265, 280.

[111] *Ellis v Loftus Iron Co* (1874) LR 10 CP 10, 12, per Lord Coleridge CJ; and see at p 13, per Brett J.

or occupied by the claimant. In fact, the continued existence of strict liability for this conduct was one good reason for not allowing claims hereunder for personal injuries.[112] As the defendant is liable though not at fault, his ability to prove lack of fault is irrelevant unless, perhaps, he can prove that the straying was involuntary.[113]

5. Actionability

There was no doubt that cattle trespass, like other forms of trespass to land, was actionable without proof of damage.[114] However, proof of a technical trespass was necessary before there could be an award of damages for consequential injury.[115] This may be illustrated by *Ellis v Loftus Iron Co.*[116] The claimant's mare was injured when the defendants' horse bit and kicked her. The two horses were each on their owners' own land, but the defendants' horse did the injury through the fence. That being so it was clear to Lord Coleridge CJ: **3.27**

> that some portion of the defendants' horse's body must have been over the boundary. That may be a very small trespass, but it is a trespass in law.[117]

The technical trespass having been proved, the claimant recovered.

Here a change was made by section 4 of the Animals Act 1971, for the statutory head of liability thereunder is not actionable per se. There must be proof of actual damage or the incurring of reasonable expenses. This makes little substantial alteration; for the rule that cattle trespass, as a form of trespass to land, was actionable per se was only of importance where there had been a possibly doubtful technical trespass to land, followed by actual damage to property thereon.[118] However, the new statutory liability is not, in so many words, based on a technical trespass to land.[119] The Animals Act 1971 talks of livestock straying on to land '*in the ownership or occupation* of another'[120] and the owner out of occupation cannot maintain an action for trespass to land.[121] Liability is based on actual injury to the land and property thereon or actual expenses incurred as a consequence of the straying. What is not clear is whether *Ellis v Loftus Iron Co*[122] would still be decided in the same **3.28**

---

[112] Law Commission Report, para 65.

[113] cf *Mitten v Faudrye* (1626) Poph 161.

[114] Except, perhaps, in the case of 'depasturing of chattels'; Williams, p 150.

[115] *Ellis v Loftus Iron Co* (1874) LR 10 CP 10; *Wiseman v Booker* (1878) 3 CPD 184; Williams, p 150.

[116] (1874) LR 10 CP 10.

[117] Ibid at p 12.

[118] eg *Ellis v Loftus Iron Co*, above.

[119] The problem arising from the fact that the marginal note to s 4 refers to 'trespassing livestock' is considered, above, para 3.08.

[120] Section 4(1), italics added.

[121] eg *Cooper v Crabtree* (1882) 20 Ch D 589.

[122] (1874) LR 10 CP 10.

way today. While there was no doubt of the injury to the property, the mare, on the claimant's land, can it be said that a horse which puts its head over a fence 'strays on to the land'?[123]

3.29 Some possible light is thrown on this question by *Wiseman v Booker*.[124] The defendant's horses had put their heads over the inadequate fence between the land of the defendant and adjoining land rented by the claimant's father from a railway company. The horses had eaten vegetables growing on the land, which growing vegetables had been sold to the claimant by his father. The defendant alleged that there was a statutory obligation on the railway company to maintain the fence, thereby protecting the land 'from trespass or the cattle of the owners or occupiers thereof from straying thereout'.[125] In other words, the railway company was under an obligation to fence out the defendant's horses. If that fencing obligation had been broken, the defendant would be relieved from liability. So the main issue was really whether horses which put their heads over or through a fence had strayed. Lindley J held that the claim failed. As the railway company was in breach of its duty to the defendant to maintain the fences, the defendant could not be made responsible to the railway company's tenant for injury resulting from breach of the fencing obligation. In the course of his judgment, Lindley J stated:

> The structure is to be sufficient to keep the cattle of the adjoining owners from straying on to the land of the company. *The horses here were straying within the fair meaning of those words*; and this it was the duty of the company to prevent.[126]

3.30 While one must always be wary of applying decisions interpreting one statute to the interpretation of another, it would appear that this case provides persuasive authority for liability being imposed under section 4 of the Animals Act 1971 in the *Ellis v Loftus Iron Co* type of situation. If, of course, the defendant's livestock are lawfully on the land where they cause damage, as under a contract of agistment,[127] they cannot be said to have strayed and there will be no liability under section 4. There is, however, the problem of livestock which were lawfully on the claimant's land, but then outstay their welcome by remaining on the land longer than the permitted period. Such conduct constitutes a trespass and could well have given rise to liability for cattle trespass.[128] It is difficult to see, however, how such livestock can be said to have strayed.

[123] In their report, the Law Commission recommended that liability should be based on a 'trespass'. This led to their recommendation that there should cease to be liability for 'depasturing chattels'; Report, para 68.

[124] (1878) 3 CPD 184.

[125] Railways Clauses Consolidation Act 1845, s 68.

[126] (1878) 3 CPD 184, at p 188, italics added.

[127] eg *Manton v Brocklebank* [1923] 2 KB 212; and see *Mathieson v G Stuckey & Co Ltd* [1921] VLR 637, 641.

[128] *Stodden v Harvey* (1608) Cro Jac 204; Williams, pp 150–52.

6. Remoteness of Damage

Although it has been argued that cattle trespass should have ceased to be a tort of strict liability,[129] it did remain such a tort. Thus, it appeared to fall within the general statement that the test of remoteness of damage based on reasonable foresight, as laid down in *The Wagon Mound*,[130] was not intended to apply to torts of strict liability.[131] However, the House of Lords has since held[132] that claims under the strict liability rule in *Rylands v Fletcher*[133] should be subject to a foreseeability test of remoteness, and it has been suggested[134] that it should follow that statutory schemes of strict liability, of which claims under section 4 of the Animals Act 1971 appear to be one, should also be subject to a foreseeability test.[135] Were it to be decided, nevertheless, that the test to be applied to claims under section 4 of the Animals Act 1971 were not to be the subject of a foreseeability test of remoteness, then the applicable test would be one of direct consequences.[136] The application of this test can be illustrated by decisions under the old law of cattle trespass, where it has been held that if a trespassing horse kicks or bites the claimant's horse, this damage is the 'natural and direct consequence of the trespass committed'.[137] The same can be said if the defendant's diseased sheep, trespassing on the claimant's land, infect the latter's sheep,[138] and if a trespassing cow gored and killed the claimant's horse.[139] **3.31**

The issue of whether or not damages can be recovered if the injury is not natural to the species has been discussed,[140] but the application of that rule to cattle trespass meant that all damage natural to the species was recoverable, and one could say that **3.32**

---

[129] Williams (1961) 77 LQR 179, 211–12; and see Dias [1962] CLJ 178, 195–6.

[130] [1961] AC 388.

[131] Ibid, at pp 426–7; and see A Tettenborn, *The Law of Damages*, 2nd edn (2010), paras 6.70 et seq; cf *Brook v Cook* (1961) 105 Sol Jo 684 and see ibid, at p 1095; although in *The Wagon Mound (No 2)* [1967] 1 AC 617 such a remoteness rule was applied to the whole of the law of nuisance, including elements of strict liability though, apparently, excluding 'cases like *Wringe v Cohen*' [1954] 1 KB 229; see Lord Reid: [1967] 1 AC 617, 639.

[132] *Cambridge Water Co Ltd v Eastern Counties Leather plc* [1994] AC 264.

[133] (1868) LR 3 HL 330.

[134] Tettenborn, above, paras 6.70–6.76; and see WH Rogers, *Winfield and Jolowicz on Tort*, 18th edn (2010), para 16.12.

[135] See, eg *Blue Circle Industries plc v Ministry of Defence* [1999] Ch 289; *The Sea Empress* [2002] EWHC 1095; [2003] Lloyd's Rep 123.

[136] *Re Polemis and Furness Withy & Co* [1921] 3 KB 560; and see Williams, pp 157–73.

[137] *Ellis v Loftus Iron Co* (1874) LR 10 CP 10, 12; and see *Lee v Riley* (1865) 18 CBNS 722; or if a trespassing cow injures the claimant's cow: *Ryan v Glover* [1939] Ir Jur Rep 65.

[138] *Theyer v Purnell* [1918] 2 KB 333, 336, 340–41.

[139] *McCabe v Delany* [1951] Ir Jur Rep 10; and see *Wormald v Cole* [1954] 1 QB 614; cf *Bradley v Wallaces Ltd* [1913] 3 KB 629; but see *Harrison v Armstrong* (1917) 51 ILTR 38—apparently a negligence case.

[140] Above, paras 3.24–3.25.

other damage was irrecoverable because it was too remote.[141] If damage not natural to the species was regarded as too remote for the purposes of the law of cattle trespass, the same might well be true of liability under section 4 of the Animals Act 1971.[142] In practice, if liability is restricted to injuries natural to the species of the straying animal, this will come very close to a test of liability for consequences which the defendant ought to have foreseen.[143] With the abolition of liability for personal injuries caused by straying livestock, the problem may well be academic.

7. Defences

3.33 The abolition by the Animals Act 1971 of the common law action for cattle trespass carried with it the corollary of the abolition of all the defences thereto.[144] It would appear, therefore, that the only defences available to an action under section 4 are those provided by the Animals Act 1971. This object is achieved by the provision in section 4(1) that the possessor of the straying livestock shall be liable 'except as otherwise provided by this Act'. No defences apply other than those laid down in the Act. There appear to be *four* such defences:

(1) Contributory negligence of the claimant

3.34 It was stated, by the Law Commission,[145] that contributory negligence on the part of the claimant should remain a defence as under the law of cattle trespass. This is achieved in the Act by what may be recalled[146] as a rather involved process. Section 10[147] provides that:

> For the purpose of . . . the Law Reform (Contributory Negligence) Act 1945 . . . any damage for which a person is liable under sections 2 to 4 of this Act shall be treated as due to his fault.

Thus, although the liability under section 4 is, in fact, strict liability, the defence of contributory negligence as provided by the 1945 Act will be available, as has been confirmed by the Court of Appeal.[148] It would seem that decisions under the law of cattle trespass will be relevant still in examining allegations of contributory negligence in claims brought under section 4. There was no doubt that contributory

[141] eg *Cox v Burbidge* (1863) 13 CBNS 430, 436–7, 438; *Manton v Brocklebank* [1923] 2 KB 212, 223, 225.

[142] See WH Rogers, *Winfield and Jolowicz on Tort*, 18th edn (2010), para 16.12.

[143] J Fleming, *Torts*, 9th edn (1998), p 398.

[144] *McLoughlin v Cooper* [1999] NIJB 90, 91.

[145] Law Commission Report, para 67(ii).

[146] Above, paras 2.159–2.164.

[147] Which has been described as 'a rather inelegant piece of legislation by reference': 312 HL Deb (1970), c 201; and see Art 12 of the Animals (Northern Ireland) Order, SI 1976/1040.

[148] *Matthews v Wicks* (1987) CA, Unreported, 22 May.

negligence could constitute a defence to cattle trespass.[149] Thus, if the claimant was licensed to build a haystack on the defendant's land,[150] and the defendant's cattle ate the hay, the failure of the claimant to fence off his haystack was evidence of his contributory negligence.[151] However, failure to put a spring on a gate through which sheep strayed on to the claimant's land has been held not to constitute contributory negligence.[152]

3.35 If an occupier finds livestock straying on his land, he should take steps to drive them out and if, in the process, he suffers damage to his land or property on it, the possessor of the straying livestock will not be able to plead that the conduct of the claimant in driving the cattle out was, in itself, evidence of contributory negligence.[153]

(2) Damage due wholly to the fault of the claimant

3.36 This defence, which is similar in nature to that of contributory negligence, is provided by section 5(1):[154]

> A person is not liable under sections 2 to 4 of this Act for any damage which is due wholly to the fault of the person suffering it.

As 'fault' is defined[155] by reference to the definition in the Law Reform (Contributory Negligence) Act 1945,[156] this means that the claimant is unable to sue for damage done by straying livestock if it has been caused wholly by his own negligence, breach of statutory duty, breach of contract,[157] or any other act or omission which would give rise to the defence of contributory negligence.[158] This is wider than the recommendation by the Law Commission[159] that the defence should apply where the claimant was solely responsible for the damage 'by reason of his negligence'.

3.37 At common law there was a defence to an action of cattle trespass if the damage was done by the 'leave and licence' of the claimant. Thus, in *Park v J Jobson and Son*,[160] the defendants' cattle strayed on to the claimant's allotment and it was argued that the allotment fence had been damaged by the allotment holders of whom the claimant was one and that therefore the claimant had licensed the presence of the cattle on his allotment. The defence failed, as the defendants failed to prove that the claimant's

---

149 Williams, pp 178–80; G Williams, *Joint Torts & Contributory Negligence* (1951), pp 209, 286.
150 Of course, the claimant will fail under s 4(1), unless he is shown to be an occupier of the land.
151 cf *Plummer v Webb* (1619) Noy 98.
152 *Matthews v Wicks*, above.
153 Williams, pp 179–80; cf *Waugh v Montgomery* (1882) 8 VLR 290.
154 And see Art 6(1) of the Animals (Northern Ireland) Order 1976, SI 1976/1040.
155 See s 11.
156 1945 Act, s 4.
157 See *Quinn v Burch Bros (Builders) Ltd* [1966] 2 QB 370.
158 G Williams, *Joint Torts & Contributory Negligence* (1951), p 318.
159 Law Commission Report, para 67(ii).
160 [1945] 1 All ER 222; discussed below, ch 4, paras 4.21–4.22 on the question of who is liable for failure to fence.

act had caused the cattle to stray and they failed, therefore, to prove any licence by the claimant. Nevertheless, the Court of Appeal accepted that the defence of consent was applicable to cattle trespass in appropriate circumstances, for Lord Greene MR said:

> I do not think the proposition is likely to be disputed that a person who gives leave, expressly or impliedly, to his neighbours' cattle to trespass on his land cannot complain, and that such leave and licence can be inferred from the circumstances of a particular case.[161]

Whether the leaving open of a gate or other such gaps in the fencing was leave and licence was difficult to assess, for generally there is no duty to fence out your neighbour's cattle. To leave a gap is not necessarily to license cattle to come through it.[162]

3.38 It will be necessary to determine what circumstances which fell under the common law defence now fall within section 5(1). The most likely situation is that where the claimant leaves a gate open or leaves gaps in his fences through which the livestock stray. While it was debatable at common law whether leaving such a gap amounted to a licence for cattle to come through it, such straying would seem normally to be due wholly to the fault of the claimant, within the meaning of section 5(1).

(3) The claimant's failure to fence

3.39 This statutory defence is provided by section 5(6),[163] which states that:

> In determining whether any liability for damage under section 4 of this Act is excluded by subsection (1) of this section the damage shall not be treated as due to the fault of the person suffering it by reason only that he could have prevented it by fencing;[164] but a person is not liable under that section where it is proved that the straying of the livestock on to the land would not have occurred but for a breach by any other person, being a person having an interest in the land, of a duty to fence.

This statutory defence is discussed in Chapter 4.[165]

(4) Straying from the highway

3.40 It is provided by section 5(5) that:

> A person is not liable under section 4 of this Act where the livestock strayed from a highway and its presence there was a lawful use of the highway.[166]

---

[161] [1945] 1 All ER 222, 224.

[162] *Swift v Ellis* [1939] LJNCCR 384, 389; cf *Wellaway v Courtier* [1918] 1 KB 200, 203; Williams, pp 180–81.

[163] And see the Animals (Northern Ireland) Order 1976, SI 1976/1040, Art 6(5).

[164] 'Fencing' includes 'the construction of any obstacle designed to prevent animals from straying': s 11.

[165] Below, paras 4.16–4.41.

[166] And see the Animals (Northern Ireland) Order 1976, SI 1976/1040, Art 6(4).

This defence is dependent on the use of the highway[167] by the livestock being lawful. If the livestock had been turned out to graze on the highway, this would constitute a trespass against the occupier of the highway;[168] the user would be unlawful; and there would be liability for damage done when the livestock strayed off the highway. Again, if the livestock strayed on to the highway in the first place, their presence thereon is not a lawful use of the highway,[169] for in these circumstances a claim under section 4 could have been brought by the owner or occupier of the highway. That would be so even if the livestock strayed onto the highway as a result of malicious damage to the defendant's fences.[170]

Matthews v Wicks[171] illustrates the problem which may arise from livestock straying from common land onto the highway and then into neighbouring gardens. In this case, sheep had long been run in the Forest of Dean, which was common land, but frequently strayed through the streets of Cinderford and then into gardens, setting up a long-standing conflict between the Commoners Association and the residents of Cinderford. The Court of Appeal concluded that, when the sheep strayed into neighbouring gardens, the owner of the sheep was liable under section 4 of the Animals Act 1971 unless a good defence was provided by section 5. Gibson LJ made clear that: **3.41**

> The statutory defence requires not only that the presence of the straying livestock on the highway be lawful . . . but that the presence of the straying livestock on the highway was a lawful use of the highway . . . I see no reason to suppose that Parliament intended that the defence provided by section 5(5), based on 'lawful use of the highway' should necessarily exist in any case in which the animals or livestock, which stray from the highway into land in the occupation of another, had previously strayed onto the highway from other common land etc on which the defendant had a right to place the animals. If such had been the intention of Parliament, again I have no doubt that words apt to achieve that purpose would have been used.

Lawful user of a highway is based on a right of passage and repassage.[172] However, **3.42**

> the right of the public to pass and repass on a highway is subject to all those reasonable extensions which may from time to time be recognized as necessary to its exercise in

[167] No definition of 'highway' is provided by the Animals Act 1971; see below, para 5.27. It is suggested that the meaning of 'highway' for the purposes of s 5(5) is the general common law meaning of 'all portions of land over which every subject of the Crown may lawfully pass': J Pratt et al, *Pratt and Mackenzie's Law of Highways*, 21st edn (1967), p 3; and see S Sauvain, *Highway Law*, 4th edn (2009), paras 1.01–1.21. This will include not only ordinary roads, but also footpaths, bridleways, and driftways.

[168] *Stevens v Whistler* (1809) 11 East 51.

[169] eg *Manchester, Sheffield and Lincolnshire Rail Co v Wallis* (1854) 14 CB 213; *Luscombe v Great Western Rail Co* [1899] 2 QB 313; *Creasy v Abell* [1945] LJRCC 148; *Morris v Curtis* [1947] LJNCCR 284; and see *Rayner v Shearing* [1926] SASR 313.

[170] *McLoughlin v Cooper* [1999] NIJB 90, 92.

[171] (1987) CA, Unreported, 22 May.

[172] *Dovaston v Payne* (1795) 2 Hy Bl 527; *R v Pratt* (1855) 4 E & B 860; *Mayhew v Wardley* (1863) 14 CBNS 550; *Harrison v Duke of Rutland* [1893] 1 QB 142; *Hickman v Maisey* [1900] 1 QB 752.

accordance with the enlarged notions of people in a country becoming more populous and highly civilized.[173]

Such reasonable user was given quite a liberal interpretation by Phillimore J in *Hadwell v Righton*,[174] a case concerned with chickens straying on to the highway:

> In the first place, I think that members of the public, in addition to using it eundo et redeundo, are also entitled to use it morando for a short time. And I doubt whether, even with that addition, the lawful uses are thereby exhausted. For instance, if fowls are kept near a highway, and there is a corn stubble belonging to their owner on the other side of the road to which they might naturally and properly go, I am not prepared to say that to allow them to go there by themselves would be an unlawful use of the highway by their owner simply because they might while so doing run or fly into someone who was riding a bicycle.

If an animal has strayed on to the highway so that its presence is unlawful, then once the owner takes control of it to drive it home along the highway, such user becomes lawful.[175] It may even be that it is lawfully on the highway before it is recaptured, provided its owner is in pursuit.[176]

3.43 If the act of a third party is not to be a defence to the statutory action under section 4,[177] this strengthens the authority of those decisions at common law[178] which indicated that cattle were not lawfully on the highway even though their straying thereon resulted from the act of a third party in, for example, leaving a gate open. This defence does not, of course, exclude liability for negligence in appropriate circumstances.

3.44 There is no limitation to be placed on the defence under section 5(5) dependent on the site of the claimant's land. It does not matter whether the claimant's land adjoins the highway or not.[179] This is justified on the grounds that, if animals get on to the claimant's land from the highway, the claimant occupies such land on the basis that it imposes on him the burden of assuming the risk of accidental trespass.[180] This means that in a country like England, with a complex road network, the majority of occupiers are considered to accept the risk of such straying. There is no requirement in this statutory defence, similar to that which may have existed in the common law defence, that the person in charge of the animals should have pursued them within a reasonable time.[181]

---

[173] *Hickman v Maisey*, above, pp 757–8; and see, eg, *Randall v Tarrant* [1955] 1 All ER 600.
[174] [1907] 2 KB 345, 348.
[175] *Midland Rail Co v Daykin* (1855) 17 CB 126; cf *Street v Craig* (1920) 56 DLR 105.
[176] cf *Spurr v Dominion Atlantic Rly* (1903) 40 NSR 417.
[177] Below, para 3.46.
[178] *Manchester, Sheffield and Lincolnshire Rail Co v Wallis* (1854) 14 CB 213; approved, albeit reluctantly, by Lord Esher MR in *Charman v South Eastern Rail Co* (1888) 21 QBD 524, 527–8.
[179] Law Commission Report, para 67, n 97.
[180] Williams, p 375.
[181] cf *Goodwyn v Cheveley* (1859) 4 H & N 631, below, paras 5.32–5.33; Williams, pp 374–5.

This defence is the statutory replacement of a similar defence to an action of cattle trespass. That common law defence was justified on the ground that occupiers accept the risk of accidental injury caused by cattle straying from a highway.[182] It is worth noting that, although the continued existence of such a defence can only be justified on the basis of assumption of risk, the Law Commission did not recommend the retention of the general defence of consent or 'leave and licence'[183] except and in so far as circumstances falling within that head could also be classed as circumstances where the claimant is wholly responsible by his fault for his injuries.[184] It should be stressed that the defence under section 5(5) is only applicable where the livestock are lawfully using the highway before they stray. If they may be regarded as trespassers thereon, then liability will exist under section 4. **3.45**

(5) Inapplicable defences

It is significant that a number of other defences applicable to cattle trespass do not apply under the Animals Act 1971 to liability under section 4. The defence of Act of God, though still a defence to a common law action based on a failure to fence,[185] does not provide a defence to an action under section 4,[186] nor does the defence of consent save in so far as it falls within section 5(1).[187] The defence of act of third party, although accepted in both England[188] and Ireland[189] as a defence to an action of cattle trespass, is inapplicable to a claim under section 4. Thus, if a third party leaves a gate open so that the defendant's livestock stray on to the claimant's land, that act of a third party is no defence to an action under section 4.[190] If, however, a third party *drove* the defendant's livestock on to the claimant's land, then it is suggested that there would be no liability on the part of the defendant, for his livestock had not 'strayed'. The third party might well be liable in such a case for trespass to land.[191] **3.46**

[182] eg *Fletcher v Rylands* (1866) LR 1 Exch 265, 286; *River Wear Commissioners v Adamson* (1877) 2 App Cas 743, 767; *Tillett v Ward* (1882) 10 QBD 17, 20; *Gayler and Pope Ltd v B Davies and Son Ltd* [1924] 2 KB 75, 82–4; *Wormald v Cole* [1954] 1 QB 614, 626.

[183] It is retained for liability under s 2; see s 5(2), above, paras 2.129–2.139.

[184] Above, paras 3.36–3.38.

[185] *Lawrence v Jenkins* (1873) LR 8 QB 274, 278; see ch 4, para 4.12, below.

[186] Although it probably did provide a defence to an action of cattle trespass: *Fletcher v Rylands* (1866) LR 1 Exch 265, 279–80; *Nichols v Marsland* (1875) LR 10 Exch 255; and see *Sharp v Harvey* [1935] LJNCCR 261, 265; *Poupart v Brazil* [1941] LJCCR 223, 224.

[187] Above, paras 3.36–3.38.

[188] *Sutcliffe v Holmes* [1947] KB 147; and see *Sharp v Harvey*, above; *Morris v Curtis* [1947] LJNCCR 284, 287; see also *Singleton v Williamson* (1861) 7 H & N 410, 416; cf *Cooke v Skinner* (1948) 98 L Jo 38.

[189] *McGibbon v McCurry* (1909) 43 ILTR 132; *Moloney v Stephens* [1945] Ir Jur Rep 37.

[190] *AVC Telling Ltd v Sheppey* (1982) CA, Unreported, 5 February; and see also *Park v J Jobson & Son* [1945] 1 All ER 222, 225. Nor would there be any defence if the defendant's livestock were stampeded on to the claimant's land through fright from low-flying aircraft. See 305 HL Deb (1969), c 1450.

[191] See ch 6 below, paras 6.02–6.06.

8. Detention of Straying Livestock[192]

3.47 At common law if the claimant had distrained the defendant's trespassing cattle damage feasant,[193] then any action for cattle trespass by the claimant was barred.[194] This only applied to the actual animals distrained[195] and the action revived if the cattle distrained died, escaped, or were stolen without the fault of the distrainor.[196] By section 7(1) of the Animals Act 1971, the right to seize and detain any animal by way of distress damage feasant was abolished.[197] This constituted abolition of the right of distress damage feasant in the case of *all* animals and not just those falling within the head of 'cattle' or 'livestock', although one must agree with the Law Commission that the exercise of the right in the case of other animals 'has fallen into complete desuetude'.[198] A new right to detain livestock was created by section 7(2):[199]

> Where any livestock strays on to any land and is not then under the control of any person the occupier of the land may detain it, subject to subsection (3) of this section, unless ordered to return it by a court.

This may be illustrated by *Morris v Blaenau Gwent District Council*,[200] where the local authority had to tackle a continual problem of livestock, which were lawfully pastured on common land by the defendant amongst others, then straying into adjoining properties owned by the council. So serious was the problem that the council had to construct a pound and employ animal catchers to deal with the issue. The Court of Appeal held that the council had acted lawfully in detaining the defendant's ponies in the pound, under section 7, and could claim their expenses for doing so, under section 4(1)(b).

3.48 The restriction of the right of detention under section 7 to cases of straying livestock, which is defined in the same way as in relation to the action for straying livestock provided by section 4,[201] is likely to be of any significance only in the case

---

[192] See G Gadsden, *The Law of Commons* (1988), paras 10.14–10.32.

[193] Williams, p 195; on the general law of distress damage feasant, see Williams, Pt I.

[194] *Vaspor v Edwards* (1702) 12 Mod Rep 658; and see *Boden v Roscoe* [1894] 1 QB 608.

[195] *Vaspor v Edwards*, above, at p 660.

[196] *Williams v Price* (1832) 3 B & Ad 695. The position where these events occurred as a result of the claimant's negligence is unclear: Williams, p 195.

[197] Although the remedy of distress damage feasant has not been abolished for other purposes: *Arthur v Anker* [1997] QB 564.

[198] Law Commission Report, para 69, n 104.

[199] Provision similar to s 7 is made by the Animals (Northern Ireland) Order 1976, SI 1976/1040, Art 9, but, in addition, in Art 10, provision is made for the police to impound any animal found wandering on a public road where the owner is unknown. In Scotland, s 3 of the Animals (Scotland) Act 1987 confers a general power for the occupier of land to detain any animal, not under the control of any person, for the purposes of preventing injury or damage by it.

[200] (1982) 80 LGR 793; and see *Matthews v Wicks* (1987) CA, Unreported, 22 May.

[201] See above, paras 3.04–3.06.

of cats and dogs. There is no statutory right to detain them and the common law right of distress with regard to them has been abolished.[202]

One or two points should be made about section 7. The only person entitled to detain straying livestock is the occupier of the land on to which they strayed. This is so even though the owner out of occupation of the land is also able to maintain an action under section 4. At common law, there is some evidence to suggest that an owner out of occupation could distrain animals damage feasant, at least if there was injury to his reversionary interest.[203] So far as the statutory right is concerned, provided the owner out of occupation has a right to enter the property on to which the animals strayed, it would seem desirable to have allowed him to detain livestock and, if necessary, to sell them and offset the price against any claim *he* might have under section 4. **3.49**

The right to detain under section 7(2) is dependent on the livestock not being under the control of any person. This reiterates the common law view as to distress in that an animal actually in use might not be distrained, in order to avoid possible breaches of the peace. So a horse which is being ridden at the time the damage is caused[204] falls outside the provision. It might also be argued that, where a horse and rider enter the claimant's land, the horse can hardly be said to have 'strayed' thereon and so both section 4 and section 7(2) would be inapplicable on that ground. A difficulty may arise if the defendant drives his livestock on to the claimant's land. It seems most desirable that the claimant should have a right to detain it, but this will only be so if the phrase 'where any livestock *strays*'[205] is given a broad enough interpretation to include an intentional trespass. This then raises an issue as to the scope of section 7 similar to the problem, already considered,[206] of the scope of section 4. The general heading of, and marginal note to, section 7 refer to 'Detention and sale of trespassing livestock'.[207] Section 7(2), the main substantive subsection, refers, as has been seen, to the situation 'where any livestock *strays* on to land'.[208] If 'stray' means 'trespass', then it is surprising that the latter well-known technical phrase was not used; but unless 'stray' does mean 'trespass', it is hard to see how section 7 can cover the case of the person who intentionally drives his livestock on to the detainor's land.[209] **3.50**

---

[202] Section 9 deals with a person's rights to kill or injure dogs which are worrying livestock; see below, ch 7.

[203] *Hoskins v Robins* (1671) 2 Saund 324, 328.

[204] *Storey v Robinson* (1795) 6 Term Rep 138; *Field v Adames* (1840) 12 Ad & El 649.

[205] Section 7(2), italics added: and see s 4(1).

[206] Above, para 3.08.

[207] Headings may be used in the construction of an Act: D Greenberg, *Craies on Legislation*, 9th edn (2008), paras 26.1.8–26.1.11.2.

[208] Italics added.

[209] The heading to Art 9 of the Animals (Northern Ireland) Order 1976, SI 1976/1040 clearly refers to the 'Detention and sale of *straying* livestock' (italics added).

3.51 When livestock has been detained under section 7(2), the right to detain it ceases after 48 hours unless within that time notice of the detention is given to the police, and, if known, to the person to whom the livestock belongs.[210] The right to detain ceases also if there is a tender of amends to the person detaining the livestock sufficient to satisfy a claim based, under section 4, on the straying of the livestock.[211] If the person detaining has no claim,[212] the right to detain ceases when the animals are claimed by the person entitled to their possession.[213]

3.52 After the detention of livestock for not less than 14 days,[214] the person detaining has a power of sale under section 7(4). The sale must be at a market or a public auction.[215] Furthermore, no such sale may take place if proceedings are pending for damages under section 4 for their straying, or for the return of the livestock. This latter situation might be illustrated by a claim in conversion[216] in the case of livestock whose straying gives rise to no valid claim under section 4. If the detainor is in breach of an obligation to fence owed to the possessor of the livestock, he may detain any livestock that stray on to his land, but he must, under section 7(3)(c), release them when claimed by their possessor. If the detainor refuses to release them and the possessor brings proceedings to claim them, then such proceedings will bar any right of sale under section 7(4).

3.53 A general effect of section 7(2) and section 7(3) is that the right to claim damages for straying livestock is not to be barred by the exercise of the right of detention, whereas an action for cattle trespass was barred by distraint. The justification for allowing an action under section 4 even though the livestock is being detained, rather than only after it has been sold, is that 'it would seem unreasonable to compel [the claimant] to proceed to sale if, for example, he knows that the damage caused far exceeds the value of the animal'.[217]

---

[210] See s 7(3)(a).

[211] See s 7(3)(b); see *Morris v Blaenau Gwent District Council* (1982) 80 LGR 793.

[212] This could be, eg, because the person on to whose land they strayed was in breach of a duty to fence: s 5(6).

[213] See s 7(3)(c). In Northern Ireland, it is an offence to prevent someone with a right to do so from detaining an animal or to rescue or cause a detained animal to escape: Animal (Northern Ireland) Order 1976, SI 1976/1040, Art 11.

[214] The question of whether the period should be 3, 14, or 21 days caused a great deal of debate during the passage of the Animals Act 1971: 305 HL Deb (1969), c 536; 317 HL Deb (1971), c 595; HC Standing Committee A, 18 March 1971, cc 14–15, 16–19, 21–2; 815 HC Deb (1971), cc 600–602, 606–7, 608–9.

[215] Despite a fear that farmers would create a 'ring' at markets or auctions, private sales were excluded because sale in a market or at an auction would ensure publicity so that a fair price would be obtained and a balance struck between the interests of the owner of the livestock and of the seller. HC Standing Committee A, 18 March 1971, cc 15–16, 18–19, 22–6; 810 HC Deb (1971), cc 761–2.

[216] And see s 2 of the Torts (Interference with Goods) Act 1977; WH Rogers, *Winfield and Jolowicz on Tort*, 18th edn (2010), paras 17.2, 17.4.

[217] Law Commission Report, para 72.

If, however, the detainor does choose to exercise his power of sale, then the proceeds of sale must be disposed of in accordance with section 7(5), which provides that: **3.54**

> Where any livestock is sold in the exercise of the right conferred by this section and the proceeds of the sale, less the costs thereof and any costs incurred in connection with it, exceed the amount of any claim under section 4 of this Act which the vendor had in respect of the livestock, the excess shall be recoverable from him by the person who would be entitled to the possession of the livestock but for the sale.

In the normal case this is quite straightforward. Where the claimant in an action for straying livestock under section 4 chooses to detain and sell the livestock, he may apply the proceeds to any claim he may have under section 4. If the amount realized by the sale is greater than that required to satisfy his claim, he must pay the excess over to the original possessor of the livestock less any costs of the sale. There are, however, at least two other situations involving sale of straying livestock for which express provision does not appear to have been made. The first is the case where the detainor has a right of action under section 4 for straying livestock but the damage done is greater than the value of the livestock detained. It has been seen that this situation has been used to justify the conclusion that the detainor may sue under section 4 even while detaining, but what happens if he sells the livestock? Although he cannot do this if proceedings are pending under section 4,[218] he may not wish to bring proceedings under section 4 until he discovers what the proceeds of sale are. If he sells the livestock and then decides to bring proceedings under section 4, no provision is made in section 7 either for the disposal of the proceeds of sale or to determine whether the detainor may still claim under section 4. The only provision in section 7 relating to the proceeds of sale is section 7(5), which deals with the specific case of the proceeds exceeding any claim under section 4. Where the proceeds are less than the damages claim under section 4, the desirable solution would be to allow the claimant to claim under section 4 such sum as amounts to his total loss, less the net proceeds of sale, having deducted the costs of sale.

The second situation to consider here is that of the detainor who has no claim under section 4 at all because, for example, the damage is due wholly to his own fault.[219] There is no doubt that section 7 confers on him a right to detain and sell straying livestock, for section 7(3)(c) envisages detention by a person with no claim under section 4.[220] Such a detainor may choose to exercise his power of sale under section 7(4), as in the case where livestock have strayed on to his land as a result of his failure to fence and he does not know to whom they belong. Once he has detained them for 14 days and the owner has not been found, the detainor will want to be rid of them as soon as possible. If they are then sold at a market or a public auction, what happens to the proceeds? Again, no provision is made in section 7(5); for that **3.55**

---

218 See s 7(4).
219 See s 5(1).
220 Notwithstanding the use of the phrase 'trespassing livestock' in the heading to s 7.

subsection envisages sale by a person who has a claim under section 4. It would appear that the seller, the detainor, ought to hold the proceeds to the use of the original owner who ought to be able to claim restitution of the proceeds of the sale. Whether the seller can deduct the costs of the sale or any costs for looking after the livestock once a reasonable period has elapsed for the original owner to reclaim them is just not considered in section 7. The common law is of no assistance, for the law of distress damage feasant is abolished by section 7(1) and, in any event, did not permit distress by someone who had no right of action. The most reasonable solution would appear to be to require the detainor in such cases to pay over the gross proceeds of sale unless the original owner has delayed unreasonably in claiming his livestock. In that latter event, the detainor should deduct the costs of sale and of maintaining the livestock after such a period has elapsed. It must not be forgotten that there is no statutory warrant for such conclusions, but as section 7 gives such a person a power of sale, the common law will have to decide what is to be done with the proceeds.

3.56 It will be recalled that the right to bring an action for straying livestock under section 4 is not affected by the fact that the claimant has detained the livestock. It appears that such an action for straying livestock is not affected by the fact that the livestock detained either has died or has escaped through the negligence of the claimant.[221] However, the defendant may be able to counterclaim for any loss which stems from the claimant's failure to take reasonable care of the livestock detained, for section 7(6) provides:

> A person detaining any livestock in pursuance of this section is liable for any damage caused to it by a failure to treat it with reasonable care and supply it with adequate food and water while it is so detained.

3.57 Any references in section 7 to a claim for damages for straying livestock under section 4 do not include any claim under section 4 for damage done or expenses incurred in respect of the livestock before the straying in connection with which it is detained under section 7.[222] Thus, if the defendant's livestock have strayed onto the claimant's land on several occasions, the claimant cannot, when seizing the animals on their last intrusion, sell them under the powers given by section 7(4) and then, under section 7(5), set the proceeds of sale off against his claims under section 4 for all the different acts of straying. He can only deduct from the sale price damages due for damage or expenses incurred during the straying incident in which the detention was made.

3.58 It should not be forgotten that, if a detainor chooses not to exercise his power of sale, no change in the ownership of the livestock takes place. The livestock still

---

[221] The effect of this on a claimant's position in an action of cattle trespass was quite unclear: Williams, p 195.

[222] See s 7(7).

belongs to the original owner; although the longer the period before the latter reclaims, the greater the claim for the expenses of the livestock's keep, under section 4(1)(b), he can expect to face.

The varied provisions of section 7 raise some difficulty with regard to the general scope of the right to detain straying livestock. It has been seen, already, that it is a right to detain 'livestock' and not 'animals', as was the case under the common law of distress damage feasant. Another comparison is that the common law right to distrain applied to causes of action other than cattle trespass,[223] although some cause of action had to be open and probably one relating to infringement of rights over land. It would apply, for example, to cases of nuisance.[224] This was relevant where the distrainor had insufficient interest to maintain cattle trespass but could maintain the latter. The new provision under section 7 is drafted in terms applicable specifically to the statutory right of action under section 4. However, it also applies where there is no claim under section 4 and so it would appear to apply in all cases where livestock stray on to another's land irrespective of the cause of action thereby created or whether there is any cause of action at all. Nevertheless, it should be borne in mind that the right to detain is only open to the occupier of the land[225] and so it is most unlikely that anyone with a right to detain would wish to utilize it in the context of an action other than one under section 4. **3.59**

In conclusion, the practical implications of the inter-relation of section 4 and section 7 might be considered. It is a tidy theoretical proposition to state that, if another's livestock stray on to your land, you may detain them provided that the police are notified and that, if they are not claimed within 14 days, you may sell them and apply the proceeds of sale to compensate for any damage you may have suffered. Undoubtedly, this is a sensible and practical proposition where the livestock stray on to the land of another farmer who has the facilities for detaining and feeding them. The position is very different if a sheep or a pony strays into a suburban garden and there does a good deal of damage. If the damage is greater than the value of the livestock, its owner will keep quiet and not claim it. The victim of the straying is, in such a case, protected by section 7, but he must catch, secure, and feed the animal for 14 days before he can sell it to recoup some of his loss. This will, all too often, be quite impracticable. It is better to drive the unidentified animal out and away with little hope of any redress. The nature of the problem has been exemplified thus: **3.60**

> If a man who owns a terrace house finds that his garden has been completely ruined as a result of the entry of a sheep which is still in his garden, can it be reasonable to suggest that he—in a garden of very small proportions and totally lacking in the facilities which a farmer would have—having notified the police, should be required to keep

223 Williams, pp 65–76.
224 Ibid, pp 65–6.
225 See s 7(2).

> that sheep tethered in his back garden, if he has one? Many terraced houses have no garden. Often the sheep is not merely in the garden; it has come in and caused damage in the outbuildings and the house itself.[226]

The problem is really one of balancing the two interests at stake—to provide security for the person who has suffered the damage and to protect the property interest of the owner of the straying livestock. It appears that the Act does this quite well in the case of neighbouring farmers, but it may well be that a right to detain is, in the case of the urban claimant, of very little practical value.[227] If he knows whose animal it is, he will claim rather than detain. It is only where the owner is unknown that he will want the right to detain, but then he has nowhere to keep the animal.

[226] HC Standing Committee A, 16 March 1971, c 14; and see 810 HC Deb (1971), cc 747–8, 773. See, eg *Matthews v Wicks* (1987) CA, Unreported, 22 May; *McLoughlin v Cooper* [1999] NIJB 90.

[227] The remedy under s 7 has been described as 'cumbersome and unrealistic in practice'; Powell-Smith (1971) 121 NLJ 584, 585.

4

FENCING AND STRAYING ANIMALS[1]

A common reason for animals, and particularly livestock, straying on to another's land is that of a defective fence. The obligation of a person to fence his land is relevant in a number of ways to tortious liability affecting animals. Failure to fence may both provide a cause of action to one party and a defence to another. Before examining the effects of a failure to fence, the nature of the obligation itself must be considered. **4.01**

1. The Obligation to Fence

Although there is no general obligation on a landowner to fence his land against either his neighbour[2] or the public,[3] an obligation to fence may be established in a **4.02**

[1] G Williams, *Liability for Animals* (1939), Pt III.

[2] *Star v Rookesby* (1710) 1 Salk 335; *Hilton v Ankesson* (1872) 27 LT 519; *Co-operative Wholesale Society Ltd v British Railways Board* (1995) CA, The Times, 20 December.

[3] *Cornwell v Metropolitan Sewers Commissioners* (1855) 10 Exch 771, 773; *British Railways Board v Herrington* [1972] AC 877.

variety of ways. It can be established by agreement,[4] although this has given rise to debate as to whether an 'easement of fencing'[5] is thereby created or whether the obligation is personal to the parties.[6] This problem appears to have been resolved in *Jones v Price*,[7] where the Court of Appeal held that a contractual obligation to maintain a boundary fence bound only the parties to the contract and did not run with the land.[8]

4.03 More commonly, the obligation, described as a 'quasi-easement'[9] or a 'spurious easement',[10] will be created by prescription.[11] Thus, in *Lawrence v Jenkins*,[12] the claimant's cow strayed on to the defendant's land through a gap in the fence caused by the defendant's felling a tree. The cow died through eating yew tree leaves on the defendant's land. As there was a prescriptive obligation on the defendant, acquired over the previous 40 years, to repair the fence, the claimant was able to recover for the loss of his cow and would also have been able to resist a claim in cattle trespass and would now be able to resist a claim based on statutory liability for straying livestock under section 4 of the Animals Act 1971.[13] To maintain a claim to a prescriptive right, it must be shown that the fence or hedge has been maintained and repaired by the occupier[14] of the 'quasi-servient' tenement as a matter of obligation and not just in his own interests of containing his own animals.[15] The best method

---

[4] J Hunt, *Hunt's Law of Boundaries, Walls and Fences*, 6th edn (1912), pp 97–8; Lord Mackay of Clashfern (ed.), *Halsbury's Laws of England*, 4th edn (2002), Vol 4(1), para 952; eg *Holgate v Bleazard* [1917] 1 KB 443; *Park v J Jobson & Son* [1945] 1 All ER 222. It is significant to note the inference from these two cases that the contractual obligation binds only the parties to it and cannot be relied on by a third party.

[5] J Gaunt, *Gale on Easements*, 18th edn (2008), paras 1.75–1.85, on the nature of the obligation to fence; and see C Harpum, *Megarry and Wade, The Law of Real Property*, 7th edn (2008), para 30.022.

[6] Williams, pp 210–11; cf *Gale on Easements*, op cit, para 1.78.

[7] [1965] 2 QB 618.

[8] [1965] 2 QB 618, 633, 639, 644–7, on the authority of *Hilton v Ankesson* (1827) 27 LT 519; *Austerberry v Oldham Corpn* (1885) 29 Ch D 750; and see *E & G C Ltd v Bates* (1935) 79 L Jo 203; *Egerton v Harding* [1975] QB 62, 68. There have been various proposals for reform of this rule, but 'nothing has been done': *Rhone v Stephens* [1994] AC 310, 321; see *Megarry and Wade*, op cit, paras 32-017–32.018.

[9] *Jones v Price* [1965] 2 QB 618. It has been said to 'rest uneasily as an easement': *Sugarman v Porter* [2006] EWHC 331, para 47; [2006] All ER (D) 117.

[10] *Lawrence v Jenkins* (1873) LR 8 QB 274, 279; *Coaker v Willcocks* [1911] 2 KB 124, 131; and see *Crow v Wood* [1971] 1 QB 77, 84–5, 86. It was described as 'anomalous' in the Report of the Committee on Positive Covenants affecting Land (1965) Cmnd 2719, para 8(v).

[11] *Egerton v Harding* [1975] QB 62, 68; Williams, pp 203–10; *Hunt's Law of Boundaries, Walls and Fences*, n 4 above, pp 100–9; *Halsbury's Laws of England*, n 4 above, Vol 4(2), paras 951–2.

[12] (1873) LR 8 QB 274. See also *Anon* (1675) 1 Vent 264; *Star v Rookesby* (1710) 1 Salk 335; *Rooth v Wilson* (1817) 1 B & Ald 59; *Boyle v Tamlin* (1827) 6 B & C 329; *Powell v Salisbury* (1828) 2 Y & J 391; *Coaker v Willcocks* [1911] 2 KB 124.

[13] Discussed in ch 3, above.

[14] The obligation is on the occupier and not on the owner out of occupation: *Cheetham v Hampson* (1791) 4 Term Rep 318.

[15] *Jones v Price* [1965] 2 QB 618, 634–6; *Hunt's Law of Boundaries, Walls and Fences*, n 4 above, p 109; cf Williams, pp 203–8.

of proof of this, although perhaps not the only method of proof,[16] is to show that the repairs were done at the request of the occupier of the 'quasi-dominant' tenement.[17] The obligation to fence can only be created by prescription in the case of adjoining owners. It does not arise where all the lands in question have, until recently, been held in common ownership.[18]

It would seem, therefore, that the right to an 'easement of fencing' may be acquired by immemorial user,[19] by presumption of lost grant,[20] and by grant.[21] This last situation was considered by the Court of Appeal in *Crow v Wood*.[22] A large Yorkshire moor had, with adjoining farms, remained in common ownership for many years. The tenants of the various farms had been granted the right to stray their sheep on the moor and the tenants agreed to maintain their fences and walls in good repair. One of these farms was sold to the claimant and another to the defendant's landlord. The claimant did not let any sheep stray on the moor and she did not maintain her fences so as to keep out the sheep of other farmers pastured on the moor. Some of the defendant's sheep strayed from the moor on to the claimant's land causing damage for which the claimant sought damages for cattle trespass. The defendant argued that his sheep strayed because the claimant had failed in her duty to fence them out. Was there such an obligation upon which the defendant could rely? The Court of Appeal concluded that: **4.04**

> a right to have your neighbour keep up the fences is a right in the nature of an easement which is capable of being granted by law so as to run with the land and to be binding on successors. It is a right which lies in grant and is of such a nature that it can pass under section 62 of the Law of Property Act 1925.[23]

Each farmer adjoining the moor had the right to pasture his sheep thereon and the duty to fence against the moor. These were rights and advantages, under section 62,

---

[16] *Boyle v Tamlin* (1827) 6 B & C 329; *Barber v Whiteley* (1865) 34 LJQB 212; *Jones v Price* [1965] 2 QB 618, 636.

[17] *Lawrence v Jenkins* (1873) LR 8 QB 274; cf *Hilton v Ankesson* (1872) 27 LT 519; *Jones v Price* [1965] 2 QB 618, 645 per Willmer LJ.

[18] *Kilgour v Gaddes* [1904] 1 KB 457; *Crow v Wood* [1971] 1 QB 77, 83.

[19] *Lawrence v Jenkins* (1873) LR 8 QB 274; *Jones v Price* [1965] 2 QB 618, 634–6.

[20] *Barber v Whiteley* (1865) 34 LJQB 212 and see *Boyle v Tamlin* (1827) 6 B & C 329; *Sharp v Harvey* [1935] LJCCR 261, 266. Cf *Sutcliffe v Holmes* [1947] 1 KB 147; *Jones v Price* [1965] 2 QB 618, 636–7. Willmer LJ, at [1965] 2 QB 618, 647, suggested that the earlier cases 'are in a special category'; and see Hunt, *Hunt's Law of Boundaries, Walls and Fences*, n 4 above, pp 103–4; Williams, p 209; C Sara, *Boundaries and Easements*, 4th edn (2008), para 22.08. The 'special circumstances' may well be based on the original enclosure of the land from the common: Gale, op cit, para 1.78.

[21] *Crow v Wood* [1971] 1 QB 77, 84, 87; *Megarry and Wade*, op cit, para 30.022; cf *Jones v Price*, above, at p 640.

[22] [1971] 1 QB 77; PVB (1971) 87 LQR 13; Wilkinson (1971) 34 MLR 223.

[23] [1971] 1 QB 77, 84–5. Section 62(1) of the Law of Property Act 1925 provides: 'A conveyance of land shall be deemed to include and shall by virtue of this Act operate to convey, with the land, all . . . easements, rights and advantages whatsoever, appertaining or reputed to appertain to the land, or any part thereof, or, at the time of conveyance, demised, occupied, or enjoyed with, or reputed or known as part or parcel of or appurtenant to the land or any part thereof.'

which had been enjoyed by the previous owner of the defendant's farm and which passed on conveyance of the farm; and so the claimant failed. This decision indicates, quite clearly, that an 'easement of fencing' can be created by grant, either express or implied.[24]

4.05 There are also a number of cases where the obligation to fence is placed on an occupier by common law rules, as with the obligation of mine and quarry owners or licensees to fence off their property.[25] In the case of the occupier of property adjoining the highway, he does not have an obligation to fence against the highway such that he can be made responsible for the erection or maintenance of fences; but he cannot succeed in a claim for damage done by straying livestock if livestock stray on to his land from the highway,[26] provided that their presence on the highway was a lawful use thereof; and he cannot lawfully resist the entry on to his land of the driver of the cattle to retake his animals.[27] On the other hand, the occupier will not be held responsible for injury to animals which stray on to his property from the highway.[28] In the case of unfenced common land, no obligation to fence can be held to arise from the fact that someone with a right to graze livestock on the land had put livestock on the land from which they strayed. Indeed, the owner of the livestock may have no right to fence the land.[29]

4.06 Finally, the obligation to fence may be created by statute,[30] as in the case of the obligation of railways[31] to fence adjoining land and level crossings, and mines and quarries legislation.[32] It may also be created by an enclosure award[33] and by custom,[34]

[24] But not where there is merely a covenant to fence: *Sugarman v Porter* [2006] EWHC 331, paras 45–52; [2006] All ER (D) 117.

[25] Williams, pp 211–12; Hunt, *Hunt's Law of Boundaries, Walls and Fences*, n 4 above, pp 109–13; *Halsbury's Laws of England*, n 4 above, Vol 4(1), para 949; *Churchill v Evans* (1809) 1 Taunt 529; *Groucott v Williams* (1863) 4 B & S 149; *Hawken v Shearer* (1887) 56 LJQB 284; and see *M'Morrow v Layden* [1919] 2 IR 398; *Harrison v M'Culvey* (1840) 2 Craw & D 1.

[26] Animals Act 1971, s 5(5); above, paras 3.40–3.45.

[27] Williams, p 372.

[28] *Blithe v Topham* (1607) Cro Jac 158; Williams, p 373. Cf the general rule, discussed below, para 4.12.

[29] *Davies v Davies* [1975] QB 172, 177, 179; *Ridyard v Owen* (1980) CA, Unreported,16 May.

[30] *Hunt's Law of Boundaries, Walls and Fences*, n 4 above, pp 113–18; *Halsbury's Laws of England*, n 4 above, Vol 4(1), para 950.

[31] Railway Clauses Consolidation Act 1845, s 68; see, eg *Ricketts v East and West India Docks etc Rail Co* (1852) 2 CB 160; *Dawson v Midland Rail Co* (1872) LR 8 Exch 8; *Child v Hearn* (1874) LR 9 Exch 176; *Wiseman v Booker* (1878) 3 CPD 184; *Dixon v Great Western Rail Co* [1897] 1 QB 300; and see *Hunt's Law of Boundaries, Walls and Fences*, n 4 above, pp 113–15; Williams, pp 212, 219, n 5; cf *Cooper v Railway Executive* [1953] 1 All ER 477. It has been held that the nature of the fencing obligation imposed by the 1845 Act is the same as it would be at common law under a prescriptive obligation to fence: *Ricketts*, above; *Manchester, Sheffield and Lincolnshire Rail Co v Wallis* (1854) 14 CB 213, 223–4.

[32] *Hunt's Law of Boundaries, Walls and Fences*, n 4 above, pp 116–18; Williams, p 212; G Gadsden, *The Law of Commons* (1988), para 9.02.

[33] *Singleton v Williamson* (1861) 7 H & N 410.

[34] *Egerton v Harding* [1975] QB 62, 70, rejecting dicta to the contrary in *Jones v Price* [1965] 2 QB 618, 639, 646–7; *Crow v Wood* [1971] 1 QB 77, 83–4. For extinction of the obligation, see Williams, pp 212–13.

provided that it is 'of immemorial origin, reasonable, continued without interruption, and certain', and provided that the duty to fence 'could have arisen from a lawful origin'.[35]

2. Standard of the Obligation

The duty to fence 'is only to keep reasonable fences to prevent the escape of ordinary cattle in ordinary circumstances',[36] for the obligation is one to fence against ordinary livestock, rather than other animals or children. The obligation is, however, not only to prevent the livestock of the owner of the 'quasi-servient' tenement from straying on to the 'quasi-dominant' tenement, but also to prevent the latter's livestock from straying on to and being injured on the former's land.[37] The fences must be maintained, by any means, in such a way as to make them proof against livestock in ordinary circumstances. Thus, the duty is broken if a hole is left in a hedge through which sheep could pass[38] or if a gate is left open. If the fence is defective, it does not matter whether this is as a result of the positive act of the 'quasi-servient' tenant[39] or the result of neglect.[40] **4.07**

If the animals in question are peculiarly prone to straying or act in an unusual manner, then provided that there are reasonable fences, there is no breach of the obligation if the animals break through them. Thus, in the case of a pig, the obligation is to erect 'such a fence that a pig not of a peculiarly wandering disposition, nor under any excessive temptation, will not get through it'.[41] In *Coaker v Willcocks*,[42] the defendant occupied a farm which had been enclosed from land forming part of the Forest of Dartmoor and it was agreed that the defendant was bound to fence his land against moorland sheep. The defendant seized some of the claimant's sheep, which had strayed on to his land from the commonable land. It was held that, although there was an obligation on the defendant to fence against commonable animals, this did not extend to the claimant's peculiar Scottish sheep, for as Darling J said:[43] **4.08**

> these Scotch sheep are of a peculiarly wandering and saltative disposition, straying and jumping in a way which distinguishes them from sheep which have hitherto been

[35] *Egerton v Harding* [1975] QB 62, 69, 71; *Matthews v Wicks* (1987) CA, Unreported, 22 May.
[36] Williams, p 214; see *Hoskin v Rogers* (1985), The Times, 25 January.
[37] *Hunt's Law of Boundaries, Walls and Fences*, n 4 above, p 100.
[38] *Bessant v Great Western Rail Co* (1860) 8 CBNS 368; and see *Page v Great Eastern Rail Co* (1871) 24 LT 585.
[39] eg *Lawrence v Jenkins* (1873) LR 8 QB 274.
[40] eg *Barber v Whiteley* (1865) 34 LJQB 212.
[41] *Child v Hearn* (1874) LR 9 Exch 176, 182.
[42] [1911] 1 KB 649. See also *Spry v Mortimore* [1946] LJCCR 83, 86.
[43] Ibid, at p 654.

> turned on to the unenclosed land, wandering as other sheep do not and jumping as other sheep cannot. In my judgment the defendant was not bound to fence his land from sheep of this description; it was the duty of the plaintiff, if he chose to own such sheep, to keep them from trespassing on the defendant's land.

4.09 Apart from the relevance of the disposition of the animal in question, the fence need only be reasonably secure; for the courts have not decreed 'that there must be a fence so close and strong that no pig could push through it, or so high that no horse or bullock could leap it'.[44] In *Cooper v Railway Executive*,[45] the claimant's cattle broke through a railway fence on to the defendants' railway line and three of them were killed when hit by a train, which was itself derailed. The defendants were under a duty to fence[46] and the claimant alleged breach of that duty and claimed damages for the death of his cattle, but the defendants counter-claimed, alleging cattle trespass. The cattle were in a state of excitement because the calves had been separated from the cows and the court found that the fence

> was as strong as any ordinary farm fence could be to offer protection against the ordinary behaviour of cattle. Indeed, it was a great deal stronger, being made of concrete posts and strong chain link fencing.[47]

As the fence was strong enough to 'prevail against the ordinary forcible behaviour of cattle in ordinary circumstances', the defendants had satisfied the obligation to fence and succeeded in their counter-claim for cattle trespass. A fence which allows animals to put their heads over the top and cause damage or be injured, for example by eating yew tree leaves,[48] would be insufficient.[49]

4.10 It seems probable that the obligation to fence is strict in that no enquiry should be made into the reasonableness of the conduct of the servient tenant so far as maintenance is concerned. This has been considered to apply even in the case of an action for damages brought by the dominant tenant for injury to his cattle on the servient tenement.[50] It can be argued that the defences of Act of God,[51] act of third party,[52] and inevitable accident should be open to the servient tenant in such cases.[53]

---

[44] *Child v Hearn* (1874) LR 9 Exch 176, 181–2.
[45] [1953] 1 All ER 477, and see *Dobbie v Henderson* 1970 SLT (Sh Ct) 27.
[46] Under the Railways Clauses Consolidation Act 1845, s 68.
[47] [1953] 1 All ER 477, 479.
[48] eg *Lawrence v Jenkins* (1873) LR 8 QB 274; cf *Wilson v Newberry* (1871) LR 7 QB 31.
[49] cf *Wiseman v Booker* (1878) 3 CPD 184, 188.
[50] *Lawrence v Jenkins* (1873) LR 8 QB 274, 278.
[51] Ibid, at p 278.
[52] Williams, pp 223, 225; cf *Sutcliffe v Holmes* [1947] KB 147; and see *Singleton v Williamson* (1861) 7 H & N 410, 416.
[53] Williams, p 225.

3. Effects of the Failure to Fence[54]

(1) Repair of the fence

The dominant tenant can compel the repair of the fence by the servient tenant. The claim will lie between adjoining possessors of land,[55] rather than between adjoining freeholders.[56] It cannot, apparently, be brought by a commoner,[57] although this restriction seems difficult to justify. There can be no obligation on the servient tenant to maintain a hedge on the dominant tenement not forming the boundary between the two.[58] **4.11**

(2) Injury to livestock

Where the dominant tenant's livestock stray on to the servient tenement, the dominant tenant can recover damages for the failure to fence,[59] but more commonly will wish to seek damages for injury to his livestock suffered on the servient tenement.[60] When the dominant tenant's cattle died through eating yew tree leaves on the servient tenant's land on to which they had escaped through a gap in the fence, the servient tenant was held liable for the loss.[61] The result would be the same if the livestock had been killed by, for example, a falling haystack,[62] through falling into a ditch,[63] by being hit by a passing train,[64] by drinking contaminated water in a mine,[65] by hitting their heads against a viaduct[66] or through falling into a quarry.[67] Furthermore, if the dominant tenant's livestock stray on to the servient tenement and then on to a third person's land where they are injured, the servient tenant will be liable.[68] Where the animals on the dominant tenement are lawfully there but do **4.12**

[54] Williams, pp 215–25.

[55] eg *Cheetham v Hampson* (1791) 4 Term Rep 318.

[56] *Cheetham v Hampson*, above; *Russell v Shenton* (1842) 3 QB 449.

[57] *Smith v Burton* (1674) 1 Freem KB 145.

[58] *Jones v Price* [1965] 2 QB 618, 623, 642.

[59] *Egerton v Harding* [1975] QB 62.

[60] If the defect in the fence is such that decayed pieces thereof fall on to the dominant tenement and are there eaten by the dominant tenant's cattle, an action will lie for the consequent death of the cattle: *Firth v Bowling Iron Co* (1878) 3 CPD 254.

[61] *Lawrence v Jenkins* (1873) LR 8 QB 274, 275; cf *Ponting v Noakes* [1894] 2 QB 281.

[62] *Powell v Salisbury* (1828) 2 Y & J 391.

[63] *Anon* (1675) 1 Vent 264; and see *Rooth v Wilson* (1817) 1 B & Ald 59; *Corry v Great Western Rail Co* (1881) 7 QBD 322.

[64] eg *Bessant v Great Western Rail Co* (1860) 8 CBNS 368; *Dawson v Midland Rail Co* (1872) LR 8 Exch 8; *Luscombe v Great Western Rail Co* [1899] 2 QB 313; *Saunders & Son v Railway Executive* [1947–51] CLC 8233; and see *Symons v Southern Rail Co* (1935) 153 LT 98.

[65] *Harrison v M'Culvey* (1840) 2 Craw & D 1.

[66] *Dixon v Great Western Rail Co* [1897] 1 QB 300.

[67] *Williams v Groucott* (1863) 4 B & S 149; *Hawken v Shearer* (1887) 56 LJQB 284; *M'Morrow v Layden* [1919] 2 IR 398.

[68] *Singleton v Williamson* (1816) 7 H & N 410, 416.

not belong to the dominant tenant, the latter may maintain a claim for injury done to them on the servient tenement if he is responsible to their owner for their safety, as where he is a bailee.[69] It would appear, furthermore, that when such animals lawfully on the dominant tenement stray onto the servient tenement as the result of the servient tenant's failure to fence, the latter will be liable to the owner for any injuries to the animals suffered on the servient tenement, even though the owner is not the dominant tenant.[70] If, however, the animals were unlawfully on the dominant tenement and they then stray on to and are injured on the servient tenement, they are regarded as being unlawfully on the servient tenement even though the servient tenant is in breach of an obligation to fence owed to the dominant tenant. That being so, the servient tenant can resist any claim based on injury to the animals on his land.[71] Furthermore, if animals stray from A's land to B's land as a result of A's defective fences and then they stray on to C's land as a result of C's failure to fence against B, A cannot recover for injuries to his animals suffered on C's land, because the animals were unlawfully on B's land.[72]

(3) Damage to the land

4.13 The dominant tenant may claim damages for damage to his land caused by animals straying on to it from the servient tenement. This would seem to be a claim separate from that for cattle trespass and from one based on the statutory liability under section 4 of the Animals Act 1971 for straying livestock.[73] It lies not only if the livestock are in the possession of the servient tenant,[74] but also, probably, even if they are not.[75] This head of liability does not affect any other possible liability on the part of the owner of the animals.[76] It appears, therefore, that the servient tenant will be liable in damages for failure to repair his fences if animals straying on to his land then strayed on to the dominant tenement through the defective fence. This is so even though no statutory claim under section 4 of the 1971 Act can be brought by the dominant tenant against the servient tenant in such circumstances, because of the servient tenant's lack of control of the livestock. It may be recalled that, in order for proceedings to be brought under the 1971 Act, the livestock must 'belong' to

[69] *Rooth v Wilson* (1817) 1 B & Ald 58.

[70] eg *Dawson v Midland Rail Co* (1872) LR 8 Exch 8; and see *Anon* (1675) 1 Vent 264.

[71] *Manchester, Sheffield and Lincolnshire Rail Co v Wallis* (1854) 14 CB 213; *Luscombe v Great Western Rail Co* [1899] 2 QB 313.

[72] *Ricketts v East and West India Docks etc Rail Co* (1852) 12 CB 160.

[73] See ch 3, above.

[74] *Star v Rookesby* (1710) 1 Salk 335. No doubt a statutory claim for straying livestock would be available here also.

[75] Williams, p 216, n 12; and see *Winter v Charter* (1829) 3 Y & J 308. Cf liability under the Animals Act 1971, s 4, above, paras 3.12–3.15.

[76] *Hunt's Law of Boundaries, Walls and Fences*, n 4 above, p 249.

the defendant and for the purposes of section 4 'any livestock belongs to the person in whose possession it is'.[77]

It would also appear that, if the dominant tenant suffers loss when, because of defective fences, livestock stray from his land onto the servient tenement and then stray through the servient tenement onto other land belonging to the dominant tenant, a claim for damages will lie against the servient tenant if that other land of the dominant tenant is damaged by the incursions thereon of his own livestock.[78] Furthermore, if as a result of the servient tenant's failure to fence, the dominant tenant's livestock stray on to the land of a third party, the dominant tenant may well be statutorily liable to that third party, under section 4 of the Animals Act 1971, for any damage to that third party's property.[79] In such a case, the dominant tenant ought to be able to claim an indemnity from the servient tenant.[80] **4.14**

(4) Recapture of straying livestock

The dominant tenant may enter the servient tenement to recapture his straying animals, provided that they strayed as a result of the defective fences;[81] although there is no general right to enter another's land to reclaim straying animals. The servient tenant on to whose land the animals have strayed has the right to eject them, but this is coupled with an obligation to return them to the land from which they have strayed,[82] and it is not a right just to turn them out onto the highway. If, however, the occupier of the land on to which the animals stray is under no obligation to repair his fences, then he is permitted to drive the straying animals out of his land,[83] even on to the highway.[84] Where animals stray as a result of a failure to fence, then it is arguable that the dominant tenant has an obligation to retake his animals within a reasonable time of notice of their escape, or he may find himself liable to the servient tenant, despite the latter's failure to fence, for any damage suffered by the servient tenant from the delay in recovery of the animals.[85] **4.15**

[77] Animals Act 1971, s 4(2).

[78] *Brox v Edmonton, Yukon and Pacific Rail Co* (1909) 2 Alta LR 379; Williams, p 217.

[79] No defence is provided in such circumstances by the Animals Act 1971, s 5(6).

[80] Williams, pp 222–3.

[81] Williams, pp 180, 217; *Baker v Andrews* (1652) Style 357; *Sorlie v McKee* [1927] 1 DLR 249, 251, 254.

[82] *Carruthers v Hollis* (1838) 8 Ad & E 1 113; *Hunt's Law of Boundaries, Walls and Fences*, n 4 above, pp 248–9.

[83] *Tyrringham's Case* (1584) 4 Co Rep 36b, 38b.

[84] Williams, pp 90–92. One might query whether this does not constitute trespass to the highway, as to which the possessor of the straying animals should be liable to indemnify the person onto whose land they originally strayed; see above.

[85] Williams, pp 223–4. The statutory right to detain straying livestock, under the Animals Act 1971, s 7, is discussed, above, paras 3.47–3.60.

(5) Defence to a claim under the Animals Act 1971

4.16 The dominant tenant may resist a claim relating to straying livestock which may be brought by the servient tenant under section 4 of the Animals Act 1971 if the former's livestock have strayed on to the latter's land through the defective fences,[86] or even if the straying livestock have damaged other land belonging to the servient tenant.[87] This defence to a claim under section 4 of the Act is provided as a result of the combined effects of sections 5(1) and 5(6) of the Act.[88] The first subsection provides that a person is not liable for any damage which is due wholly to the fault of the person suffering it. It is then provided by section 5(6) that:

> In determining whether any liability for damage under section 4 of this Act is excluded by subsection (1) of this section the damage shall not be treated as due to the fault of the person suffering it by reason only that he could have prevented it by fencing;[89] but a person is not liable under that section where it is proved that the straying of the livestock on to the land would not have occurred but for a breach by any other person, being a person having an interest in the land, of a duty to fence.

4.17 The effect of these subsections is to embody two principles:

(i) If there is no obligation on the claimant, in a claim relating to straying livestock, to fence his neighbour's livestock out, the claimant is not at fault within the meaning of section 5(1) if he fails to do so, even though such fencing could have prevented the straying; he may still maintain the statutory claim; and

(ii) there is to be no liability if the defendant's livestock strayed on to the claimant's land as the result of a breach of an obligation to fence by any person other than the defendant, provided that person had an interest in the land strayed upon.

4.18 Although, as has been seen, the general law of fencing is quite complex,[90] the provisions of section 5(6) would seem to affect only that part of it which is relevant to a claim for straying livestock and they leave untouched that which relates to the other effects of the failure to fence.[91] This singling out of only part of the law of fencing for treatment in the Animals Act 1971 causes no difficulty where the dominant

---

[86] eg *Wiseman v Booker* (1878) 3 CPD 184.

[87] *Singleton v Williams* (1861) 7 H & N 410, 416.

[88] For Northern Ireland, see the Animals (Northern Ireland) Order 1976, SI 1976/1040, Art 6(1) and (5).

[89] Fencing includes 'the construction of any obstacle designed to prevent animals from straying': Animals Act 1971, s 11. This will mean that fencing will include not only fences, but also, for example, ditches, although only where the purpose of the ditch is to contain livestock, and not where its sole purpose is to carry away water.

[90] The Law Commission Report, para 67, n 98, expressly declined to examine fencing obligations other than in the context of the provision of a defence to liability for straying livestock. During the House of Lords debates on the Animals Bill, Lord Denning indicated that it was a defect in the Act that nowhere did it indicate what the duty to fence is. Indeed, he thought the law relating to the obligation to fence was so complex that that was why the Law Commission had not stated it: 312 HL Deb (1970), c 228, and see 810 HC Deb (1971), c 765.

[91] Above, paras 4.11–4.14.

tenant's livestock stray on to the servient tenant's land as a result of the latter's breach of the duty to fence; these will be the majority of cases of liability for straying livestock. Problems do arise, however, where the parties between whom the obligation to fence exists are not the same as those in the claim for straying livestock.

In order to understand how the Animals Act 1971 has affected the situation in this context, it is helpful to examine the common law position, as well as that under the 1971 Act, and to consider them both in relation to a number of separate problems. There are three main issues to be considered here. Two arise from the fact that nothing is said in section 5(6) as to the person to whom the duty to fence must be owed in order for the defence of failure to fence to be applicable.[92] The third is concerned with an obligation owed to the defendant, but by a person other than the claimant. Finally, certain problems arising from multiple fencing obligations will be considered. **4.19**

(a) A fencing obligation owed by the claimant to a person other than the defendant from whose land the livestock have strayed

While the normal fencing obligation will be owed by a servient tenant to a neighbouring dominant tenant, this will not always be the case. Two examples will be considered. **4.20**

(i) Tenancies

A tenant of a farm may owe a contractual obligation to his landlord to erect and maintain the farm fences. This may have nothing whatsoever to do with any obligation owed by either the landlord or the tenant to a neighbouring occupier of land. Indeed, there may well be no such obligation. This situation may be illustrated by the common law decision in *Park v J Jobson & Son*.[93] Here, tenants of allotments which adjoined a farm agreed with their landlord to maintain the fences against the farm. In fact, their landlord was also the landlord of the farm, but this is not significant for present purposes. When cattle from the farm strayed on to the allotments, the tenant of one of the allotments sued the farmer in cattle trespass. The fence was in disrepair and the livestock would not otherwise have strayed. Could the defendant farmer resist an action for cattle trespass on the ground that the claimant was in breach of his fencing obligations? This was, therefore, a case where the claimant was under an obligation to fence, but the obligation was owed to a third party and not to the defendant. As the claimant's obligation to fence was a contractual one owed to his landlord, his breach of that obligation was no defence to an action of **4.21**

[92] A suggestion was made in the House of Lords that the duty should be owed to a person with an interest in the land from which the livestock strayed. This amendment was withdrawn after considerable debate and opposition: 312 HL Deb (1970), cc 203–5, 227–31, 857–63; 313 HL Deb (1970), cc 447–52; 810 HC Deb (1971), cc 739–40.

[93] [1945] 1 All ER 222; and see *Holgate v Bleazard* [1917] 1 KB 443, which was not cited in the former case.

cattle trespass against the farmer from whose land the cattle had strayed. The latter could not rely on a fencing obligation owed by the claimant to a third party. As has been said by Ridley J:

> The obligation [to fence] upon the plaintiff... is a secondary one and is an obligation as between himself and the landlord, but there is an obligation upon the defendant if he brings cattle upon his land to keep them from straying, and he cannot take advantage of the plaintiff's breach of contract with the landlord by claiming a right to let his cattle escape through the gaps in the fence and trespass on the plaintiff's land.[94]

4.22 Could a tenant of the allotments succeed today in a claim under section 4 of the Animals Act 1971 based on liability for straying livestock, or could the farmer successfully raise the defence of failure to fence under section 5(6)? The claimant was an occupier of the allotment, and so satisfied section 4. It is assumed that he let the fence get into disrepair and so was in breach of his fencing obligation, owed to his landlord. The livestock would not have strayed but for the breach by the claimant of his duty to fence. The fact that it is owed to his landlord and not to the defendant is, within the meaning of section 5(6), irrelevant. That being so, the defence of failure to fence is made out and the decision would now be different from that at common law.[95]

(ii) Fencing against common or unenclosed land

4.23 It is often the case where a farm adjoins open moorland that there is an obligation on the farmer to fence his land against the moor and to fence out the livestock of those who have rights to pasture such livestock on the moor. This might be illustrated by *Crow v Wood*.[96] It may be recalled that a large sheep moor in Yorkshire and its adjoining farms had been held in common ownership. One of the farms was sold to the claimant along with rights to pasture sheep on the moor, which rights she never exercised. A neighbouring farm with similar sheep rights over the moor had earlier been sold to a third party and the rights, appurtenant to that farm, to pasture sheep on the moor were let by the new owners of the farm to the defendant. The claimant in more recent years had failed to maintain her fences against the moor and the defendant's sheep, straying on the moor, strayed on to the claimant's land. The claimant sought damages for cattle trespass and the defendant pleaded as a defence that the claimant was in breach of her obligations to fence against the moor. Much of the judgments in the Court of Appeal are concerned with the question of whether the claimant was under any obligation to fence against the moor. The court concluded that there was a right to have the occupier of the claimant's farm

[94] *Holgate v Bleazard*, above, at p 447. On the question of the failure of a third party to fence, see *Sutcliffe v Holmes* [1947] KB 147, below, para 4.34.

[95] Similarly abrogated is the decision on this point in *Holgate v Bleazard*, above.

[96] [1971] 1 QB 77, above, para 4.04.

maintain the fences against the moor and that right had passed to the owners of the neighbouring farm.[97] As Lord Denning MR said:

> All the tenants of the common owner had previously enjoyed this right. The custom of the moor was that each farmer enjoyed this right. It was obviously enjoyed with the land and reputed to appertain to it. The result is that, in my opinion, each farmer next to Bilsdale West Moor had, on the one hand, a right to put so many sheep on the moor to stray: and each farmer, on the other hand, was under a duty to keep up his own walls and fences so as to keep the sheep of the other owners out.[98]

Having decided that the claimant was in breach of her fencing obligation, the Court of Appeal had no hesitation in finding for the defendant. There is an assumption in the judgments that the defendant could rely on the breach of the claimant's fencing obligation owed to the owner of the farm from whom the defendant had acquired his rights to stray sheep on the moor.

This common law position is unaltered by the Animals Act 1971.[99] There is no requirement in section 5(6) that the person to whom the fencing obligation is owed should be the defendant or should be a person who has any interest in the land from which the livestock have strayed.[100] So long as the claimant is in breach of the fencing obligation, whether or not owed to the defendant, the defence under section 5(6) is available. The general conclusion to be drawn is that the decision not to indicate in section 5(6) *to* whom the obligation to fence must be owed, provided it is owed *by* a person with an interest in the land strayed upon, will mean that a defendant can claim the benefit of a breach of a contractual or other fencing obligation to which he is not a party. **4.24**

(b) A fencing obligation owed by the claimant to the dominant tenant, but relied on by a third party

The basic situation to consider here is that where livestock other than those belonging to the dominant tenant are on the dominant tenement and stray from there on to the servient tenement. Furthermore, it is assumed that straying is as a result of the servient tenant's breach of his fencing obligation owed to the dominant tenant. Does that breach of the fencing obligation affect the servient tenant's right to claim under section 4 of the Animals Act 1971 against the possessor of the livestock? It is proposed to examine separately the cases where the livestock is either lawfully or unlawfully present on the dominant tenement and to look, briefly, at the common law position before examining the effects of the Animals Act 1971. **4.25**

---

[97] By reason of the Law of Property Act 1925, s 62(1). This aspect of the decision is discussed above, para 4.04.

[98] [1971] 1 QB 77, 85.

[99] See *Egerton v Harding* [1975] QB 62; *Matthews v Wicks* (1987) CA, Unreported, 22 May.

[100] It was disputed in the House of Lords debates on s 5(6) whether the defendant in *Crow v Wood*, above, did have any such interest: 312 HL Deb (1970), cc 858–60; 313 HL Deb (1970), cc 449–51.

(i) Livestock lawfully present on the dominant tenement with the consent of the owner thereof

4.26 If his livestock were lawfully present on the dominant tenement, the owner would appear, at common law, to have been able to rely on the fencing obligations owed by the servient tenant to the dominant tenant.[101] Lawful presence includes various instances of the right to put livestock on the dominant tenement, such as the rights of the tenant of that land,[102] the person who has a right of common over it,[103] the rights of a licensee on the land,[104] and the lawful user of a highway.[105] Such a person may resist a statutory action for straying livestock under section 4 of the Animals Act 1971 if his livestock, lawfully on the dominant tenement, stray onto the servient tenement as a result of the servient tenant's failure to fence. A valid defence exists under section 5(6), for that subsection merely requires that the claimant's fencing obligation be owed *by* a person with an interest in the land strayed upon. There is no requirement that the obligation be owed to the defendant or to a person with an interest in the land from which the livestock strayed.

(ii) Livestock unlawfully present on the dominant tenement

4.27 It was the case at common law that a servient tenant on to whose land cattle, trespassing on the dominant tenement, had strayed as a result of the servient tenant's breach of his obligation to fence could maintain an action of cattle trespass against the owner of such cattle. The defendant could not rely on the servient tenant's breach of his obligation to fence, for it was not owed to him nor to anyone under whom he claimed.[106] The position was summed up by Wilmot CJ:

> If a man turn his cattle into Blackacre, where he has no right, and they escape and stray into my fields for want of fences, he cannot excuse himself, or justify for his cattle trespassing in my field.[107]

4.28 Turning to the Animals Act 1971, it will be recalled that nothing is said in section 5(6) as to the person to whom the duty to fence must be owed in order for the defence of failure to fence, ie the defence under section 5(1) that the damage was due wholly to the fault of the claimant, to operate. It will also be recalled that, so far as the defendant in a claim relating to straying livestock is concerned, section 4

[101] *Pomfret v Ricroft* (1669) 1 Saund 321, 322(c); *Ricketts v East and West India Docks etc Co* (1852) 12 CB 160, 174, 176.

[102] *Faldo v Ridge* (1605) Yelv 74, 75.

[103] *Sir Francis Leke's Case* (1579) 3 Dyer 365a.

[104] *Dawson v Midland Rail Co* (1872) LR 8 Exch 8; and see *Sir Francis Leke's Case,* above, at p 365b.

[105] eg *Dovaston v Payne* (1795) 2 Hy Bl 527; *Midland Rail Co v Daykin* (1855) 17 CB 126; the lawfulness of user of the highway is discussed in ch 3, above, paras 3.40–3.45.

[106] This may have been because the obligation existed, at least originally, only between neighbouring and contiguous tenements: *King v Rose* (1673) Freem KB 347; and see ibid, p 356; *Right v Baynard* (1674) Freem KB 379; *Sutcliffe v Holmes* [1947] KB 147, 154.

[107] *Anon* (1770) 3 Wils 126; and see *Dovaston v Payne* (1795) 2 Hy Bl 527.

refers to the liability of the possessor of the livestock. He may be either the dominant tenant, or he may be a third party whose livestock are either lawfully on[108] or are trespassing on the dominant tenement. Under the common law of cattle trespass, as has been seen, the first two but not the third could rely on the breach by the servient tenant of his fencing obligation to the dominant tenant as a defence. The Animals Act 1971 is silent on this matter. It cannot be resolved by reference to the specific fencing provisions of section 5(6) save to suggest that, as there is no indication in that subsection of to whom the fencing obligation must be owed, a trespasser can shelter behind it.

It may be, however, that section 5(1) takes the matter further. Can it be said that damage is due wholly to the fault of the claimant, the servient tenant who is in breach of his obligation to fence owed to the dominant tenant, when the livestock which stray from the dominant tenement are those which are there unlawfully? If not, then section 5(1) will provide a defence. However, the lawfulness of the presence of the defendant's livestock on the dominant tenement would appear to be quite irrelevant to the fault of the servient tenant in failing to maintain his fences. The livestock would have strayed through the defective fences whether they were lawfully or unlawfully present on the dominant tenement. If that argument is accepted, then the 1971 Act has produced a change in the common law and a person with no interest in, or lawful presence on, the dominant tenement may rely on the servient tenant's failure to fence against the dominant tenement as a defence to liability for straying livestock. In other words, the defence does not operate against the dominant tenant, but against any possessor of livestock which stray from the dominant tenement. This is difficult to justify in the case of so unmeritorious a defendant as the person whose livestock are unlawfully present on the dominant tenement. This conclusion can only be avoided in such a case by holding that the claimant's injury is not due wholly to his own fault within the meaning of section 5(1). **4.29**

Finally, it has been assumed so far that it is clear when livestock are unlawfully on the dominant tenement. Any livestock present without the consent of the dominant tenant or without some other lawful authority would seem to fall within the above discussion. One case worthy of special mention concerns common land. If a commoner has a right to turn out a fixed number of animals on to the common, he is liable in a claim by other commoners if he turns out more than his allotted number and surcharges the common land.[109] If he turns out too many animals and some then stray on to a neighbour's land as a result of that neighbour's failure to **4.30**

[108] Discussed, above, para 4.26.

[109] See G Gadsden, *The Law of Commons* (1988), paras 8.28–8.38; N Ubhi and B Denyer-Green, *Law of Commons and of Town and Village Greens*, 2nd edn (2006), paras 6.7.1–6.7.5.

fence, the excessive number of animals on the common are not considered to be there unlawfully *vis à vis* the claimant.[110]

(c) A fencing obligation owed to the dominant tenant by a person other than the claimant

4.31 At common law, not only did breach of an obligation to fence by the occupier of the servient tenement provide a defence to an action of cattle trespass, but breach of such an obligation by the owner out of occupation could also have this effect. If, as in *Wiseman v Booker*,[111] a landlord was under an obligation to fence, then if this obligation was broken, his tenant could not maintain an action of cattle trespass against the occupier of the dominant tenement whose horses 'trespassed'[112] on to the servient tenement occupied by the tenant and there damaged his crops. The tenant could be in no better position than the landlord.[113] If, however, the claimant was an employee on whose employer the obligation to fence was placed, then the former could not maintain an action of cattle trespass against the owner of pigs which strayed through the defective fence on to his employer's property and there injured him.[114] The employee had no interest in the land such as to maintain an action of cattle trespass,[115] but an action might lie against his employer or the owner of the pigs on proof of negligence.[116]

4.32 Turning to the effect of the Animals Act 1971 in this context, it is provided by section 5(6) that the defence of failure to fence thereunder depends on 'a breach by any other person, being a person having an interest in the land, of a duty to fence'. There are two conditions here. First, the person who is in breach of his fencing obligation must be someone other than the defendant, but there is no requirement that it must be the claimant. Second, that other person must both have a duty to fence and have an interest in the land whereon he is to fence.

4.33 The first comment to make on this provision is the obvious one that breach of an obligation to fence by the occupier of the servient tenement, the duty to fence being owed by him, will bar his right to make a claim under section 4 if the dominant tenant's livestock stray on to the servient tenement. Assuming that the duty to fence is placed on the owner of the servient tenement, it must next be asked what the position of his tenant is. Can the tenant make a claim if the dominant tenant's livestock stray on to the servient tenement? It would appear that he cannot. There has been a breach of a duty to fence by a person, other than the defendant, who has an

[110] *Vivian v Dalton* (1896) 41 Sol Jo 129; this was, in fact, a case of cattle trespass and distress damage feasant.

[111] (1878) 3 CPD 184, above, para 3.29.

[112] This was no more than a technical trespass, for the horses just put their heads over the fence.

[113] (1878) 3 CPD 184, 188.

[114] *Child v Hearn* (1874) LR 9 Exch 176.

[115] Above, ch 3, paras 3.07–3.11.

[116] Common law liability is discussed, below, ch 6.

interest in the land strayed upon, ie the owner of the servient tenement. It appears, therefore, that a landlord's breach of his obligation to fence will deprive his tenant of a right to claim under section 4, and so the common law position as exemplified by *Wiseman v Booker*[117] is unaltered.

4.34 Of course, section 5(6) does not apply just to the situation where the servient tenant is a landlord and the actual occupier of the land is his tenant, but that is the most likely situation where land is occupied by someone other than the person on whom the fencing obligation is placed. It should not be forgotten that a claim under section 4 can only be brought by the owner or occupier of the land upon which the animals stray.[118] A case which might be considered in this context is *Sutcliffe v Holmes*.[119] The defendants' livestock strayed from the defendants' land on to that of a local authority as a result of the latter's failure to fence. They went from that land on to the claimant's land, the claimant being under no fencing obligation. The claimant's action for cattle trespass, at common law, would have failed on the basis of the defence of act of third party had the Court of Appeal not held that the defendants should have foreseen and guarded against it. That defence is not available, in any event, under section 4. Is the statutory 'fencing' defence under section 5(6) available in such circumstances? There was a duty to fence owed to the person, the defendant, from whose land the livestock strayed, but no duty to fence was owed by the claimant on to whose land the livestock eventually strayed. Within the meaning of section 5(6), there was a breach of a fencing obligation by a person other than the defendant, and that person had an interest in the land he was obliged to fence. However, the phrase in section 5(6) 'a person having an interest in the land' must be taken to refer to 'the land of the claimant's which has been strayed upon'.[120] In that case, the defence under section 5(6) will not apply to facts such as those in *Sutcliffe v Holmes*, nor will it apply to any case where the fencing obligation is broken by a third party.[121]

4.35 Finally, one general comment should be made on the scope of the defence provided by section 5(6). It is only operative where it is proved that the straying would not have occurred but for a breach of a fencing obligation. What of the situation where the claimant is under an obligation to fence which he satisfies by the provision of a reasonable fence[122] and yet the defendant's livestock stray on to his land? In this case, the defendant is liable under section 4. If the claimant is in breach of his fencing obligation but the circumstances are such that, even had he fenced as required,

[117] (1878) 3 CPD 184, above, paras 3.29, 4.31.

[118] Hence an employee will still be unable to sue under s 4.

[119] [1947] KB 147; and see *Redfern & Son Ltd v Storey* [1969] NZLR 945.

[120] This is because s 5(6) is dependent on s 4, which refers to the claimant as the person in occupation of the land strayed upon.

[121] eg *Sharp v Harvey* [1935] LJCCR 261; and see *Cooke v Skinner* (1948) 98 L Jo 38.

[122] Above, paras 4.07–4.10.

he could not have kept the defendant's particular livestock out, as where they are sheep 'of a peculiarly wandering and saltative disposition',[123] then the failure to fence does not appear to constitute a defence. The position seems to be the same as that where there was an adequate fence and yet, nevertheless, the livestock strayed; for in such a case they would have strayed even without the breach by the claimant of his fencing obligation.

It should not be forgotten that, if neither of the occupiers of adjoining land is under an obligation to fence, then both occupiers owe a duty to prevent their livestock from straying,[124] and neither can recover for injuries to their livestock on the other's land.[125]

(d) Multiple obligations to fence

4.36 The situation envisaged here is that, where Blackacre, Whiteacre, and Greenacre are contiguous, G, the owner of Greenacre, is bound to fence against Whiteacre and W, the owner of Whiteacre, is bound to fence against Blackacre. Livestock belonging to B, the owner of Blackacre, stray on to Whiteacre as a result of W's failure to fence[126] and then, as a result of G's failure to fence, they stray on to Greenacre. What are the consequences of this straying as between B and G?

4.37 (a) B is not statutorily liable for straying livestock. Although there was authority at common law to support the view that B could not rely on G's failure to fence as a defence to an action for cattle trespass because the duty to fence was owed to W and not to B,[127] the statutory position would appear to be that B can rely on the breach of a fencing obligation owed to a third party. B's livestock would not have strayed on to Greenacre but for the breach by G of his fencing obligation. As G is a person who has an interest in the land strayed upon, the conditions of section 5(6) appear to be satisfied and B has a good defence. There is no requirement in section 5(6) that the fencing obligation which has been broken should have been owed to the defendant.

4.38 (b) B may be unable to sue G for injury done to his livestock on Greenacre. Such a conclusion would follow if the cases at common law holding B liable for cattle trespass[128] are to be applied by analogy here. This is an undesirable result for, as Williams

[123] *Coaker v Willcocks* [1911] 1 KB 649, 654, above, para 4.08.

[124] cf, eg, *Kempston v Butler* (1861) 12 ICLR 516.

[125] *Ponting v Noakes* [1894] 2 QB 281; and see *Roberts v Great Western Rail Co* (1858) 4 CBNS 506.

[126] The situation where they stray as a result of B's failure to fence has already been discussed, above, paras 4.27–4.30.

[127] *Anon* (1482) Jenk 161; *Right v Baynard* (1674) Freem KB 379; and see *Harvey v Gulson* (1604) Noy 107; these decisions are criticized by Williams, pp 220–21.

[128] See, above, n 127.

has pointed out in the cattle trespass context,[129] it may well be that B can sue W for the consequences of W's failure to fence and W may then sue G for the damages paid to B, this latter claim being based on G's breach of his fencing obligation to W. Circuity of action would be avoided by allowing B to sue G for the damage done to B's livestock. If G's obligation to fence is to fence against livestock lawfully on Whiteacre, it is hard to classify cattle thereon as a result of W's failure to fence, other than as being lawfully there.

A variation of this general problem of multiple fencing obligations might properly be considered here. Again, Blackacre, Whiteacre and Greenacre are contiguous. W, the owner of Whiteacre, is obliged to fence against Blackacre, but G, the owner of Greenacre, is not obliged to fence against Whiteacre. Livestock belonging to B, the owner of Blackacre, stray from Blackacre on to Whiteacre as a result of W's defective fences. They then stray from there on to Greenacre. What are B's rights and obligations in this type of case? **4.39**

(a) If B's livestock are injured on Greenacre, B can claim damages from W; for the animals would not have strayed in the first place but for W's breach of his fencing obligations to B.[130] No liability based on breach of an obligation to fence exists between G and B. **4.40**

(b) If B's livestock cause damage to Greenacre and G sues B under section 4 of the Animals Act 1971, can B rely on the protection of section 5(6)? There is no doubt that the livestock strayed in the first instance as the result of the breach of a duty to fence owed by W to B. However, B cannot claim under section 5(6) that the straying would not have occurred but for a breach of a fencing obligation by a person who has an interest in Greenacre, and so B would be liable to G under section 4. Furthermore, B is unable under the Animals Act 1971 to plead the common law defence of act of third party[131] in that the livestock would not have strayed on to Greenacre but for W's failure to fence them out of Whiteacre. There does, then, remain the question of whether B can obtain some redress from W for his statutory liability to G. There is authority, both academic[132] and judicial,[133] to support a claim by B against W for damages for breach of W's fencing obligation owed to B. It has been argued by Williams[134] that to allow G to recover damages from B based, now, on a statutory claim for straying livestock and then to allow B to recover an indemnity as to those damages from W, based on breach of a fencing obligation, **4.41**

[129] Williams, p 221.

[130] *Singleton v Williamson* (1861) 7 H & N 410, 416.

[131] See ch 3, above, para 3.46; cf *Sutcliffe v Holmes* [1947] KB 147; and see also *Sharp v Harvey* [1935] LJCCR 261.

[132] Williams, pp 222–3.

[133] eg *Holbach v Warner* (1623) Cro Jac 665; *Right v Baynard* (1674) Freem KB 379, 380; and see *Dunlop v Troy* [1915] VLR 639, where, however, the action had a contractual basis.

[134] Williams, p 223.

promotes circuity of claims and that a far better solution would be to deny G a claim against B, but to give him a claim in negligence against W. Not only has this argument been considered judicially at common law and rejected,[135] but there is no justification within the terms of the Animals Act 1971 for denying G his statutory right to claim against B under section 4.

135 *Sutcliffe v Holmes* [1947] KB 147, 156.

5

ANIMALS AND THE HIGHWAY

There are various bases of liability which concern harm done by animals which have **5.01** strayed onto or from a highway, or have caused injuries or damage while lawfully on the highway. Indeed, it has been seen already that the fact that livestock was lawfully on a highway before it strayed is a defence to an action under section 4 of the Animals Act 1971.[1] The purpose of this chapter is to gather together the examination of the various bases of liability for harm done by animals in connection with their use of the highway. While liability in nuisance and in trespass does exist in such cases and will be considered in due course, the prime area for examination is that of liability in negligence, especially because of substantial changes in such liability brought about by section 8 of the Animals Act 1971.

1. Negligence

There are three factual situations in which discussion of liability in negligence is **5.02** relevant. They are the cases of: animals straying on to the highway as the result of negligence and there causing injury or other damage to users of the highway; damage or injury caused by an animal which has been lawfully taken onto the highway but whose keeper has acted negligently in permitting it to cause harm to persons

[1] Above, paras 3.40–3.45.

using the highway; and the related case of such harm being caused by animals straying from the highway.

(1) Animals straying onto the highway

(a) Rule in Searle v Wallbank

5.03 The general rule at common law[2] was that an occupier of land was under no duty to erect or maintain fences so as to fence his land off from the highway[3] and was under no liability if his domestic animals strayed onto the highway and there injured a user of the highway, whether the straying was caused by his negligent failure to build or maintain fences or by some other factor. This rule was confirmed in the House of Lords decision in *Searle v Wallbank.*[4] Here, a cyclist collided with the defendant's horse which was on the highway, having escaped from an adjoining field where the defendant had put it. The claimant's claim in negligence failed, for the court held that there was no general duty on the defendant to use reasonable care to prevent the horse from straying.

5.04 To this general rule there were a number of possible exceptions, although they were exceptions that were more often explained than applied. First, if the owner of a domestic animal brought it onto the highway and it there caused damage to persons or property on or adjoining the highway, then he would, and will,[5] be liable provided that negligence can be proved.[6] Second, if an animal with a known vicious propensity was allowed to stray onto the highway or if there were other special circumstances concerning the characteristics of the animal which took the case out of the general rule, then the owner might be held liable in negligence for injuries caused by the animal,[7] as where a dog tended to act like 'a missile',[8] but not just where it was blind.[9] There was a third probable exception, namely where there were special circumstances which imposed liability, other than the propensities of the animal, such as the peculiar topography[10] or the fact that the animal was engaged in an activity which could only be carried on under a high degree of human control,[11] but not, perhaps, the circumstances of darkness.[12]

---

[2] G Williams, *Liability for Animals* (1939), Pt 6; Bentham (1958) 3 U Qd LJ 222; Toohey (1966) 7 UWALR 490.

[3] *Potter v Perry* (1859) 23 JP 644.

[4] [1947] AC 341.

[5] Below, paras 5.28–5.29.

[6] eg *Deen v Davies* [1935] 2 KB 282; *Gomberg v Smith* [1963] 1 QB 25.

[7] *Searle v Wallbank* [1947] AC 341, 356–7, 359–60; *Wright v Callwood* [1950] 2 KB 515, 527–8, 529–30; *Brock v Richards* [1951] 1 KB 529, 536–8; *Ellis v Johnstone* [1963] 2 QB 8, 21–3, 25–6, 28–32; *Gomberg v Smith* [1963] 1 QB 25, 32–4, 37; *Bativala v West* [1970] 1 QB 716.

[8] *Ellis v Johnstone,* above, at pp 25–6.

[9] *Millns v Garrett* (1906), The Times, 6 March.

[10] *Ellis v Johnstone,* above, at pp 21, 25–6.

[11] *Bativala v West* [1970] 1 QB 716.

[12] *Anderson v Wilson's Trustees* 1965 SLT (Sh Ct) 35, 36.

The general rule in *Searle v Wallbank* excluding liability in negligence was subjected to vigorous and sustained criticism,[13] being described as 'an outrageous subsidy shamelessly exacted by the farming lobby at the expense of public safety'.[14] There had long been considerable debate on this issue in other common law jurisdictions and, although approval of the rule had been expressed in Ireland,[15] Australia,[16] and New Zealand,[17] it was disapproved of in Scotland[18] and in Canada.[19] More recently, the rule has been abolished by statute in a number of jurisdictions,[20] for example, Australia,[21] New Zealand,[22] Northern Ireland,[23] and Ireland.[24] Much of this legislation is modelled on the Animals Act 1971. **5.05**

(b) Animals Act 1971, section 8

Various attempts had been made in England to abolish the rule,[25] culminating in the provisions of the Animals Act 1971, section 8 of which states: **5.06**

(1) So much of the rules of the common law relating to liability for negligence as excludes or restricts the duty which a person might owe to others to take such care as is reasonable to see that damage[26] is not caused by animals straying on to a highway is hereby abolished.

(2) Where damage is caused by animals straying from unfenced land to a highway a person who placed them on the land shall not be regarded as having committed a breach of the duty to take care by reason only of placing them there if—

(a) the land is common land, or is land situated in an area where fencing is not customary, or is a town or village green; and

(b) he had a right to place the animals on that land.[27]

---

[13] eg *Gomberg v Smith*, above, at pp 31, 39–40; *Ellis v Johnstone*, above, at p 27; *Bativala v West*, above, at p 724.

[14] J Fleming, *Introduction to the Law of Torts*, 2nd edn (1985), p 162.

[15] *Gibb v Comerford* [1942] IR 294; cf *Dunphy v Bryan* (1962) 97 ILTR 4; *Gillick v O'Reilly* (1984) 4 ILRM 402.

[16] *State Government Insurance Commission v Trigwell* (1979) 142 CLR 617; cf *Reyn v Scott* (1968) 2 DCR (NSW) 13.

[17] *Simeon v Avery* [1959] NZLR 1345; *Ross v McCarthy* [1970] NZLR 449.

[18] *Gardiner v Miller* 1967 SLT 29; *Wormald v HJ Walker & Co* 2004 SCLR 733; *Davidson v McIrvine* 2007 SLT (Sh Ct) 71; and see *O'Connor v McRobb* 1975 SLT (Sh Ct) 42.

[19] *Fleming v Atkinson* (1959) 18 DLR (2d) 81; G Fridman, *The Law of Torts in Canada*, 2nd edn (2002), pp 269–71; L Klar, *Tort Law*, 4th edn (2008), pp 644–5.

[20] See above, paras 1.24, 1.26, 1.27.

[21] eg Animals Act 1977 (NSW), s 7; and see *Brown v Tooey* (1994) 35 NSWLR 417; J Fleming, *Torts*, 9th edn (1998), pp 407–8; F Trindade, P Cane, and M Lunney, *The Law of Torts in Australia*, 4th edn (2007), p 660; but not in Queensland: *Smith v Williams* [2006] Aus Torts Rep 81-863.

[22] Animals Law Reform Act 1989, s 5; see S Todd, *The Law of Torts in New Zealand*, 5th edn (2009), para 6.10.02.

[23] Animals (Northern Ireland) Order 1976 SI 1976/1040, Art 7.

[24] Animals Act 1985, s 2(1); see *O'Reilly v Lavelle* [1990] 2 IR 372; *O'Shea v Anhold* (1996) 15 ILT (NS) 128; *Murray v Millar* (2002) 20 ILT (NS) 252.

[25] North, (1966) 30 Conv (NS) 44.

[26] Damage is defined here, as elsewhere in the Act, so as to include 'the death of, or injury to, any person (including any disease and any impairment of physical or mental condition)': Animals Act 1971, s 11.

[27] And see the Animals (Northern Ireland) Order 1976, SI 1976/1040, Art 7.

5.07 This section of the Animals Act 1971 generated more Parliamentary debate than any other, indeed almost as much as all of the other sections combined. The rule abolished by this section was said to be:

> rooted in the social conditions of an earlier age when pastoral land in England was not normally fenced, and consequently straying animals on the highway were a normal hazard of the highway which any traveller on the highway had to expect and be prepared to meet. Nowadays such conditions only survive in relatively remote parts of the country; Dartmoor springs to mind as an example. Over the major part of England and Wales the relevant social conditions are vastly different.[28]

Nevertheless, it was strongly urged that to impose liability in negligence for straying animals was an intolerable burden to place on farmers, in terms of fencing and insurance. On the other side, it was argued that the Act, in section 8(2), goes too far in the protection of farmers, especially in the case of animals straying from unfenced or common land. The end result is a compromise between the interest of the farmer and of the motorist, which is 'to some extent a judgment of Solomon'.[29] In the past, the scales had been weighed far too heavily against the motorist. As Lord Gardiner LC said:

> Really, the farmers have been very lucky. The historical truth of the matter is that, whereas in nearly every walk of life we are all under a duty to take care to see that we do not injure our neighbours, their position has always been a complete exception. Farmers have been lucky to be in this exceptional position from the start; the dead and the injured have been unlucky.[30]

5.08 The basic effect of section 8(1) is to treat the case of animals straying onto a highway in no way different from other liability in negligence.[31] It did not put the owner or keeper of the animals in a peculiarly disadvantageous position. It merely removed a peculiar advantage. The effect of section 8(2) is to indicate that there is no presumption of negligence when animals stray from unfenced land. No peculiar benefit is conferred on the farmer who places animals on unfenced land. He is merely protected against an abnormal disadvantage.[32] The effects of these two subsections will now be considered in more detail.

(i) Effects of section 8(1)

5.09 In abrogating the rule in *Searle v Wallbank*, section 8(1) has rendered otiose any discussion of the scope of that rule; and, indeed, the same might be said of any

---

[28] *Bativala v West* [1970] 1 QB 716, 724.

[29] 312 HL Deb (1970), c 200.

[30] 305 HL Deb (1969), c 562; cf *Ross v McCarthy* [1970] NZLR 449, 456.

[31] Liability under s 8 applies to the Crown: Animals Act 1971, s 12, discussed, above, para 2.32.

[32] The Attorney-General would appear to have stated the position too widely when he said that s 8(2) 'ensures that no liability shall fall on a person who grazes an animal on unfenced land in open parts of the country': 815 HC Deb (1971), c 603; cf the Solicitor-General, HC Standing Committee A, 18 March 1971, c 65.

discussion of the scope of section 8(1) itself for, when *Searle v Wallbank* did not apply, the common law of negligence did. Once *Searle v Wallbank* had gone, it was clear that the common law of negligence applies throughout. There is no restriction on the generality of the application of negligence principles based on either the types of animals which strayed, or on the type of highway—for example, footpath, bridle path, main road, or motorway—onto which they strayed.[33] In all cases, liability depends on general negligence principles. The law is the same for straying dogs as for straying cattle[34] or sheep.[35] Indeed, it might be said that not only are the former as great an evil and danger as the latter, but that section 8(1) has as great an effect on the urban dog keeper as on the rural farmer.

Some indication of the types of conduct which may or may not connote negligence in the case of animals straying from a highway may be drawn from Canadian experience. Judson J in the Supreme Court of Canada held, in *Fleming v Atkinson*,[36] that the rule in *Searle v Wallbank* did not apply in Ontario and that **5.10**

> there can be no difficulty in the application of the ordinary rules of negligence to the facts in this type of case and the matter should be left to the tribunal of fact to determine, with due regard to all the circumstances, including the nature of the highway and the amount and nature of the traffic that might reasonably be expected to be upon it, whether or not it would be negligent to allow a domestic animal to be at large.[37]

This judgment as to the law of Ontario has been adopted in several other,[38] though not all,[39] Canadian Provinces with the effect that a corpus of decisions, essentially factual, has been built up on what constitutes negligence on the part of a farmer whose animals stray onto the highway. This body of case law may provide some guidance, by analogy, to the interpretation of section 8(1) of the Animals Act 1971. Thus, it is not a case of negligence if animals break through an ordinary reasonable fence, especially if it is a new fence.[40] In many circumstances, a fence will be **5.11**

---

33 Law Commission Report, paras 45–54.

34 eg *O'Reilly v Lavelle* [1990] 2 IR 372; *O'Dwyer v Dalgliesh* [1993] DCR 986 (NZ); *Heywood v May* [1995] DCR 211 (NZ); *O'Shea v Anhold* (1996) 15 ILT (NS) 128; *Murray v Millar* (2001) 20 ILT (NS) 252; *Wilson v Donaldson* [2004] EWCA Civ 972.

35 eg *Davies v Davies* [1975] QB 172; *Ridyard v Owen* (1980) CA, Unreported, 16 May.

36 (1959) 18 DLR (2d) 81.

37 Ibid, at p 102.

38 eg Alberta—*Cooper v Matteotti* (1968) 66 DLR (2d) 338; British Columbia—*Staul v Crawford* (1968) 64 WWR 568; Manitoba—*Manitoba Public Insurance Corp v Lamb* [2006] 2 WWR 136; Newfoundland—*Rowe v Canning* (1994) 117 Nfld & PEIR 383; Nova Scotia—*Crosby v Curry* (1970) 7 DLR (3d) 188; Saskatchewan—*Windrem v Hamill* [1979] 1 WWR 767; *Reynoldson v Simmons* (1982) 14 Sask R 257; and in the Canadian Exchequer Court in the case of an accident occurring in New Brunswick—*R v DeWitt* [1968] 1 Ex CR 156.

39 It has been rejected in New Brunswick: *Mussens Ltd v Lean* (1968) 190 NBR (2d) 161; *Cormier v McCarthy* (1969) 1 NBR (2d) 866; but see *Haley v Reade* (2000) 228 NBR (2d) 359.

40 *Cormier v McCarthy*, above, at p 870.

adequate even though insufficient to contain an animal which is determined to escape; but it has been suggested that if the defendant's land adjoined

> a heavily travelled, high speed road, he might well be required to use fencing, however expensive, through which his cattle could not possibly escape.[41] I do not think that one can require that when the land adjoins a gravel market road, which is lightly travelled.[42]

There is no negligence when cattle are contained by an electric fence in good order and charged with current at all material times and yet a cow gets onto the highway in some inexplicable way,[43] or where a horse escapes through a well-maintained fence.[44] Similarly, the use of a four-foot fence to contain heifers in heat was reasonable, even though heifers in such a condition may become unruly and jump fences. As the judge said:

> It would surely not be reasonable to ask farmers whose properties are adjacent to a public highway to erect eight-foot fences or such fences that no animal at any time would ever be able to break out of. Cows are persistent, and in spite of their apparent stupidity, are very resourceful when they wish to go from point A to point B.[45]

5.12 Examples might, on the other hand, be given of conduct which has been considered to amount to common law negligence. The most dramatic example is provided by *Fleming v Atkinson*[46] itself, where the defendant made no attempt to contain his cattle at all, the fences of his land being in a very poor state of repair, and his cattle were regularly allowed to range over the highway. Again, to allow horses to roam over land adjoining a highway without any attempt to fence them in has been held to amount to negligence;[47] but even where animals are fenced in, a farmer may be at fault if he does not regularly check the security of his fences, at least where they adjoin a busy road.[48] It has even been held that, where A's land adjoins B's and B is under an obligation to fence, then if A knows that the fence is defective, A will be held liable in negligence if he puts animals into such an inadequately fenced field so that they stray from his land, onto B's land, and thence onto a highway; although B may be liable to A for any injury to A's animals caused by a collision on the highway.[49] It has been held to be negligence where a farmer left cattle feed so close to an

---

[41] While this may be an excessively high standard, it has been accepted that the heavier the traffic, the higher the duty of care: *R v DeWitt* [1968] Ex CR 156.

[42] *Penner v Allan* (1963) 43 WWR 244, 245.

[43] *Crosby v Curry* (1970) 7 DLR (3d) 188.

[44] *Reynoldson v Simmons* (1982) 14 Sask 257; and see *Rozon v Patenaude* (1982) 35 OR (2d) 619; *Pellizzari v Miller* (1981) 35 OR (2d) 700.

[45] *Staul v Crawford* (1968) 64 WWR 568, 573.

[46] (1959) 18 DLR (2d) 81.

[47] *Bonany and Bonany v Gratton* (1960) 23 DLR (2d) 591.

[48] *Gash v Wood* (1960) 22 DLR (2d) 625; and see *Stelter v Stross Management Ltd* (1977) 4 Alta LR (2d) 284.

[49] *Colonial Coach Lines Ltd v Bennett* [1968] 1 OR 333.

electric fence that his cattle were enticed to break through the fence,[50] to put a dog in a pen out of which it could jump,[51] or to exercise a dog off the leash close to an urban road.[52]

Although these common law decisions are no more than illustrative of the application of the general and inherently flexible rule of negligence liability[53] to the particular case of animals straying onto a highway, they give some indication of the types of issues to which the application of section 8(1) of the Animals Act 1971 may give rise, and of the types of factors which the court will weigh in considering whether the defendant has been negligent. If it is reasonable for him to fence, then, subject to section 8(2),[54] he may well be considered at fault in failing to do so. However, his fences need only be reasonable ones. The fact that an animal got through or over a normally satisfactory fence is not, as such, conclusive of negligence. Again, some intervening cause may have rendered the fence inadequate;[55] a trespasser may have left a gate open; a motorist may have knocked part of it down; the electricity supply in an electric fence may have failed. None of these, unless foreseeable or ignored, would indicate fault on the part of the farmer.[56] If, however, the fencing is 'erected and maintained to a standard well below that required by the common practice in the locality for containing cattle', then the defendant will be liable.[57] **5.13**

It does appear that in areas of heavy traffic, of fields well stocked with animals, or of high population, the obligation imposed by section 8(1) may only be met by the provision of reasonably adequate fences. In *Wilson v Donaldson*,[58] a farmer was held liable in negligence when cattle escaped from his land, through another neglected farm, and then onto a road where they collided with the claimant's car. There was a well-used public footpath through the defendant's land and the adjoining property, with a gate between the two. The cattle escaped through this gate which was insecure, and the defendant was held liable in negligence for failing to address the risk of the gate being left open and of his cattle escaping onto the highway. Indeed, in a decision under the New Zealand equivalent[59] of the Animals Act 1971, it has been **5.14**

---

[50] *Haley v Reade* (2000) 228 NBR (2d) 359.
[51] *Ruckheim v Robinson* [1995] 4 WWR 284.
[52] *Spanton v Laviolette* (1977) 19 OR (2d) 21.
[53] Twelfth Report of the Law Reform Committee for Scotland, (1963), para 12; Report of the New South Wales Law Reform Commission (1970), LRC 8, para 21.
[54] Discussed, below, paras 5.18–5.27.
[55] *Heywood v May* [1995] DCR 211 (NZ); *Wilson v Donaldson* [2004] EWCA Civ 972.
[56] But see the discussion of *res ipsa loquitur*, below, para 5.16.
[57] *O'Dwyer v Dalgliesh* [1993] DCR 986, a decision on s 5 of the New Zealand Animals Law Reform Act 1989.
[58] Above; and see *Hoskin v Rogers* [1985] TLR 42; *Gardner v Wharton* (2004), M Pether et al, *Bingham & Berryman's Personal Injury and Motor Claims Cases*, 13th edn (2010), para 18.35.
[59] Animals Law Reform Act 1989.

held that a defective latch on an otherwise sound fence may lead to liability.[60] However, in *Brown v Tooey*,[61] a decision under the New South Wales Animals Act 1977,[62] the New South Wales Court of Appeal made clear that, in considering the issue of liability for a road accident caused by sheep straying through a fence damaged by a falling tree, the court had to balance the rights and obligations of the landowner and a passing motorist:

> It involves the balancing of 'the magnitude of the risk and the degree of the probability of its occurrence' against the expense, difficulty and inconvenience of finding and repairing the fence soon enough to prevent the escape of the sheep . . . A reasonable person would not see the landowner as obliged to patrol his fences constantly and would allow some time for the landowner to discover and repair a damaged fence. During that time, the passing motorist would, in practical sense, bear the risk of escaping sheep.[63]

5.15 If an unidentified person let or drove horses onto a road, their owner would not be regarded as negligent;[64] nor was there held to be negligence when a cow escaped onto the highway 'by jumping or clambering over a six barred livestock gate'.[65] It has been said, in New Zealand, that the reasonableness of the defendant's behaviour will depend on the location of his property:

> In a mixed residential, industrial, pastoral and horticultural area . . . where the common practice is to fence farm animals in so that they cannot stray at all, reasonable care to prevent cattle straying onto the highway must obviously include proper supervision of the cattle and proper means of restraining them from straying.[66]

The need for adequate precaution will be particularly true in the case of liability for accidents in urban areas caused by dogs. Where a dog is allowed out onto the highway without a lead, or no adequate steps are taken to prevent it getting onto a highway, it will be very difficult to rebut an allegation of negligence.

5.16 It has been held in Ireland, in *O'Reilly v Lavelle*,[67] that section 2(1) of the Animals Act 1985, which is in the same terms as section 8(1) of the Animals Act 1971, in some way embodies what has been described as the doctrine of *res ipsa loquitur*,[68] so as to shift the burden of proof onto the defendant to show that he took reasonable

---

[60] *Heywood v May* [1995] DCR 212. Cf *Ali v Allen* (1987) Unreported, 22 October, where the owner of a dog was held not liable for an accident caused by its escape after his children may have failed adequately to close a garden gate.

[61] (1992) 35 NSWLR 417.

[62] See s 7.

[63] (1992) 35 NSWLR 417, 425.

[64] *Jaundrill v Gillett* (1996), The Times, 30 January; and see *Hole v Ross-Skinner* [2003] EWCA Civ 774; [2003] All ER (D) 272.

[65] *McKenny v Foster* [2008] EWCA Civ 173.

[66] *O'Dwyer v Dalgliesh* [1993] DCR 986, 995; and see *Heywood v May*, above.

[67] [1990] 2 IR 372; and see *McCaffrey v Lundy* (1988) 6 ILT (NS) 245; *Murray v Millar* (2001) 20 ILT (NS) 252. Contrast *O'Shea v Anhold* (1996) 15 ILT (NS) 128, where the defendant was held, by the Irish Supreme Court, to have discharged his burden of proof as to the adequacy of his fencing.

[68] cf *Roe v Minister of Health* [1954] 2 QB 66, 87.

care of his animals. In this case, a number of cattle escaped onto the highway, where one was hit by the claimant's car. The cattle had escaped from the defendant's field, but the roadside fences showed no sign of defects and the gate was securely bolted. Given that there was clear evidence that the cattle, which belonged to the defendant, had escaped, it was held that the defendant had failed to discharge the burden of proof on him to show that his fencing was not defective. However, it is hard to see in the legislation any justification for that conclusion. Nevertheless, animal owners put under a risk of liability by section 8(1) will find it prudent to insure, thereby spreading the burden over a wider sector of the community than its imposition on the victim of their negligence under the *Searle v Wallbank* rule.

No definition of 'animals' is provided in the Animals Act 1971. That being so, it must be furnished by the common law, and it would appear that there may now be liability in negligence where not only cows, horses, and sheep stray onto a highway, but also where dogs, cats, and even poultry do so.[69] There is no restriction on the type of creature whose straying may involve liability in negligence,[70] and it is suggested that 'animals' is apposite in this context to include poultry.[71] **5.17**

(ii) Protection under section 8(2)

Some protection for the keeper of animals is provided by section 8(2) of the Animals Act 1971, but only, it may be recalled, to the extent that there is to be no presumption of negligence from the fact that the animals strayed from unfenced land where such fencing is not customary and the defendant had a right to put his animals there. The subsection states: **5.18**

> Where damage is caused by animals straying from unfenced land to a highway a person who placed them on the land shall not be regarded as having committed a breach of the duty to take care by reason only of placing them there if—
>
> (a) the land is common land, or is land situated in an area where fencing is not customary, or is a town or village green; and
>
> (b) he had a right to place the animals on that land.[72]

One general comment on this subsection is that it applies to all cases of alleged liability for injury or other damage done by animals straying onto a highway and not just to such liability as was introduced by section 8(1) following the abrogation **5.19**

---

[69] And, in appropriate circumstances, deer: Law Commission Report, para 53.

[70] cf the doubts in the various Private Member's Bills on this topic; see North (1966) 30 Conv (NS) 44, 55–7.

[71] Although, undoubtedly, one factor in determining whether there is liability for allowing poultry to escape would be 'the extreme difficulty of preventing poultry escaping on to the road': Twelfth Report of the Law Reform Committee for Scotland (1963), para 12. The same might be said of cats: see Law Commission Report, para 54.

[72] A rather broader approach has been taken in New Zealand, where the Animals Law Reform Act 1989, s 5(2), states that, in determining whether the defendant has been negligent, consideration should be given to the common practice in the locality with regard to fencing and whether measures were taken to warn of the likely presence of animals on the highway.

of the rule in *Searle v Wallbank*. Section 8(2) is drafted in terms wide enough also to apply to any cases of liability which, at common law, fell outside the constricting effects of that rule, for the very scope of the rule had been 'subject to qualifications of uncertain extent and authority'.[73] So all liability in negligence for harm done by animals straying onto the highway, no matter what its provenance, is subject to section 8(2).

(iii) Definition issues

5.20 Both subsections 8(1) and 8(2) raise a number of detailed issues of definition.

5.21 (*a*) *Fencing*. The land to which section 8(2) applies must be 'unfenced land' and, furthermore, one of the further possible conditions under section 8(2)(a) is that it is land where 'fencing is not customary'. Fencing is defined in section 11 of the Animals Act 1971 as to include 'the construction of any obstacle designed to prevent animals from straying'. This includes not only fences, but also ditches whose object is not solely drainage but also the retention of animals. It would also include cattle grids. So, land which has no fences but which has some other obstacle, such as a wide, stock-proof ditch, will not be regarded as unfenced land. It may not always be easy to determine whether there is, in fact, any fencing as where, for example, there are 'rough stone walls' between common land and the highway.[74] A further unresolved issue is whether, in the case of a large area of common, section 8(2) applies to protect the defendant if the area from which his livestock strayed is unfenced, although other areas of the common are fenced.[75]

5.22 (*b*) *Types of unfenced land*. Three types of unfenced land are referred to in section 8(2), all of which raise issues of definition. The first is 'common land'.[76] This is defined as:[77]

> (a) land[78] registered as common land in a register of common land kept under Part 1 of the Commons Act 2006;
> (b) land to which Part 1 of that Act does not apply and which is subject to rights of common within the meaning of that Act.

One reason for the inclusion of common land in the categories of unfenced land is that a commoner has, normally, no right to fence the land and, under the Commons Act 2006, section 38, the consent of the 'appropriate national authority' is required before common land may be fenced.

[73] Law Commission Report, para 30.
[74] See *Ridyard v Owen* (1980) CA, Unreported, 16 May.
[75] Ibid.
[76] eg *Davies v Davies* [1975] QB 172; *Matthews v Wicks* (1987) CA, Unreported, 22 May.
[77] Animals Act 1971, s 11, as amended by the Commons Act, s 52, Sch 5.
[78] Defined by s 6(1) of the Commons Act 2006 to include 'land covered with water'.

The second type of unfenced land is a 'town or village green', and, again, this is defined[79] by reference to the Commons Act 2006, which says that it means 'land registered as a town or village green in a register of town or village greens kept under Part 1 of the Commons Act 2006'. It should be noted that, in relation to both common land and a town or village green, registration under the Act is conclusive of the matter registered,[80] with the consequence that the registered right cannot be challenged under section 8(2) of the 1971 Act.[81] **5.23**

The third category is that of 'land situated in an area where fencing is not customary'. **5.24** There is no definition of this provided by the Animals Act 1971 and its general vagueness may well be the source of considerable difficulty. The custom is that of the area and not that of the particular land in question. If it is customary to fence in the area, then the fact that the defendant's land has never been fenced may not bring the protection of section 8(2) into play; although it is difficult to assess the ambit of 'area', for it can mean 'anything from a couple of farms to Cumberland or South-East England'.[82] Underlying this provision is the fact that some account must be taken of the circumstance that, in some areas of the country, highways run through unenclosed land, especially moorland, and it would be unreasonable to consider that a farmer who exercised his rights to graze sheep on such moorland should be held to be negligent merely because they strayed onto a road running across the moor. Whether fencing is 'customary' will have to be decided according to the general usages of the area in question. An area of decaying walls and rotting fences is, probably, an area where fencing is customary.[83] However, it may be that section 8(2) could act as a deterrent against the very fencing that section 8 is designed, in part, to encourage. No farmer will wish to upset a local custom of leaving land unfenced if no liability necessarily accrues from the failure to fence. If a farmer then does fence, he will have to maintain his fences and may be held liable if his animals stray as a result of the disrepair of his fences. There is no provision for those areas, often on the edge of moorland, where 'bad or inadequate fencing is customary'. Furthermore, no provision is made for the fact that it may be customary not to fence, although it is widely agreed that the custom, in that area, is bad.

(*c*) *Right to place animals on unfenced land.* In order for there to be no presumption **5.25** of negligence when animals stray from unfenced land, the defendant must have had a right to put his animals on that land. A variety of persons will have rights to pasture animals on unfenced land. They will include the owner or occupier of the land,

[79] Animals Act 1971, s 11, as amended by the Commons Act 2006, s 52, Sch 5.
[80] Commons Act 2006, s 18.
[81] *Ridyard v Owen* (1980) CA, Unreported, 16 May, decided under the Commons Registration Act 1965, s 10, the predecessor of the 2006 Act.
[82] 313 HL Deb (1970), c 460.
[83] See *Ridyard v Owen*, above.

a person with a contractual right as under a contract of agistment, a non-contractual licensee, and, as with much unfenced land, a person with rights of common over the land. In *Davies v Davies*,[84] sheep strayed onto the highway from common land and the claimant in his car collided with them at night. The defendant's parents had the right to graze sheep on the common, but the sheep in question belonged to their son, the defendant, who grazed his sheep on the common with his parents' agreement. The Court of Appeal held that the defendant could claim the protection of section 8(2) because the subsection protects 'any person licensed by the owner to put the animals on the common land',[85] provided that the number of sheep put on the common did not exceed the number entitled to be grazed there under the right of pasture. Furthermore, the right to put animals on the common land, and thus to claim the protection of section 8(2), does not appear to be excluded by the fact that 'the grazing available to the animals is limited'.[86]

5.26 It might be asked what the effect on liability is, under section 8, of animals straying from unfenced land where they had no right to be or where the right has been exceeded.[87] What section 8(2) indicates is that there is no presumption of negligence 'by reason only' of animals being placed on unfenced land if there was a right to do so. It does not also say that there is a presumption of negligence if there was no right to place them there. Indeed, it is difficult to see how the mere fact that animals are kept on unfenced land for one day longer than they are contractually permitted to be there makes it any more foreseeable that they will stray onto a highway and cause injury or other damage. Perhaps the most that can be said for section 8(2) is that it excludes any operation of the doctrine of *res ipsa loquitur*[88] in determining the negligence of someone who has a right to pasture his animals on unfenced land. Section 8(2) will not protect a defendant where there is some further evidence of possible negligence other than failure to fence the common land, as where, for example, he 'negligently drove an animal from the common into the path of an oncoming car'.[89]

5.27 (*d*) *Highway*. No definition of a 'highway' is provided in the Animals Act 1971. The rule in *Searle v Wallbank* had been applied not only to highways where there was a right of passage for vehicular traffic, but also to public footpaths.[90] It is suggested that the meaning of 'highway' for the purposes of section 8 is the general common law meaning of 'all portions of land over which every subject of the Crown may

[84] [1975] QB 172.

[85] Ibid, at p 176.

[86] Ibid, at p 177.

[87] It could be exceeded, for example, by the animals being kept on the land for too long a period or by too many being pastured on the land: see *Davies v Davies*, above.

[88] And see, above, para 5.16.

[89] *Ridyard v Owen* (1980) CA, Unreported, 16 May.

[90] *Fitzgerald v ED & AD Cooke Bourne (Farms) Ltd* [1964] 1 QB 249.

lawfully pass'.[91] This is an unlimited definition which would include footpaths and bridleways, as well as all public roads.[92] This has the result that, not only will a farmer be under a duty of care in relation to his animals straying onto roads, but he will also owe a duty of care to those persons who use a highway, such as a footpath, across his land. If that footpath crosses a field in which animals are pastured and those animals injure users of the highway, then the farmer will be held liable if such injuries are the result of his negligence. He will, however, only be liable if he has been negligent, and it has been suggested that:

> it would be too much to expect that an 'ordinarily careful' owner of fillies should refrain from keeping them in a field where there is a public highway merely because there is a chance that one of the fillies in a playful mood might . . . come in contact with and injure someone lawfully walking along the highway.[93]

(2) Animals lawfully on the highway causing injury or damage there

It has been settled since the seventeenth century that an obligation of care is imposed on anyone who takes a horse out onto a highway.[94] This is a general obligation which is, in fact, applicable to all who take any animals onto the highway.[95] For example, if a horse bolts and knocks a cyclist over;[96] if a pony is insecurely tethered so that it escapes and injures a pedestrian;[97] if a pony is left unattended for so long that it becomes restive and causes injury;[98] if a large St Bernard dog escapes and collides with a car,[99] then in all of these cases there will be liability for such damage or injury if negligence is proved. **5.28**

It is undoubtedly true, as in all negligence cases, 'that what constitutes "reasonable care" is a question of fact in each case'.[100] All that one can do is to point to a variety of factors which may be relevant in deciding whether adequate care has been taken. The standard of care may vary as between town and country,[101] and as between day and night.[102] Other factors would be the number[103] and age[104] of the animals **5.29**

---

[91] J Pratt et al, *Pratt & Mackenzie's Law of Highways*, 21st edn (1967), p 3; and see S Sauvain, *Highway Law*, 4th edn (2009), paras 1.01–1.21.

[92] And see para 5.09, above.

[93] *Fitzgerald v ED & AD Cooke Bourne (Farms) Ltd*, above, at p 265.

[94] *Mitchil v Alestree* (1676) 1 Vent 295.

[95] Lawful use of the highway is discussed, in ch 3, paras 3.40–3.45 above, in the context of liability for straying 'livestock'. However, it is also lawful to take other animals, including dogs, onto the highway, and that includes hounds: *Adam v Chiddingfield Farmers Foxhounds* (1955), The Times, 5 November.

[96] *Turner v Coates* [1917] 1 KB 670.

[97] *Deen v Davies* [1935] 2 KB 282.

[98] *Aldham v United Dairies (London) Ltd* [1940] 1 KB 507.

[99] *Gomberg v Smith* [1963] 1 QB 25; and see *Weld v McMyn* (1972) 28 DLR (3d) 253.

[100] Ibid, at p 30.

[101] *Gomberg v Smith*, above; and see *Deen v Davies*, above, at pp 286, 299.

[102] *Turner v Coates*, above; *Griffith v Turner* [1955] NZLR 1035.

[103] *Paul v Rome* (1904) 24 NZLR 641; *Furlong v Curran* (1959) 25 Ir Jur 30.

[104] *Turner v Coates*, above.

involved, the extent to which they were used to traffic conditions,[105] the speed at which they were driven,[106] the nature of the road,[107] the ability or age and experience of the person in charge of them,[108] the number of people available to control them,[109] the steps taken to warn drivers,[110] whether they were driven loose[111] or turned loose,[112] the measures taken to secure unattended animals,[113] whether the animals were adequately lit at night,[114] the weather conditions,[115] or even the width of the road.[116] Not only may there be liability in negligence for harm done by animals which are lawfully being taken or driven along a highway, but, for example, there may also be liability in negligence for injuries caused by animals which are kept in a parked car on the highway.[117] Again, however, liability depends on the facts of the particular case.[118]

(3) Animals straying from the highway

5.30 There was no liability in cattle trespass where animals lawfully on the highway strayed from the highway onto the claimant's land.[119] Similarly, there is no liability for damage done by straying livestock under section 4 of the Animals Act 1971 if such animals stray from the highway. This is because of the special defence provided by section 5(5) of that Act to protect the owner of livestock lawfully on the highway from such liability.[120] Thus, 'a bull may stray from the highway into a china shop without imposing liability on its owner'.[121] In the leading case of *Tillett v Ward*,[122] an ox strayed into an ironmonger's shop from the highway. No negligence was proved. There was no liability.

[105] Ibid; and see *Purdon v Scott* [1968] NZLR 83.

[106] *Barrett v Hardie and Thompson* [1923] NZLR 228.

[107] *George Graham (1960) Ltd v Crawford* [1964] NZLR 668; *Berry v John Remus Transport Ltd* [1989] DCR (NZ) 448.

[108] *Desmond v Scott* [1951] 3 DLR 418.

[109] *Hill v Clark* [1969] 2 NSWR 733.

[110] *Harrison v Jackson* (1947) 14 LJNCCR 242; *Matthews v Taylor* (1995), M Pether et al, *Bingham & Berryman's Personal Injury and Motor Claims Cases*, 13th edn (2010), para 18.31.

[111] *Allen v Borough of St Kilda* (1912) 31 NZLR 265; and see *George Graham (1960) Ltd v Crawford*, above.

[112] *Lysnar v Binnie* (1901) 24 NZLR 241; and see *Bujold v Dempsey* (1996) 181 NBR (2d) 111.

[113] *Gayler and Pope Ltd v B Davies & Son Ltd* [1924] 2 KB 75; *St Pierre v Savoie* (1994) 153 NBR (2d) 326.

[114] *Turnbull v Wieland* (1916) 33 TLR 143; *Furlong v Curran* (1959) 25 Ir Jur 30; *Gardner v Delia Santa* [1968] SASR 345; *Andrews v Watts* [1971] RTR 484; cf *Catchpole v Minster* (1913) 30 TLR 111.

[115] *E J Lett & Co v Air Contracts Ltd* (1968) 12 MCD 360; *Eales v James* (1977) 17 Nfld & PEIR 242.

[116] *Nickells v Melbourne Corp* (1938) 56 CLR 219.

[117] *Sycamore v Ley* (1932) 147 LT 342, 345.

[118] *Fardon v Harcourt-Rivington* (1932) 146 LT 391; *Sycamore v Ley*, above.

[119] *Tillett v Ward* (1882) 10 QBD 17; *Goldston v Bradshaw* [1934] LJNCCR 355; *Esso Petroleum Co Ltd v Southport Corp* [1956] AC 218, 244.

[120] Above, paras 3.40–3.45.

[121] *Manton v Brocklebank* [1923] 2 KB 212, 231.

[122] (1882) 10 QBD 17.

Although occupiers of land adjoining a highway are deemed to assume the risks of livestock straying from the highway where there is no fault on the part of the defendant,[123] the position is quite different where that straying is caused by negligence. The leading authority is *Gayler and Pope Ltd v B Davies & Co Ltd*.[124] The defendants' pony and milk van had been left unattended in the street. The pony bolted and crashed through the claimants' shop window, causing a good deal of damage to the goods inside the claimants' drapers shop. Although a claim in trespass failed, McCardie J held that 'when a pony and van, wholly unattended, dash into a plaintiff's shop window adjoining a highway there is a prima facie case of negligence'.[125] The defendants were held liable in negligence. **5.31**

While there is no liability under section 4 of the Animals Act 1971 when livestock stray from the highway onto the claimant's land,[126] a problem may arise when such animals do stray and are not removed by their owner. Under the Animals Act 1971 this failure to remove them does not affect their owner's non-liability under section 4. It is possible, however, that an action might lie against him in negligence. The problem arose, at common law, in *Goodwyn v Cheveley*.[127] The claimant's drover was driving cattle along the highway when some strayed onto the defendant's land. The drover left them where they were and took the remaining cattle to their destination for the night and returned an hour later for the errant ones. By that time, the defendant had impounded them. The claimant sued in trespass and, in defence, it was argued that as the claimant had not removed his cattle within a reasonable time, the defendant was justified in impounding them. The court held that it was for the jury to decide what constituted a reasonable time in all the circumstances of the case, which included not only time to remove the straying cattle, but also time to make the others safe. Nevertheless, it is clear that where cattle strayed from a highway onto the defendant's land, although this gave rise to no action in cattle trespass, the defendant could impound them if they were left on his land for an unreasonable length of time. Presumably, the basis for this right is dependent on the fact that, once the reasonable period had elapsed, a right of action in cattle trespass arose. **5.32**

When one turns to the statutory position under the Animals Act, it will be recalled[128] that the defence to an action under section 4 of the Animals Act 1971 is provided by section 5(5) of that Act, ie animals lawfully on the highway straying onto the claimant's land, has no requirement or qualification that the animals be removed within a reasonable time. Nevertheless, there could be great inconvenience caused **5.33**

---

[123] *Fletcher v Rylands* (1866) LR 1 Exch 265, 286; *Tillett v Ward* (1882) 10 QBD 17, 20; *Gayler and Pope Ltd v B Davies & Son Ltd* [1924] 2 KB 75, 82–4; Animals Act 1971, s 5(5).

[124] [1924] 2 KB 75.

[125] Ibid, at p 87.

[126] See s 5(5), above, paras 3.40–3.45.

[127] (1859) 4 H & N 631; see also *Butcher v Smith* (1868) 5 WW & a'B 223; *Bourchier v Mitchell* (1891) 17 VLR 27.

[128] Above, paras 3.40–3.45.

to an occupier of land adjoining the highway if livestock straying there from the highway were left to graze on his land for any great length of time. The right to detain straying livestock, under section 7 of the Animals Act 1971,[129] is of little real assistance; for, if the person onto whose land they have strayed had no claim under section 4, the right to detain until the livestock is claimed by the claimant[130] is worthless in terms of recompense for the damage resulting from the inordinate delay in the claimant's collecting them. If he has no claim under section 4, he cannot keep the proceeds of any sale in exercise of his rights under section 7 to offset his expenses and loss.[131] One possible solution to this dilemma is to adapt the principle of *Goodwyn v Cheveley*[132] to present circumstances and hold that he who unreasonably leaves his animals on another's land after they have strayed from the highway will be liable in negligence for any harm that they do as a result of the unreasonable delay. In other words, although there is no liability under section 4 of the Animals Act 1971 for allowing them to stray from the highway, this should not preclude liability, at common law, in negligence for unreasonable delay in removing them.

2. Nuisance

5.34 If animals stray onto the highway in such numbers that their presence causes an obstruction, then it is probable that that constitutes an actionable public nuisance if it interferes with the right of free passage.[133] The presence, however, of a single animal,[134] or even of a few animals,[135] is much less likely to be considered to constitute a nuisance.[136] For, as Lord du Parcq has said:

> The stray horse on the road does not seriously interfere with the exercise of a common right, and is no more a nuisance in law, merely by reason of its presence there, than the fallen carthorse or its modern analogue, the lorry which has temporarily broken down.[137]

5.35 If a dog or some other animal escapes while on the highway or, perhaps, escapes onto the highway, this may well constitute a nuisance if the animal poses some

---

[129] Above, paras 3.47–3.60.

[130] Animals Act 1971, s 7(3)(c).

[131] Animals Act 1971, s 7(5), above, para 3.55.

[132] (1859) 4 H & N 631.

[133] *Ellis v Banyard* (1911) 106 LT 51, 52, 53; *Cunningham v Whelan* (1917) 52 ILTR 67; *Hall v Wightman* [1926] NI 92, esp at pp 102–3; *Gillick v O'Reilly* [1984] ILRM 402; and see *Price v Godfrey* (1884) 2 NZLR 300, 302; *State Government Insurance Commission v Trigwell* (1979) CLR 617, 638.

[134] *Higgins v Searle* (1909) 100 LT 280, 281; cf Williams, pp 384–5; *Howarth v Straver* (1953); *Bingham & Berryman's Personal Injury and Motor Claims Cases*, 13th edn (2010), para 18.16.

[135] *Maddy v Rutter* [1934] LJCCR 259; *State Government Insurance Commission v Trigwell*, above, at p 638.

[136] Given the need for there to be an obstruction which removes access to the whole or part of the highway in order to constitute a nuisance: *Trevett v Lee* [1955] 1 WLR 113, 117.

[137] *Searle v Wallbank* [1947] AC 341, 361; cf *Cox v Burbidge* (1863) 32 LJCP 89, 92 (the report in 13 CBNS 430, 441 is slightly different); *Wood v Madders* [1935] LJCCR 253, 254 (this last case would probably be regarded as wrongly decided in the light of *Searle v Wallbank*).

hazard additional to that of its mere presence. In *Pitcher v Martin*,[138] it was held that a dog running on the highway with a long lead trailing from its collar constituted an actionable nuisance.[139] The dog had escaped while being taken for a walk on the highway and its lead had become entangled with the claimant's legs causing her to fall and injure herself. It is a nuisance to leave a dead animal on the street for an unreasonable length of time[140] and, therefore, it is possible that an owner who allows his animals to stray onto the highway where they are later killed may be liable in nuisance for failure to remove their corpses.

3. Trespass and Liability for Straying Livestock

As with negligence, there are three different situations to examine here in relation to liability in trespass for animals straying onto or from a highway. **5.36**

(1) Animals straying onto the highway

If an animal falling within the definition of 'livestock'[141] strays onto a highway, then the owner or occupier of the highway would appear to be able to maintain an action under the Animals Act 1971, section 4, for any damage done to the land or property thereon in the ownership or possession of the claimant.[142] It appears clear that, at common law, an action of cattle trespass[143] would lie in such circumstances.[144] Certainly, an action lay at the suit of the occupier of the highway[145] against a person who had put his animal out to graze on the highway.[146] It may well be that this latter right of action is more properly classified as ordinary trespass to land, rather than as cattle trespass.[147] If that is so, it remains unaffected by the fact that the Animals Act 1971 has abolished the tort of cattle trespass[148] and replaced it with liability, under section 4, for harm done by straying livestock. Moreover, such action for trespass to land applies to all animals, whether 'cattle', 'livestock', or anything else. **5.37**

---

[138] [1937] 3 All ER 918.

[139] It was decided by Atkinson J that there was also liability in negligence.

[140] *Percy Bros v Fly and Young* [1917] NZLR 451.

[141] Animals Act 1971, s 11.

[142] Liability for straying livestock is discussed in ch 3, above.

[143] *Durand v Child* (1611) 1 Bulst 157, per Croke J; *Cox v Burbidge* (1863) 13 CBNS 430, 435, 441; *Hadwell v Righton* [1907] 2 KB 345, 349; *Higgins v Searle* (1909) 100 LT 280, 280–81; *Heath's Garage Ltd v Hodges* [1916] 2 KB 370, 377; Williams, pp 367–9; and see *Hayes v Shire of Fitzroy* (1913) 7 QJPR 42.

[144] It was also possible to distrain such animals damage feasant: *Dovaston v Payne* (1795) 2 Hy Bl 527. See now Animals Act 1971, s 7, above, paras 3.47–3.60.

[145] cf *Haigh v West* [1893] 2 QB 19; and see *Lade v Shepherd* (1734) 2 Stra 1004.

[146] *Stevens v Whistler* (1809) 11 East 51.

[147] *R v Pratt* (1855) 4 E & B 860; *Hunt v Shanks* [1918] SALR 254, 261–2; and see *Buckle v Holmes* (1925) 42 TLR 147, 148.

[148] Animals Act 1971, s 1(1)(c).

5.38 No action of cattle trespass lay, nor will an action lie under section 4 of the Animals Act 1971, at the suit of a *user* of the highway against the person to whom an animal which has strayed onto the highway belongs. This is because the highway user's rights are limited to rights of passage and he has no necessary interest, unless he is the owner or occupier,[149] in the highway.[150]

(2) Animals straying from the highway onto the claimant's land

5.39 It may be recalled[151] that, provided that the use of the highway by the defendant is lawful, no action will lie under section 4 of the Animals Act 1971 at the suit of an owner or occupier of land onto whose property livestock stray from the highway.[152] If, however, the defendant's use of the highway is unlawful,[153] then not only is he liable to an action under section 4, at the suit of the occupier of the highway, but also at the suit of the occupier or owner of land onto which the livestock stray from the highway. If a lawful user of the highway, without authority, sends or takes his animals, including those other than 'livestock', such as dogs, from the highway onto the claimant's land, then an action will lie against the defendant for trespass to land.[154] There is also liability for damage done by animals straying from the highway on proof of negligence.[155]

(3) Animals straying onto the highway and thence onto the claimant's land

5.40 In these circumstances, there would seem to be no reason why an action should not lie under section 4 of the Animals Act 1971 in the case of straying 'livestock', just as an action lay at common law for cattle trespass[156] in this type of case. No defence is available under section 5(5)[157] to a claim under section 4 of the Animals Act 1971 based on use of the highway, for the use of the highway would not appear to be lawful in this type of case. However, it does seem anomalous that:

> a person who puts his stock on a highway is not liable for their trespasses in the absence of negligence though, if they stray out to the highway without negligence on his part, [and thence stray onto other land] he is.[158]

[149] Animals Act 1971, s 4(1).

[150] *Cox v Burbidge* (1863) 13 CBNS 430; *Hadwell v Righton* [1907] 2 KB 345; *Higgins v Searle* (1909) 100 LT 280; and see *Heath's Garage Ltd v Hodges* [1916] 2 KB 370.

[151] Above, ch 3, paras 3.40–3.45.

[152] Animals Act 1971, s 5(5).

[153] See, above, paras 3.40–3.43.

[154] *R v Pratt* (1855) 4 E & B 860, 864, 868.

[155] eg *Tillett v Ward* (1882) 10 QBD 17, above, para 5.30.

[156] *D'Agruima v Seymour* (1951) 69 WN (NSW) 15; and see *Poupart v Brazil* [1941] LJCCR 223; *Creasy v Abell* [1945] LJCCR 148; *Morris v Curtis* [1947] LJCCR 284; *Cooke v Skinner* (1948) 98 L Jo 38.

[157] Discussed, above, paras 3.40–3.45.

[158] *D'Agruima v Seymour* (1951) 69 WN (NSW) 15, 17.

The justification that adjoining landowners take the risk of accidental straying from the highway, provided that the animals are lawfully thereon, is rather hollow in the light of the fact that they do not assume the risk of animals straying from neighbouring fields even though lawfully there. As Fleming has said: 'None of this makes a great deal of sense.'[159]

4. Breach of Statutory Duty

There has been a history of statutory provisions[160] making it a criminal offence to allow various classes of animals to stray onto the highway.[161] However, such criminal liability is most unlikely to give rise to any civil liability for breach of statutory duty.[162] Neville J has said, of such provisions, that they: **5.41**

> do not, in my opinion, impose any civil liability in respect of animals trespassing upon the highway. So far as I know they have never been held so to do, and from their form I do not think they could have been intended to do so.[163]

It has been held, furthermore, that breach of bye-laws relating to London parks and open spaces does not give rise to a cause of action for injury caused by a dog.[164]

---

[159] J Fleming, *Torts*, 9th edn (1998), p 397.

[160] eg the Highways Act 1959, s 135(1); *Rees v Morgan* [1976] Crim LR 252. See North (1966) Conv (NS) 44, 46; Law Commission Report, paras 42, 49.

[161] See now the Road Traffic Act 1988, s 27, in relation to dogs.

[162] *Cox v Burbidge* (1863) 13 CBNS 430, 435–6; *Heath's Garage Ltd v Hodges* [1916] 2 KB 370, 376, 383–4; *Searle v Wallbank* [1947] AC 341, 362; *Davies v Davies* [1975] QB 172; and see *Maddy v Rutter* [1934] LJNCCR 259; *Creasy v Abell* [1945] LJCCR 148, 154–5. A similar view has been taken in New Zealand: *Simeon v Avery* [1959] NZLR 1345, 1346; *Ross v McCarthy* [1969] NZLR 691, affirmed [1970] NZLR 449; cf *Turner v August* (1909) 11 GLR 715.

[163] *Heath's Garage Ltd v Hodges* [1916] 2 KB 370, 383–4; and see *Davies v Davies* [1975] QB 172, 178–9.

[164] *Newman v Francis* [1953] 1 WLR 402; and see *Rowan v Mann* (1959) 19 DLR (2d) 163; *Thordarson v Zastre* (1968) 65 WWR 555.

6

LIABILITY AT COMMON LAW

There is no doubt that there can be liability for harm done by animals outside the ambit of the Animals Act 1971. The Act deals primarily with the instances of strict liability for harm done by animals; but liability may also arise in the context of other heads of tortious liability. So far as the problems of liability for harm done by animals on or by straying off the highway are concerned, these other heads of liability have been considered already,[1] but it is proposed in this chapter to consider, generally, such common law liabilities as remain unaffected by the Animals Act 1971. It is quite clear that the torts of negligence, nuisance, trespass, and liability under the rule in *Rylands v Fletcher*[2] and under the rules of occupiers' liability may arise through the use or agency of animals. This fact poses no particular problems for the application of the principles of these heads of tortious liability, but it may be helpful to consider instances where there may be such liability. **6.01**

1. Trespass[3]

It is undoubtedly an actionable trespass to the person to set a dog onto the claimant, or to cause his horse to throw him off,[4] provided that it is done intentionally. In *Gloster v Chief Constable of Greater Manchester Police*,[5] Hale LJ made clear that, **6.02**

[1] See ch 5, above.
[2] (1866) LR 1 Exch 265, affirmed (1868) LR 3 HL 330.
[3] G Williams, *Liability for Animals* (1939), p 340.
[4] *Scott v Shepherd* (1773) 3 Wils KB 403, 408; *Cronin v Connor* [1913] 2 IR 119.
[5] [2000] PIQR 114.

in the case of police dogs, 'if such a trained dog is deliberately set upon a quarry without lawful justification then it will be an assault'.[6] However, the defendant may claim that he had a lawful excuse for his conduct, an issue which has arisen in the context of injury caused by a police dog in the process of assisting a police officer in making an arrest. In *Pollard v Chief Constable of West Yorkshire*,[7] a police dog handler had used his dog to arrest a number of drunken youths, one of whom, the claimant, was bitten by the dog. The claim failed because the Court of Appeal held that the defendant was entitled to use reasonable force to effect an arrest[8] and that, in the circumstances, the use of the dog was reasonable. It is a trespass to goods to set a dog onto the claimant's animals.[9]

6.03 The action of trespass to land will lie when committed through the agency of an animal. It is actionable as trespass to land intentionally to take[10] or send an animal onto the claimant's land[11] or to drive the animal onto the land, without the claimant's permission.[12] Again, to leave cattle, which have strayed onto the claimant's land, on that land for an unreasonable length of time is a common law trespass.[13] It may even be a trespass even though the cattle originally strayed as a result of the claimant's failure to fence.[14]

6.04 One particular context in which the issue of trespass to land has arisen is that of hunting.[15] It has long been held that hunting could not be carried on over a person's land without his consent.[16] The leading recent authority is *League Against Cruel Sports Ltd v Scott*.[17] The claimant owned areas of unfenced moorland in Somerset on which hunting was not permitted, as they were intended as sanctuaries for wild deer. The defendants were the joint masters of the Devon and Somerset Staghounds which hunted red deer. On a number of occasions the hunt and the hounds had entered various areas of the claimant's land. No damage was alleged to have been done, but an injunction was sought to restrain the defendants from repeating

---

[6] Ibid, at p 121.

[7] [1999] PIQR 219; applied in *Roberts v Chief Constable of Kent* [2008] EWCA Civ 588.

[8] Criminal Law Act 1967, s 3.

[9] *Baker v Webberley* (1631) Het 171.

[10] *Beckwith v Shordyke* (1767) 4 Burr 2092.

[11] *R v Pratt* (1855) 4 E & B 860, 864–5; *Buckle v Holmes* (1925) 42 TLR 147, 148; and see *Dimmock v Allenby* (1810), cited 2 Marsh, at p 582.

[12] For discussion of whether the flight of bees onto a neighbour's land constitutes trespass by the bee-keeper, see *Stormer v Ingram* (1978) 21 SASR 93, 101.

[13] *Hunt v Shanks* [1918] SALR 254.

[14] Williams, pp 223–4.

[15] It has to be borne in mind that, under the Hunting Act 2004, hunting with dogs is not, generally, permitted; but drag hunting continues, and the laying of the scent could lead to trespass onto neighbouring land. Issues of negligence can also arise from incidents in the hunting field: *Jones v Hall* (1982) Unreported, 9 November; *Breeden v Lampard* (1985) CA, Unreported, 21 March, considered above, para 2.79.

[16] *Paul v Summerhayes* (1878) 4 QBD 9, 10–11; cf *Calvert v Gosling* (1885) 5 TLR 185.

[17] [1986] QB 240.

the incursions. Park J rejected the argument that the defendants would be liable irrespective of any intention or fault on their part, saying:

> I have come . . . to the conclusion that, before a master of hounds may be held liable for trespass on land by hounds, it has to be shown that he either intended that the hounds should enter the land, or by negligence he failed to prevent them from so doing. In my judgment the law as I take it to be may be stated thus: where a master of staghounds takes out a pack of hounds and deliberately sets them in pursuit of a stag or hind, knowing that there is a real risk that in the pursuit hounds may enter or cross prohibited land, the master will be liable for trespass if he intended to cause hounds to enter such land, or if by his failure to exercise proper control over them he caused them to enter such land.[18]

On the facts, the judge found that the claims for trespass had been made out.[19]

There is an obvious affinity between the action of trespass to land through the medium of an animal, on the one hand, and the old action of cattle trespass or, as it now is, the statutory action for straying livestock under section 4 of the Animals Act 1971, on the other hand. The basic distinction between the two forms of liability has been explained thus: **6.05**

> If one's cattle stray, of their own volition, onto the land of another, without his consent, one thereby commits the tort of cattle-trespass; on the other hand if one's cattle get onto the land, not by straying, but because one deliberately drives them onto the land, one commits the ordinary tort of trespass to land. In the case of the ordinary tort of trespass to land, the cattle are merely the means whereby one commits the trespass. It would be equally ordinary trespass to land if one drove onto the land not cattle but a motor car.[20]

Important reasons for distinguishing between the statutory liability for straying livestock, under section 4 of the Animals Act 1971, and liability at common law for trespass are that the former is restricted to 'livestock', is a tort of strict liability, and is subject to only the limited statutory defences, whereas the latter can apply to all animals, its defences exist at common law, and it would appear to be based on proof of intention or of fault.[21] The nature of the distinction is put most cogently by Murray CJ in *Hunt v Shanks*:[22] **6.06**

> A man is answerable for the trespass of his cattle, if they stray without his knowledge and against his will into another person's land; but he is also answerable for his own acts of trespass, and if he unlawfully drives his cattle into another's land or permits

[18] Ibid, at pp 252–3.

[19] Where, however, a driver collided with hounds which were lawfully on the highway in pursuit of a fox, the hunt was not liable for damage to the claimant's car, given that all reasonable precautions had been taken: *Adams v Chiddingfold Farmers Foxhounds* (1955), The Times, 5 November.

[20] Report of the New South Wales Law Reform Commission on Civil Liability for Animals, (1970) LRC 8, para 23.

[21] *National Coal Board v J E Evans & Co Cardiff Ltd* [1951] 2 KB 861; *Fowler v Lanning* [1959] 1 QB 426; *Letang v Cooper* [1965] 1 QB 232; *Wilson v Pringle* [1987] QB 237.

[22] [1918] SALR 254, 261.

them to remain there for an unreasonable time after he has become aware that they are trespassing, or breaks a fence, or opens a gate, with a view to inducing them to pass through, and they do pass through, the resulting trespass, in my opinion, is his trespass, and not merely the trespass of his cattle.

2. Nuisance[23]

6.07 It is possible that an action for public nuisance will lie for the obstruction of the highway by animals,[24] and such an action will lie for allowing roosting pigeons to foul the highway with droppings.[25] Further, an action for private nuisance may lie where animals escape from the defendant's land onto that of the claimant. This can be very relevant where, for example, a statutory action under section 4 of the Animals Act 1971 is inapplicable because the animals do not fall into the category of 'livestock', as where they are cats, dogs, or wild animals. Thus, the owner of a dog which escapes onto his neighbour's property, constantly fouling it, may be liable in nuisance.[26]

6.08 If wild animals escape from the defendant's land, they may constitute a nuisance to the claimant's use and enjoyment of his land, provided that the animals in question have been brought or attracted onto the defendant's land in the first place. If they are naturally there, then the defendant is unlikely to be held liable in nuisance if they multiply and escape onto adjoining land. The basis of the liability should be that the defendant is 'liable for damage caused . . . by extraordinary, non-natural, or unreasonable action'.[27] Thus, to bring an abnormal number of pheasants onto one's land can lead to liability in nuisance if they escape;[28] but there will be no such liability if the increase in the number of pheasants is due to unusually favourable weather, rather than to any unreasonable action by the defendant.[29] If rabbits are naturally on the land, then their escape to the claimant's land should give rise to no liability in nuisance;[30] but if they are lured onto the defendant's land and then escape onto

[23] Williams, ch 14. For a discussion of statutory nuisances by animals, see R McCracken, G Jones, and J Pereira, *Statutory Nuisance*, 2nd edn (2008), paras 1.51–1.60; J Murphy, *The Law of Nuisance* (2010), paras 8.25–8.29, 8.33.

[24] See ch 5, above; and see Report of the New South Wales Law Reform Commission on Civil Liability for Animals, (1970) LRC 8, para 32.

[25] *Wandsworth London Borough Council v Railtrack plc* [2001] EWCA Civ 1236; [2002] QB 756.

[26] cf *Curtis v Thomson* (1956) 106 L Jo 61.

[27] *Peech v Best* [1931] 1 KB 1, 14; and see *Farrer v Nelson* (1885) 15 QBD 258, 260.

[28] *Farrer v Nelson*, above.

[29] *Seligman v Docker* [1949] 1 Ch 53; and see *Robson v Marquis of Londonderry* (1900) 34 ILTR 88; *Foley v Berthoud* (1903) 37 ILTR 123; although this might need to be reviewed in the light of *Goldman v Hargrave* [1967] 1 AC 645 and *Leakey v National Trust* [1980] QB 485, where the courts have been prepared to extend the law of nuisance to include natural nuisances; and see *Stockwell v State of Victoria* [2001] VSC 497; R Buckley, *The Law of Nuisance*, 2nd edn (1996), p 48.

[30] *Brady v Warren* [1900] 2 IR 632; cf *Boulston's Case* (1597) 5 Co Rep 104b.

the claimant's land, then there may well be liability in nuisance.[31] The presence on the defendant's land of heaps of bones which attracted rats which later went onto the claimant's land and ate his crops has been considered not to be unreasonable, and not an actionable nuisance.[32] Yet an unusual and excessive collection of manure which attracted flies which bred in the manure and then went onto the claimant's land has been considered to be a nuisance,[33] as has a rubbish dump which attracted seagulls which damaged the claimant's plants.[34] So far as bees are concerned, it would seem clear that their escape can constitute a nuisance.[35] However, it is only in the keeping of an excessive number of bees, or keeping them in such a place as to cause discomfort to neighbours through their escape, that there will be liability.[36]

All of the cases of nuisance considered so far have been ones where animals have interfered with the use and enjoyment of the claimant's land by escaping from the defendant's land. Just as such escapes may constitute a nuisance, so also may the conduct of animals remaining on the defendant's land. If pigs are kept on the defendant's land so that the smell from them unreasonably interferes with the claimant's enjoyment of his land, this is a nuisance;[37] and the same may be said for other smells, such as those from horses.[38] Liability in nuisance extends also to unreasonable noise made by animals on the defendant's land, as with the crowing of cockerels,[39] the barking of dogs,[40] or the noises of horses in a stable.[41] Also the noise of pigeons, both on the defendant's land and in flight over the claimant's land, may constitute a nuisance.[42] It is probable also that it is an actionable nuisance to keep **6.09**

[31] *Pratt v Young* (1952) 69 WN (NSW) 214.

[32] *Stearn v Prentice Bros Ltd* [1919] 1 KB 394.

[33] *Bland v Yates* (1914) 58 Sol Jo 612.

[34] *Plater v Town of Collingwood* (1968) 65 DLR (2d) 492.

[35] *O'Gorman v O'Gorman* [1903] 2 IR 573; *Parker v Reynolds* (1906), The Times, 17 December; cf *McStay v Morrissey* (1949) 83 ILTR 28; *Stormer v Ingram* (1979) 21 SASR 93; and see J Frimston, *Bee-Keeping and the Law* (1966), pp 7–8; K Swan, *A Receiver of Stolen Property* (1956), pp 8–9.

[36] *O'Gorman v O'Gorman*, above, at pp 581–2; *Lucas v Pettit* (1906) 12 OLR 448, 451–2; *Johnson v Martin* (1950) 100 L Jo 541; and see the county court cases cited by Frimston, op cit, p 8. For a decision on harm to bees which flew onto neighbouring land, see *Tutton v AD Walter Ltd* [1986] QB 61.

[37] *Aldred's Case* (1610) 9 Co Rep 57b; *A-G v Squire* (1906) 5 LGR 99; *Bone v Seal* [1975] 1 WLR 797; *Milner v Spencer* (1976) 239 Estates Gazette 573; *Wheeler v JJ Saunders Ltd* [1996] Ch 19.

[38] *Ball v Ray* (1873) LR 8 Ch 467; *Broder v Saillard* (1876) 2 Ch D 692; *Rapier v London Tramways Co* [1893] 2 Ch 588; *Drysdale v Dugas* (1896) 26 SCR 20; *Munro v Southern Dairies Ltd* [1955] VLR 332; and see *Treadwell v Wellington Dairy Co* (1910) 29 NZLR 906.

[39] *Leeman v Montagu* [1936] 2 All ER 1677; cf *Hunt v W H Cook Ltd* (1922) 66 Sol Jo 557; *Ruthning v Ferguson* [1930] Qd SR 325; *Randall v Harper* [1955] CLY 1940.

[40] *Mallock v Mason and Mason* [1938] LJCCR 387; *O'Connor v Higgisson* (1946) 12 Ir Jur 61; *Shanlin v Collins* 1973 SLT (Sh Ct) 21; and see Williams, pp 236–7.

[41] *Ball v Ray* (1873) 8 Ch App 467; *Broder v Saillard* (1876) 2 Ch D 692; *Rapier v London Tramways Co* [1893] 2 Ch 588; *Drysdale v Dugas* (1896) 26 SCR 20; *Painter v Reed* [1930] SASR 295; *Munro v Southern Dairies Ltd* [1955] VLR 332.

[42] *Fraser v Booth* (1949) 50 SRNSW 113; cf *Mobbs v Shephardson* [1937] LJCCR 277.

diseased animals on one's own land in circumstances such that their disease infects one's neighbour's animals, and thereby interferes with his use of his land.[43]

3. *Rylands v Fletcher* Liability[44]

6.10 The basis of liability under this head is that an occupier of land who brings onto and keeps on his land, as a non-natural user of the land, anything likely to do mischief if it escapes, is liable for all the direct consequences of such an escape.[45] He keeps it at his peril and his liability does not depend on his being negligent, but 'foreseeability of damage of the relevant type should be regarded as a pre-requisite of liability in damages under the rule'.[46] There would seem, in principle, to be no reason why there should not be liability under the rule in *Rylands v Fletcher* for harm done to the claimant by animals escaping from the defendant's land.[47] Indeed, in *Rylands v Fletcher* itself, Blackburn J[48] regarded the law of cattle trespass as merely an instance of the wider and more generalized head of liability there being laid down. Nevertheless, it remains true that authorities, both academic[49] and judicial,[50] have regarded cattle trespass and liability under *Rylands v Fletcher* as separate heads of liability. Furthermore, one could have said the same for the relationship between the *scienter* action and the rule in *Rylands v Fletcher*.[51]

6.11 While accepting that liability under *Rylands v Fletcher* was separate from liability in cattle trespass or the *scienter* action and is now separate from the strict liability

[43] cf *R v Henson* (1852) Dears CC 24; *Ruhan v Water Conservation and Irrigation Commission* (1920) 20 SRNSW 439; Williams, pp 342–3. Similarly, it may be an actionable nuisance to contaminate your neighbour's water supply with droppings from animals on your land: Report of the New South Wales Law Reform Commission on Civil Liability for Animals, (1970) LRC 8, para 32.

[44] Williams, pp 197–9, 261–2, 352–3.

[45] *Rylands v Fletcher* (1866) LR 1 Exch 265, affirmed (1868) LR 3 HL 330; although in recent years a more restrictive approach has been adopted: *Cambridge Water Co Ltd v Eastern Counties Leather plc* [1994] 2 AC 264; and see above, para 2.60.

[46] *Cambridge Water Co Ltd v Eastern Counties Leather plc*, above, at p 306.

[47] In New South Wales, s 9 of the Animals Act 1977 specifically abolished the application of the rule in *Rylands v Fletcher* to animals. Since then, the High Court of Australia has determined that the rule no longer forms part of the law of Australia: *Burnie Port Authority v General Jones Pty Ltd* (1994) 179 CLR 520; but the House of Lords has declined to follow that approach: *Transco plc v Stockport Metropolitan Borough Council* [2003] UKHL 61; [2004] 2 AC 1. Given the decision of the High Court of Australia in 1994, it seems strange that the application of the rule to cases involving animals was later abolished by statute in the Australian Capital Territory: Civil Law (Wrongs) Act 2002, s 141.

[48] (1866) LR 1 Exch 265, 280 et seq.

[49] Williams, pp 197–9; WH Rogers, *Winfield and Jolowicz on Tort*, 18th edn (2010), para 16.12; and see Report of the New South Wales Law Reform Commission, above, para 15.

[50] eg *Manton v Brocklebank* [1923] 2 KB 212, 222, 230; cf, eg *Holgate v Bleazard* [1917] 1 KB 443; *Miles v Forest Rock Granite Co (Leicestershire) Ltd* (1918) 34 TLR 500.

[51] *Winfield and Jolowicz on Tort*, above, para 16.12; Williams, pp 353–4; *Fardon v Harcourt-Rivington* (1932) 146 LT 391, 392; *Read v J Lyons & Co Ltd* [1947] AC 156, 166–7; *Behrens v Bertram Mills Circus Ltd* [1957] 2 QB 1, 21–2; cf, eg *Baker v Snell* [1908] 2 KB 825, 835–6; *Lowery v Walker* [1910] 1 KB 173, 182; *Knott v LCC* [1934] 1 KB 126, 139.

imposed by sections 2 to 4 of the Animals Act 1971, this does not mean that liability for harm done by escaping animals cannot fall within the rule in *Rylands v Fletcher*. On the other hand, it is unlikely that many cases of harm done by animals will fall within that rule. The reason for such a conclusion is that for liability to exist under the rule, not only must there be an escape of the animal from the defendant's land,[52] and a wolf was held not to have escaped when it grasped a child through the bars of its zoo cage,[53] but the keeping and accumulating there of the animal must constitute a non-natural use of the land. The pasturing of domestic livestock, as with the keeping of domestic pets, is, one assumes, a natural use of the land.[54] Furthermore, the animals which escape must fall within the class of 'dangerous things' and, again, domestic animals such as horses[55] or dogs[56] cannot normally be classified as dangerous things. To keep a wild animal such as a bear on your land would appear to be a non-natural use of the land and, if the bear, being a dangerous thing, escaped, then there could well be liability under *Rylands v Fletcher*.[57] It is possible that there might be such liability for harm caused by an escaping fox[58] or even, in appropriately unusual circumstances, by a dangerous dog.[59]

4. Negligence

There has never been any doubt since the seventeenth century[60] that an action will **6.12** lie for the negligent keeping of animals which cause harm to the claimant. There is, therefore, a common law duty to take reasonable care to prevent your animals from causing injury, whether or not they escape from your land or control. This liability was quite independent of the common law heads of liability peculiar to animals and is quite independent of any statutory liability imposed in their place by the Animals Act 1971.[61] As Lord Atkin has said:

> It is also true that, quite apart from the liability imposed upon the owner of animals or the person having control of them by reason of knowledge of their propensities, there is the ordinary duty of a person to take care either that his animal or his chattel

[52] *Read v J Lyons & Co Ltd* [1947] AC 156.

[53] *Maynes v Galicz* [1971] 1 WWR 557.

[54] cf *Stearn v Prentice Bros Ltd* [1919] 1 KB 394. *Holgate v Bleazard* [1917] 1 KB 433 must surely be wrongly decided in so far as it is based on *Rylands v Fletcher*.

[55] *Manton v Brocklebank* [1923] 2 KB 212.

[56] cf *Hines v Tousley* (1926) 95 LJKB 773.

[57] *Shaw v McCreary* (1889) 19 OR 39; and see *Behrens v Bertram Mills Circus Ltd* [1957] 2 QB 1, 22.

[58] *Brady v Warren* [1900] 2 IR 632, 651. As to the situation with regard to bees, see *Robins v Kennedy and Columb* [1931] NZLR 1134, 1142.

[59] *Hines v Tousley*, above, at p 774.

[60] *Mitchil v Alestree* (1676) 1 Vent 295.

[61] See chs 2, 3, 7.

is not put to such a use as is likely to injure his neighbour—the ordinary duty to take care in the cases put upon negligence.[62]

6.13 It is necessary for all the elements of the tort of negligence to be satisfied. There must be a duty of care owed to the claimant by the defendant, breach of that duty by the defendant, and reasonably foreseeable damage suffered by the claimant as a consequence of that breach of duty. Liability is based on foresight and not on the defendant's knowledge of the dangerous characteristics of the animal which caused the injury.[63] Thus, where a pony was left unattended in the street which, when it became restive, attacked the claimant, the defendants were held liable in negligence for such injuries, despite a finding that they did not know of the animal's propensity to injure.[64] They ought to have foreseen the likelihood of such injury from leaving the pony unattended.

6.14 A further significance of determining whether the action for injury done by an animal is one in negligence or one of strict liability under the Animals Act 1971 is that for the latter no fault on the part of the defendant needs to be proved. Liability is strict, with the one qualification of proof of knowledge under section 2(2), although this may often be equivalent to proof of fault. This distinction is well illustrated by *Draper v Hodder*,[65] decided after the 1971 Act came into force, but in relation to events occurring earlier. The infant claimant lived next door to the defendant who bred Jack Russell terriers. Seven puppies suddenly dashed onto the claimant's premises where he was playing and savagely attacked him. The trial judge rejected a claim based on *scienter* (now section 2 of the 1971 Act) because it could not be proved that the defendant knew of a vicious propensity in some, or all, of the puppies. However, the Court of Appeal upheld his decision that the defendant was liable in negligence. It was reasonably foreseeable that Jack Russell terriers, especially as a 'pack', are likely to do damage, including damage to people, and the defendant, as a breeder, should have been aware of this. There was no fence between the two properties and the defendant knew that his dogs 'were free to roam at will'.[66] It is necessary for the claimant to show:

> A propensity on the part of the animal not necessarily known to the owner or keeper but one which was such that the owner or keeper knew or ought to have known and

[62] *Fardon v Harcourt-Rivington* (1932) 48 TLR 215, 217. See also *Hinckes v Harris* (1921) 65 Sol Jo 781, 782; *Lathall v Joyce & Son* [1939] 3 All ER 854; *Brackenborough v Spalding UDC* [1942] AC 310, 321–2; *Ellis v Johnstone* [1963] 2 QB 8, 29–30; *Fitzgerald v ED & AD Cooke (Bourne) Farms Ltd* [1964] 1 QB 249.

[63] *Fardon v Harcourt-Rivington*, above; and see *Matheson v G Stuckey & Co Pty Ltd* [1921] VLR 637; *Sycamore v Ley* (1932) 147 LT 342.

[64] *Aldham v United Dairies Ltd* [1940] 1 KB 507; and see *Hinckes v Harris*, above, at p 782; and see *Earp v Faulkner* (1875) 34 LT 384, affirmed (1876) 24 WR 774; cf *Tucker v Hennessy* [1918] VLR 56.

[65] [1972] 2 QB 556; and see *Galea v Gillingham* [1987] Qd R 365; *Taller v Goldenstein* (1992) 87 BCLR (2d) 249.

[66] [1972] QB 556, 572.

therefore ought to have foreseen that there was a real risk of the injury or damage complained of being caused by the animal exhibiting that propensity.

It is not sufficient for a plaintiff to prove a failure by the defendant to guard against the possibilities that a tame animal of mild disposition will do some dangerous act contrary to its ordinary nature.[67]

A corollary of this general distinction between liability in negligence and under the Animals Act 1971 is that the rules of remoteness of damage appear to be different. It has been suggested already[68] that, just as with the *scienter* action and cattle trespass at common law, the statutory liability under sections 2 and 4 of the Animals Act 1971 attracts a test of remoteness based on direct consequences. However, the test of remoteness in negligence is now[69] that of reasonable foresight of consequences.[70] Thus, the statutory actions based on strict liability could give rise to a greater extent of liability than in negligence. **6.15**

Another basic difference between liability in negligence and under the Animals Act 1971 for harm caused by animals is that the only defendant in the latter case is the keeper of the animal. Although there may be more than one keeper,[71] liability is confined to that particular class of defendant. There are no such limitations on liability in negligence. Anyone who is negligent in the keeping or care of an animal may be liable for harm that it does. On the other hand, under the statutory actions the keeper will be liable, even though he has taken all possible care, whereas, at common law, negligence liability will depend on fault. **6.16**

It is a basic requirement of liability in negligence that the claimant's injury is caused by and is a reasonable consequence of the defendant's negligence. Without this link the claimant must fail, as is illustrated by *Bradley v Wallaces Ltd*.[72] Here the deceased was killed when passing behind a horse, which kicked him. The horse had been left unattended by the defendants in the deceased's employers' yard. As the deceased's injury was considered not to have been a natural or probable consequence of the negligence of the defendants in leaving the horse unattended, the action by his dependants failed. It is not sufficient that injury is only foreseeable as 'a possibility', as illustrated by *Whippey v Jones*.[73] The claimant was out for a run in a park area beside the River Aire when he encountered Hector, the defendant's 12-and-a-half **6.17**

[67] *Galea v Gillingham*, above, at p 375.

[68] Above, paras 2.60, 2.75, 3.31–3.32; and see M Jones and A Dugdale, *Clerk and Lindsell on Torts*, 20th edn (2010), para 2.137.

[69] cf *Aldham v United Dairies Ltd* [1940] 1 KB 507, 513.

[70] *The Wagon Mound* [1961] AC 388; *The Wagon Mound (No 2)* [1967] 1 AC 617; and see *Whycherley v Grave* [1967] CLY 91.

[71] Animals Act 1971, s 6(3).

[72] [1913] 3 KB 629; and see *Abbott v Freeman* (1876) 35 LT 783; *Lathall v Joyce* [1939] 3 All ER 854, 856; *Gallacher v St Cuthbert's Co-operative Association Ltd* 1976 SLT (Notes) 25.

[73] [2009] EWCA Civ 452; and see *Clinch v Sullivan* (1981) Unreported, 20 January; *Fairlie v Carruthers* 1996 SLT (Sh Ct) 56; *Welsh v Brady* 2008 SLT 363, affirmed on another point: 2009 SLT 747.

stone Great Dane. The dog knocked the claimant over and he broke his ankle. The defendant said that, although Hector was very gentle, he kept him on a lead when people were around because he had a tendency to run up to people and bark, which might frighten them, although he had never touched anyone. On this occasion, the defendant saw no one around and let Hector off his lead. The Court of Appeal decided that, although there was a possibility of the dog injuring someone, a reasonable person could not have anticipated that physical harm could have been caused to the claimant by the dog, given that Hector had never exhibited a tendency to jump up at people.

6.18 Just as negligence is a very flexible basis of liability, so too are the instances where there has been such liability for harm done by animals very varied. Where animals are taken out onto the highway and there cause injury as a result of the negligent conduct or lack of care on the part of the person who took them out onto the highway, there will be liability for such injury.[74] Such a duty of care on the part of the person who takes animals onto a highway has been applied to the case of leaving a dog in a parked car[75] and has been suggested on the part of the owner of animals who takes them to market.[76] Failure to keep a fierce stallion a good distance from a novice rider, when both were out riding on a road, has been held to be negligent,[77] as has failure to keep two stallions apart.[78] All the more will there be liability where the defendant does a positive act which causes the animal to injure the claimant, as with the negligent whipping of a horse, causing it to lash out.[79]

6.19 In *Smith v Prendergast*,[80] the claimant was a child who was walking past the defendant's scrapyard on her way home from school when she was bitten by an Alsatian which had 'established residence' in the yard. The dog was a stray which had walked into the yard three weeks earlier, and the defendant had fed it and decided to keep it as a guard dog. He said he had seen nothing which had made him apprehensive that the dog might bite. However, the Court of Appeal held that three weeks' experience of a stray dog was inadequate to form a view that no control of it was necessary in order to safeguard people in the street. Failure to take precautions when it is known that an Irish Wolfhound is likely to be aggressive towards someone carrying

---

[74] eg *Deen v Davies* [1935] 2 KB 282; *Brackenborough v Spalding UDC* [1942] AC 310; Williams, pp 377–8. The whole problem of liability for harm done by animals on the highway is examined in ch 5.

[75] *Fardon v Harcourt-Rivington* (1932) 48 TLR 215; *Sycamore v Ley* (1932) 147 LT 342, esp at p 345; and see *Bennett v Magera* (1993) 138 AR 75.

[76] *Brackenborough v Spalding UDC* [1942] AC 310, 331.

[77] *Acheson v Dory* (1993) 8 Alta LR (3d) 128; (1994) 24 Alta LR (3d) 187.

[78] *McDonald v Olmsted* (1982) 20 Sask LR 132.

[79] *Abbott v Freeman* (1876) 34 LT 544; reversed on a different view of the facts, 35 LT 783.

[80] (1984) CA, Unreported, 16 October.

a bag,[81] or when a large Rottweiler has a history of attacks in a shopping centre[82] has been held to be negligence.

Another situation where a duty of care might arise is where an animal has escaped from one building or part of a building to another, where it has caused the injury. Thus, in *Hines v Tousley*,[83] the claimant was injured when the defendant's dog collided with her on the staircase of a building in which she was employed. The defendant lived on the top floor of the building and the dog was coming downstairs when the incident occurred. The action failed because 'there was no evidence at all that the dog on this occasion was rushing or doing anything other than proceeding in a way in which a well-behaved dog would go downstairs'.[84] Nevertheless, the Court of Appeal was prepared to accept that there could well be circumstances where the owner of a dog would be liable for causing such injury.[85] It would not, however, appear to be a breach of the duty of care to allow a large dog, playing in a small garden, to jump over a garden wall and land on the neck of the claimant who was digging in the adjoining garden.[86] **6.20**

If the defendant's dog strays onto the claimant's land and fouls his garden, then it has been held[87] that, as there is no liability for the straying or the trespass[88] in such a case, there is no liability in negligence for failing to prevent the trespass. It might be argued, nevertheless, that although there may be no strict liability for straying livestock, yet if the animal escapes through the neglect of the defendant, there should be liability in negligence. The exclusion of dogs from the statutory definition of 'livestock' should not operate as an exclusion, also, of liability in negligence. Where a defendant whose land adjoined the claimant's mink farm allowed his dog to run at large during the whelping season, the defendant was held liable in negligence for damage done to the claimant's mink when the dog jumped into the mink pen. The defendant was at fault in that he should have known of the dangers to mink from strange dogs at that time, and he failed to take steps to control his dog.[89] On the other hand, there was no liability where a Border Collie ran into the claimant from behind, given that there was no evidence of previous collisions or of the risk of such collisions.[90] **6.21**

---

[81] *Kite v Napp* (1982) Unreported, 26 May.

[82] *Mason v Weeks* (1995) Unreported, 10 March.

[83] (1926) 95 LJKB 733.

[84] Ibid, at p 774.

[85] Ibid, at pp 774, 775.

[86] *Sanders v Teape and Swan* (1884) 51 LT 263; although it was held to be such a breach to allow a large collie dog to knock the claimant over in *Morris v Baily* (1970) 13 DLR (3d) 150.

[87] *Curtis v Thompson* (1956) 106 L Jo 61.

[88] Neither in cattle trespass at common law, for a dog is not 'cattle', nor under s 4 of the Animals Act 1971, for neither is it 'livestock'.

[89] *Caine Fur Farms v Kokolsky* (1963) 39 DLR (2d) 134; and see (1962) 31 DLR (2d) 556.

[90] *Hunt v Wallis* [1994] PIQR 128.

6.22 There may also be liability in negligence for allowing a diseased animal to escape onto neighbouring land and there infect the claimant's cattle,[91] or even the claimant. In *Earp v Faulkner*,[92] the defendant's diseased cattle escaped into the claimant's field and infected the latter's cattle with foot and mouth disease. There was evidence that the defendant's employees knew that the cattle were diseased when they were placed in a field adjoining the claimant's. It was held that such conduct amounted to negligence on the part of the defendant.[93] Further examples might be given to illustrate the scope of liability in negligence for harm done by animals. It has been held to be negligence to allow a bantam cockerel, known to be aggressive, to run loose where it injured a child.[94] It is also actionable negligence to keep bees in excessive numbers without taking due care, if such conduct causes injury to the claimant.[95]

6.23 A number of decisions have been concerned with accidents in riding schools. Where a riding school is negligent in the selection of the horse which it supplies to a rider, it will be held liable in negligence for the rider's injuries.[96] Failure to take reasonable precautions to prevent a temperamental horse from kicking the claimant who stabled her horse at the defendant's riding stables has been held to amount to negligence;[97] as has allowing Jack Russell terriers into a training ring, with the result that the infant pursuer was hurt when she fell off her horse which had been startled by the dogs.[98] However, where a 9-year-old girl was injured falling off a horse which had bolted, the owner was held not liable in negligence because she had not given the child permission to ride the horse.[99]

6.24 Camels have also featured in claims for damages for negligence. *Tutin v Mary Chipperfield Promotions Ltd*[100] was concerned with a claim by the actress, Dorothy Tutin, who was injured when she fell off a camel at Olympia. She had agreed to take part in a charity event in which various well-known people agreed to ride camels belonging to the defendants. She was injured when she fell off the camel she was

---

[91] Equally there would be liability under s 4 of the Animals Act 1971, above, para 3.22.

[92] (1875) 34 LT 284, affirmed (1876) 24 WR 774; and see *Cooke v Waring* (1863) 3 H & C 332.

[93] There is no reason to doubt that such an action will lie where the claimant's cattle are infected, even if only the disease, and not the animals, escapes: *Earp v Faulkner*, above, at p 286; cf *Weller & Co v Foot and Mouth Disease Research Institute* [1966] 1 QB 569; *D Pride and Partners v Institute of Animal Health* [2009] EWHC 685.

[94] *Kane McKenna* (1991) 1 BNIL 105, damages reduced on appeal: (1992) 2 BNIL 125.

[95] *O'Gorman v O'Gorman* [1903] 2 IR 573; *Robins v Kennedy and Columb* [1931] NZLR 1134.

[96] *Collins v Richmond Rodeo Riding Ltd* (1966) 56 DLR (2d) 428; and see *Saari v Sunshine Riding Academy Ltd* (1968) 65 DLR (2d) 92; *Harrison v Gledstone* (1987) CA, Unreported, 30 June. On negligence in organizing a gymkhana where horses got out of control, see *Evans v Waitemata District Pony Club* [1972] 1 NZLR 773; affirmed [1974] 1 NZLR 28.

[97] *Lewty v Gross* (1980) Unreported, 5 November.

[98] *Clayton Robertson v Horses in Scotland Ltd* [2007] CSOH 68.

[99] *Patton v McFarland* [2006] NIQB 16. For consideration of negligence claims in the context of hunting, see *Jones v Hall* (1982) CA, Unreported, 9 November; *Breedon v Lampard* (1985) CA, Unreported, 21 March.

[100] (1980) Unreported, 23 May. There was also a claim based on s 2 of the Animals Act 1971, see above, paras 2.43, 2.133.

riding in what turned out, to her surprise, to be a type of race, rather than just a parade of camels; but she decided nevertheless to take part. It was held that her accident arose through the fault of an employee of the defendants, who were held liable for allowing her camel to start off before the others and, indeed, before the race had begun. In Australia,[101] the operator of a camel-riding expedition has been held liable in negligence for failing to control the camels as they ran home in a bunch at the end of the day, causing the claimant to fall off and be injured.

While the defences to a claim under section 2 of the Animals Act 1971 are as provided in the Act,[102] in a claim for negligence all common law defences generally available can be relied on, such as assumption of risk[103] or contributory negligence.[104] **6.25**

5. Occupiers' Liability[105]

If the claimant is injured by the defendant's animal when visiting the defendant's premises, this poses the question of whether the special rules relating to the liability of an occupier for harm done to visitors are applicable. This issue must be examined on the alternative hypotheses that the claimant is a lawful visitor or a trespasser. **6.26**

(1) Lawful visitors

The obligations of an occupier to lawful visitors are governed by the Occupiers' Liability Act 1957, but there are few decisions thereunder concerned with injuries to visitors caused by the occupier's animals. The basic liability under the 1957 Act is that the occupier shall take reasonable care to make the premises reasonably safe for the purpose for which the lawful visitor visits them.[106] It is suggested that an occupier fails in that duty if he exposes a lawful visitor to risk of injury from an animal on the premises. Certainly, so far as the pre-1958 common law position was concerned, there seems little doubt that, not only would the *scienter* action lie when the injury occurred on the defendant's premises, but also that the specialized common law rules relating to an occupier's liability could be applied to cases of harm caused by animals on premises visited by the claimant. Thus, in *Kavanagh v Stokes*,[107] the claimant recovered on the basis of the duty owed to her as an invitee **6.27**

---

[101] *James v Fullerton* (1983) 77 FLR 321.

[102] See above, paras 2.128–2.166.

[103] *Shelfontuck v Le Page* [1938] 1 DLR 513; *Lewty v Gross* (1980) Unreported, 5 November; *Acheson v Dory* (1993) 8 Alta LR (3d) 128; (1994) 24 Alta LR (3d) 187; *Lay v Jaffary* (1995) 29 Alta LR (3d) 68.

[104] *Beattie v McConnell* [2005] NIQB 47; and see *Acheson v Dory*, above.

[105] See P North, *Occupiers' Liability* (1971), pp 91–2.

[106] Occupiers' Liability Act 1957, s 2.

[107] [1942] IR 596; and see *Gould v McAuliffe* [1941] 1 All ER 515, affirmed [1941] 2 All ER 527; *Duggan v Armstrong* [1992] 2 IR 161; *Le Blanc v Legue* (1995) 157 NBR (2d) 26; although see now, in

of the defendant when she was bitten by the defendant's dog while she was walking up the drive of the defendant's guest house; and in *Maltais-Comeau v Laliberte*,[108] a zoo keeper was held liable when a visitor was bitten by a baboon in a defective cage.

6.28 The most likely situation where the claimant would wish to base his case on the rules of occupiers' liability, rather than on strict liability under the Animals Act 1971, is the case of an injury caused by an animal of a non-dangerous species where the defendant occupier has no actual knowledge of the animal's dangerous nature, but ought to have used reasonable care for the safety of his lawful visitors.[109] The most likely animals to fall into this category will be cattle[110] and dogs.[111] However, a claim under the 1957 Act failed in *Carroll v Garford*[112] where the claimant simply tripped over a dog which had been brought into the defendants' pub. Similarly, in *Chauhan v Paul*,[113] a postman failed in his claim against the owner of a Rottweiler. The claimant was delivering letters to the defendant when he saw the dog and ran away, falling over in so doing; but there was no evidence that the dog might chase visitors. So far as dogs are concerned, it should be remembered that, if a dog bites the claimant, there will be no liability under section 3 of the Animals Act 1971, because the strict liability there laid down relates only to damage by killing or injuring livestock.[114] The basic principle of the liability of the occupier in such a case is still that expressed by Tindal CJ in *Sarch v Blackburn*:[115]

> Undoubtedly, a man has a right to keep a fierce dog for the protection of his property, but he has no right to put the dog in such a situation, in the way of access to his house, that a person innocently coming for a lawful purpose may be injured by it. I think he has no right to place a dog so near to the door of his house, that any person coming to ask for money, or on other business, might be bitten.

6.29 This general proposition can be illustrated by *Hill v Lovett*,[116] a decision under the Occupiers' Liability (Scotland) Act 1960.[117] The pursuer, who worked for a veterinary surgeon, was allowed into the private garden of her employer and his wife, the defenders, in order to clean the surgery windows; and she was bitten there by one of the defenders' two West Highland terriers. Although neither dog had bitten

---

Ireland, the Occupiers' Liability Act 1995; B McMahon and W Binchy, *Law of Torts*, 3rd edn (2000), paras 27.09–27.14.

[108] (1986) 36 CCLT 26.

[109] Such was the opinion of the Divisional Court in *Clinton v J Lyons & Co Ltd* [1912] 3 KB 198, so far as the common law obligations of an occupier to invitees were concerned; and see *Andrews v Patullo* [1955] CLY 1835; *McNeill v Frankenfeld* (1964) 44 DLR (2d) 132, 139–40.

[110] eg *McKaskie v Cameron* (2009) Unreported, 1 July.

[111] eg *Carroll v Garford*, above; *Hill v Lovett* 1992 SLT 994.

[112] (1968) 112 Sol Jo 948

[113] (1998) CA, Unreported, 19 February.

[114] See ch 7.

[115] (1830) 4 C & P 297, 300.

[116] 1992 SLT 994.

[117] Section 2(1), which is in similar terms to s 2(2) of the Occupiers' Liability Act 1957.

anyone before, the court found that these dogs had shown a dislike of strangers 'in their territory', and that such dogs 'had a tendency to nip', of which the defenders should have been aware. They were held liable because there was a foreseeable risk of harm to a visitor which the defenders should have appreciated and against which risk no steps had been taken, such as removing the dogs from the garden. Again, in *McKaskie v Cameron*,[118] the claimant was walking across the defendant farmer's field, apparently on a public footpath,[119] when she was injured by cows in the field who had calves with them. Given the fact that it is not uncommon for cows with calves to attack walkers, the defendant was held to have failed in his statutory duty of care in not taking steps to fence the footpath or move the cows.

(2) Trespassers[120]

There was very little direct authority, at common law, on the question of the liability of an occupier to a trespasser injured by animals on the land trespassed upon.[121] The general common law rule was that the occupier must not wilfully injure a trespasser or act with reckless disregard of his presence on the land; but there was no liability merely for the negligent infliction of injury on a trespasser,[122] until the decision of the House of Lords in *British Railways Board v Herrington*,[123] which decided that a trespasser was owed a limited duty of care—a duty of 'common humanity'[124]—but the extent of the duty was far from clear.[125] **6.30**

The position of the trespasser is now governed by the Occupiers' Liability Act 1984,[126] which provides[127] that an occupier owes a trespasser[128] a duty to take such care as is reasonable in all the circumstances of the case to see that the trespasser does **6.31**

---

[118] (2009) Unreported, 1 July.

[119] It is debatable whether the claimant should have been given the benefit of the duty of care under the 1957 Act, given that it does not apply to users of a public highway: see Occupiers' Liability Act 1957, s 2(6); *Greenhalgh v British Railways Board* [1969] 2 QB 286; P North, *Occupiers' Liability* (1971), pp 40–42.

[120] Liability to trespassers under s 2 of the Animals Act 1971 is discussed above, paras 2.140–2.153.

[121] See *Murphy v Zoological Society of London* [1962] CLY 68. A number of cases dealing with an occupier's liability for harm done by animals are concerned, primarily, with the issue of whether or not the claimant was a trespasser: *Lowery v Walker* [1910] 1 KB 173, reversed [1911] AC 10; *Gould v McAuliffe* [1941] 1 All ER 515, affirmed [1941] 2 All ER 527; and see *Pearson v Coleman Bros* [1948] 2 KB 359.

[122] *Robert Addie & Sons (Collieries) Ltd v Dumbreck* [1929] AC 358; *Commissioner for Railways v Quinlan* [1964] AC 1054.

[123] [1972] AC 877.

[124] Ibid, at p 909, and see at pp 922–3.

[125] In *Cummings v Granger* [1977] QB 397, it was considered that no duty of care was owed, at common law, to a trespasser bitten by a guard dog.

[126] As amended by the Countryside and Rights of Way Act 2000, 13(2), and the Marine and Coastal Access Act 2009, s 306.

[127] See s 1(1), (4).

[128] On the issue of whether a trespass was committed through the bars of a gate, see *Beattie v McConnell* [2005] NIQB 47; and see *Bates v Horkoff* (1991) 119 AR 270.

not suffer injury on the premises by reason of any danger due to the state of the premises or things done or omitted to be done on them. This duty is, however, subject to three conditions, namely that the occupier is aware of the danger or has reasonable grounds to believe that it exists, he knows or has reasonable grounds to believe that the trespasser is in the vicinity of the danger, and the risk is one against which, in all the circumstances of the case, he may reasonably be expected to offer the trespasser some protection. It ought also to be noted that people exercising private rights of way, or rights under the National Parks legislation or the Countryside and Rights of Way Act 2000, are essentially owed the same duty of care as that owed to trespassers. The duty of care to trespassers introduced by the 1984 Act covers personal injuries, but not loss of or damage to property.[129] So the common law rules will continue to apply to such claims.

6.32 If an occupier keeps on his land an animal of whose dangerous characteristics he has actual or presumed knowledge, then the occupier should not be liable under the 1984 Act for injuries to a trespasser if he had no reason to believe that a trespasser might be present. No liability should normally ensue from a trespasser being gored by a bull[130] or kicked by a horse[131] which is kept in the field into which an unexpected person trespassed. The position would be different if the claimant was exercising a right of way, because his presence might be expected.[132] Liability ought not to attach if, for example, a guard dog was put there to protect the property and deter trespassers,[133] at least if there are warnings of its presence. Similarly, if the claimant trespasses by climbing into a lion's enclosure[134] or by walking into a zebra's cage,[135] he ought not to be able to complain if he is injured, given that such folly cannot reasonably be expected.

6.33 No provision is made in the 1984 Act to address the issue of its interrelation with the Animals Act 1971 in general,[136] nor specifically with the defence to liability under section 2 which is provided by section 5(3)[137] in terms that the keeper of a dangerous animal shall not be liable for injuries to a trespassing claimant if the

---

[129] Occupiers' Liability Act 1984, s 1(8), (9).

[130] cf *Brock v Copeland* (1794) 1 Esp 203, 204; *Blackman v Simmons* (1827) 3 C & P 138, 140.

[131] *Lowery v Walker* [1910] 1 KB 173, reversed on the basis that the claimant was not a trespasser, [1911] AC 10.

[132] cf *McKaskie v Cameron* (2009) Unreported, 1 July.

[133] cf *Sarch v Blackburn* (1830) 4 C & P 297, 300; *Cummings v Granger* [1977] QB 397.

[134] *Murphy v Zoological Society of London* [1962] CLY 68; cf *Pearson v Coleman Bros* [1948] 2 KB 359.

[135] cf *Marlor v Ball* (1900) 16 TLR 239.

[136] When examining the issue of liability for animals, the Law Commission thought it inappropriate to make recommendations affecting the common law covering occupiers' liability and trespassers; but they did indicate what provisions might be made in relation to animals if general reform was introduced, as eventually it was: Law Commission Report, para 58. However, no consideration was given by the Law Commission in its Report on Liability for Damage or Injury to Trespassers and Related Questions of Occupiers' Liability, Law Com No 75 (1976), the forerunner of the 1984 Act, to the interrelation of their proposals with the provisions of the Animals Act 1971.

[137] See above, paras 2.140–2.153.

animal was not kept on the premises for the protection of persons or property or, if it was kept there for those purposes, that such keeping was not unreasonable. It can be concluded from that that a trespasser who is injured on the defendant's premises by his animal may claim for any injuries under both the 1971 Act and the 1984 Act. The fact that a claim under the 1971 Act is defeated by the defence under section 5(3) should not exclude a claim under the 1984 Act. If, for example, the defendant reasonably keeps a guard dog for the protection of his farm, he will not be liable under section 2 of the 1971 Act for injuries to a trespasser.[138] Where, however, the defendant has reasonable grounds to believe that a trespasser will, nevertheless, visit the premises and the trespasser is injured by the dog, then the defendant may be liable under the 1984 Act.

[138] *Cummings v Granger* [1977] QB 397.

7

SPECIAL PROVISIONS RELATING TO DOGS

Dogs are singled out for special treatment by the Animals Act 1971 in two different, though related, respects. Strict liability for damage caused by a dog killing or injuring livestock is imposed on its keeper by section 3. However, the owner of the livestock does not have to wait until they have been killed or maimed before taking action. Section 9 defines the circumstances in which a person may kill or injure another's dog for the protection of livestock. These two separate provisions must now be examined. **7.01**

1. Liability for Harm Done by Dogs

Dogs, it may be recalled, fall outside the statutory definition of 'livestock'[1] for the purposes of liability, under section 4 of the Animals Act 1971, for damage caused by trespassing livestock;[2] just as they fell outside the definition of 'cattle' for the purposes of the common law action of cattle trespass.[3] On the other hand, there may be strict liability for damage caused by dogs under section 2(2) of the Animals **7.02**

[1] Animals Act 1971, s 11.

[2] Above, ch 3.

[3] eg *Buckle v Holmes* [1926] 2 KB 125, 128–9, 130; *Tallents v Bell and Goddard* [1944] 2 All ER 474.

Act 1971,[4] if they cause damage of a kind which they were likely to cause as a result of abnormal characteristics known to their keeper. Similarly, there was, at common law, liability for injuries caused by dogs under the *scienter* action,[5] dogs being classed as animals *mansuetae naturae*. Furthermore, there will also be liability for harm caused by dogs under the common law of negligence[6] and nuisance.[7]

7.03 Apart from these forms of liability, it has long been thought necessary to provide some special form of strict liability in the case of certain types of injuries by dogs, such liability being imposed irrespective of proof of negligence or *scienter*. The Dogs Act 1865 imposed such general liability. This was replaced by the Dogs Act 1906,[8] as amended by the Dogs (Amendment) Act 1928,[9] which were themselves replaced in so far as they related to civil liability by the provisions of the Animals Act 1971.[10] Section 3 of the Animals Act 1971 provides that:

> Where a dog causes damage by killing or injuring livestock, any person who is a keeper of the dog is liable for the damage, except as otherwise provided by this Act.[11]

A number of elements in this head of liability merit separate discussion.

(1) Kinds of damage

7.04 Liability is imposed for 'damage by killing or injuring livestock'. Livestock is defined in terms similar to but not identical with its meaning for the purposes of liability under section 4 for damage caused by straying livestock.[12] Section 11 of the Animals Act 1971 states:

> 'livestock' means cattle, horses, asses, mules, hinnies, sheep, pigs, goats and poultry, and also deer not in the wild state and, in sections 3 and 9, also, while in captivity, pheasants, partridges and grouse.

---

[4] Above, ch 2.

[5] eg *M'Kone v Wood* (1831) 5 C & P 1; *Card v Case* (1848) 5 CB 622; *Barnes v Lucille Ltd* (1907) 96 LT 680.

[6] eg *Fardon v Harcourt-Rivington* (1932) 146 LT 391; *Gomberg v Smith* [1963] 1 QB 25; *Draper v Hodder* [1972] QB 556; *Whippey v Jones* [2009] EWCA 452.

[7] eg *Mallock v Mason and Mason* [1938] LJCCR 387; and see *O'Connor v Higgisson* (1946) 12 Ir Jur 61; *Curtis v Thompson* (1956) 106 L Jo 61; *Shanlin v Collins* 1973 SLT (Sh Ct) 21. Common law obligations which are unaffected by the Animals Act 1971 are considered in ch 6.

[8] Section 1(1)–(3).

[9] Section 1(1).

[10] Section 1(1)(b). The relevant provisions of the Dogs Acts 1906–1928 were repealed by s 13(2) of the Animals Act 1971.

[11] Similar provision is made by Art 8(1) of the Animals (Northern Ireland) Order 1976, SI 1976/1040, as amended by the Dogs (Northern Ireland) Order 1983, SI 1983/764, Sch 1. Special provision for liability for damage done by dogs is provided in New Zealand by s 63 of the Dog Control Act 1996, although it is unclear just how extensive the liability is: see S Todd, *The Law of Torts in New Zealand*, 5th edn (2009), para 6.10.03. There is widespread legislation, of varied extent, addressing the issue of damage done by dogs, in the different jurisdictions in Australia (see F Trindade, P Cane, and M Lunney, *The Law of Torts in Australia*, 4th edn (2007), para 12.4) and in Canada (see G Fridman, *The Law of Torts in Canada*, 2nd edn (2002), p 266).

[12] Discussed, above, paras 3.04–3.06.

Poultry is further defined in the same section as 'the domestic varieties of the following, that is to say, fowls, turkeys, geese, ducks, guinea-fowls, pigeons, peacocks and quails'. If the creature injured falls outside these varieties, there will be no liability under section 3.[13] It will, therefore, still be the case, as under the Dogs Acts 1906–1928, that there will be no such liability where, for example, a dog kills or injures rabbits, whether domestic or wild.[14]

The damage covered by section 3 must involve the killing or injuring of livestock by dogs. Thus, the keeper would be liable if his dog attacked a horse,[15] worried and killed sheep,[16] or chased and killed chickens.[17] Damage caused directly to people or to other property is not actionable under this provision; it falls to be dealt with under either section 2 or section 4 of the Animals Act 1971, or at common law. Section 3 of the Animals Act 1971, as with the Dogs Acts, 'placed cattle and sheep in a better position than human beings'.[18] This anomaly has been corrected in Ireland by section 21 of the Control of Dogs Act 1986, which extends also to 'damage caused in an attack on any person by the dog'.[19] **7.05**

There was also liability under the Dogs Acts 1906–1928 if a dog caused an appropriate animal to be injured even though it was not attacked. For example, it was held that it would suffice for liability if the dog merely frightened a horse so that it bolted and was thereby injured;[20] although the injury had to be to the animal in question and there could be no recovery for consequential injury to, for example, a horse's harness or the trap that the horse was pulling.[21] The question arises as to whether there is now liability under section 3 of the Animals Act 1971 for injuries caused in similar circumstances. The Dogs Acts spoke of 'injury done to any cattle by that dog'.[22] The equivalent phrase in section 3 is: 'Where a dog causes damage by killing or injuring livestock'. It would seem that a dog has as much 'caused injury to livestock' as 'done injury to cattle' by causing a horse to bolt so that it is injured. Therefore, it is suggested that there will still be strict liability, now under section 3 of the Animals Act 1971, for injuries to a horse by its being caused to bolt by a dog. **7.06**

[13] No protection would be given to a park where a dog attacked wild swans, geese, or ducks.

[14] *Tallents v Bell and Goddard* [1944] 2 All ER 474.

[15] *Wright v Pearson* (1868) LR 4 QB 582; *McKinnon v Dwyer* [1906] VLR 28; cf *Raisbeck v Desabrais* (1971) 16 DLR (3d) 447.

[16] *Grange v Silcock*, above; and see, eg *Strachan v M'Leod* (1884) 5 NSW LR 191; *Nicol v Humphreys* (1922) 18 MCR 22; *Priest v Davidson* (1922) 17 MCR 105; *Burchmore v Rawson* [1932] GLR 283.

[17] *Ives v Brewer* (1951) 95 Sol Jo 286.

[18] *Grange v Silcock* (1897) 77 LT 340, 341.

[19] See *Quinlisk v Kearney* [2004] IEHC 96; B McMahon and W Binchy, *Law of Torts*, 3rd edn (2000), paras 27.27–27.41.

[20] *Elliott v Longden* (1901) 17 TLR 648; and see *Cowell v Mumford* (1886) 3 TLR 1.

[21] *Cowell v Mumford*, above.

[22] Dogs Act 1906, s 1(1).

7.07 Will there, in such a case, be liability for damage to the horse's harness or trap? It has already been suggested that section 3 relates to injuries to livestock, rather than to people or other property. Although the marginal note to section 3 talks of 'Liability for injury done by dogs to livestock', the actual section talks of a dog which 'causes damage by killing or injuring livestock'. Undoubtedly, there must be death of or injury to livestock for liability to arise under section 3; but what if there is further damage caused by the injury? If a horse is bitten in the leg by a dog and so bolts and wrecks its trap, is the latter damage caused by the injury to the horse? To take another example: if a dog kills a man's prize pig, will the owner of the pig who has a heart attack on discovering the slaughter be able to recover for such personal injuries? There has been death or injury to livestock. There has been damage caused, for section 11 defines damage so as to include 'the death of, or injury to, any person (including any disease and any impairment of physical or mental condition)'. The one debateable issue is whether that damage is caused by the dog killing the pig. It is hard to see why it is not.

7.08 A final series of examples of the problems raised as to the scope of section 3 might be given which relate in part to the issue of who can properly complain of the damage. A variety of situations may be posed:

(i) A dog bites a cow, thereby injuring it. The owner of the cow may recover under section 3.

(ii) A dog runs at a cow, causing it to bolt and injure itself. It is suggested that the owner can recover under section 3.

(iii) A dog bites a cow, causing it to run into a car. The cow has been injured and it is, at the least, arguable that that injury has caused the damage to the car.[23] If so, then both the owner of the cow and of the car might recover under section 3. Similarly:

(iv) A dog bites a cow, causing it to bolt and knock a man off his bicycle. Both this case and case (iii) above raise the issue of whether the claimant under section 3 must be the person whose livestock is injured. There is nothing in the Animals Act 1971 to indicate that that must be the case. There is an arguable case that the injured claimant could recover under section 3 on the basis that his damage is caused by the injury to the cow.

(v) A dog barks at a cow, causing it to bolt. In running away, it collides with a car and knocks a man off his bicycle. As a result of that collision, it is injured. No doubt the owner of the cow can succeed under section 3 (as in case (ii)). Can the owner of the car or the man knocked off his bicycle recover under section 3 for their damage? Was the damage caused by the injury to the livestock? The dog injured the cow by causing it to be involved in the collision. That which actually injured the cow is part of the same incident as caused the car owner's

[23] cf *Knowlson v Solomon* [1969] NZLR 686, 690.

or cyclist's damage. Here again, it is arguable that, as the dog caused the cow to bolt and to collide with the car and the cyclist, thereby injuring the cow, the keeper of the dog is liable for the harm suffered by the car owner and the cyclist.

(vi) A dog bites another dog, or barks at it, causing it to bolt, with the result that it is injured and causes damage to the claimant in any of the ways envisaged in cases (i)–(v) above. There will be no liability under section 3, for the animal injured is not 'livestock'. It does, however, seem a little strange that to cause a cow to knock the claimant off his bicycle might involve strict liability, while to cause a dog to do so will not. One can but recall that the purpose of section 3 is, in the words of the Law Commission, 'that the opportunity should be taken to provide a clearer statement of the law'.[24]

(2) Who is liable?

Although liability under the Dogs Acts 1906–1928 was placed on the owner of the dog or the occupier of the premises where the dog was kept, unless he could prove that he was not the owner,[25] this was generally regarded as unsatisfactory.[26] Liability under section 3 of the Animals Act 1971 is imposed on the keeper of the dog. The keeper is defined, by section 6(3) and (4), in exactly the same way for the purposes of liability under section 3 as for liability under section 2, and this definition has already been examined in detail in that latter context.[27] **7.09**

Briefly, liability as a keeper will be imposed on the owner of the dog or the person who has it in his possession.[28] Also, the head of a household in which there is a keeper under the age of 16 will be a keeper.[29] If the dog has been taken into possession to prevent it causing damage or to return it to its keeper, that possession, as such, will not create the obligations of a keeper.[30] Thus, the owner of a dog will be liable for the damage it has caused, even though he was not in possession of it.[31] Conversely, the possessor will also be liable, even though he is not the owner.[32] If there is neither ownership nor possession, actual or constructive, then there will be no liability. Therefore, an employer is not liable for damage done by his employee's dog;[33] nor would the organizers of a drag hunt be held liable if the dogs, a pack of **7.10**

---

[24] Law Commission Report, para 73.

[25] Dogs Act 1906, s 1.

[26] Law Commission Report, para 74.

[27] Above, paras 2.11–2.31.

[28] Animals Act 1971, s 6(3)(a); and see *Payling v Parry* (1990) CA, Unreported, 12 June. Liability may be imposed on the Crown: Animals Act 1971, s 12, discussed, above, para 2.32.

[29] Animals Act 1971, s 6(3)(b).

[30] Ibid, s 6(4); cf *Roberts v McCready* (1921) 14 MCR 4.

[31] cf *Grigg v Murname* [1934] VLR 295.

[32] cf *Jackson v Croft* (1879) 2 SCR (NSW) (NS) 295; and see *Tobin v Dorman* [1937] NZLR 937.

[33] cf *Knott v LCC* [1934] 1 KB 126.

beagles, attacked the claimant's sheep after the end of the hunt; for, in both cases the defendants would be neither owners nor possessors of the dogs.[34]

(3) Strict liability

7.11 Liability under section 3 of the Animals Act 1971 is strict, although not absolute.[35] The keeper of the dog will be liable for damage done without proof of fault on his part. No proof of knowledge of the dog's vicious or abnormal characteristics is required; nor will proof by the defendant of lack of knowledge[36] or absence of fault[37] afford a defence. The existence of strict liability under section 3 will not affect other heads of liability, either at common law or under other provisions of the Animals Act 1971.[38]

(4) Defences

7.12 As liability under the Dogs Acts 1906–1928 was abolished by the Animals Act 1971,[39] to be replaced by the head of liability under section 3, the only defences to statutory liability under the 1971 Act are those provided by the Act. Two of these are general in that they apply not only to liability under section 3, but also to liability for dangerous animals[40] and to liability for straying livestock,[41] but the third is peculiar to liability under section 3. The first two are that a person will not be liable for any damage which is due wholly to the fault of the person suffering it,[42] and the defence of contributory negligence.[43] It might well be said that, if a dog is provoked by the owner of livestock, the ensuing damage to such livestock is due wholly to the fault of the provoker.[44] Again, if livestock is being driven negligently so that it bolts and is injured when barked at by a dog, this might well constitute contributory negligence and justify the apportionment of damages under the Law Reform (Contributory Negligence) Act 1945.[45]

7.13 The third defence provided by the Animals Act 1971, and the only one which relates solely to liability under section 3, concerns liability for injury to livestock which has strayed onto the defendant's land. It was no defence to an action under the Dogs Acts that the animals injured by the defendant's dog were trespassing on

---

[34] cf *Crean v Nolan* (1963) 97 ILTR 125.
[35] Defences are discussed below.
[36] cf *R v Hare* (1888) 14 VLR 89; *Stremple v Wilson* (1904) 7 WAR 101.
[37] cf *Knowlson v Solomon* [1969] NZLR 686, 690.
[38] cf *Ex p Finneran* (1897) 18 NSWR 353; *Torpy v Hart* (1915) 11 Tas LR 6.
[39] Animals Act 1971, s 1(1)(b), s 13(2).
[40] Animals Act 1971, s 2.
[41] Ibid, s 4.
[42] Ibid, s 5(1), discussed, above ch 2, paras 2.154–2.158.
[43] Ibid, s 10, discussed, above, ch 2, paras 2.159–2.164.
[44] cf *Elliott v Longden* (1901) 17 TLR 648, 649; and see *R v Hare* (1888) 14 VLR 89, 94.
[45] cf *Campbell v. Wilkinson* (1909) 43 ILTR 237.

the defendant's land.[46] This situation had been criticized[47] and so it is provided by section 5(4) of the Animals Act[48] that:

> A person is not liable under section 3 of this Act if the livestock was killed or injured on land to which it had strayed and either the dog belonged to the occupier or its presence on the land was authorised by the occupier.[49]

There are three main elements in this defence. First, the livestock must have strayed onto the land where they were injured or killed. There will be no problem where the livestock are trespassing, ie where there is no doubt that their straying is wrongful. There is, however, no suggestion in the Animals Act that this defence is inapplicable where the livestock have strayed as a result of the fault of the defendant. Such a case might be where the defendant was under an obligation to fence the livestock out. If he is in breach of that obligation, he will be unable to maintain an action, under section 4, for damage done by straying livestock;[50] but it appears that he will have a good defence, under section 5(4), to any claim under section 3 for damage to the livestock done by his dog. This may be of little real help to him, for there is no reason why he should not be liable, independently of section 3, for harm caused to the livestock as a result of his breach of his fencing obligation and it is suggested that exposure to injury from his dog could lead to such liability.[51] **7.14**

The other two elements are really alternatives. The first is that the dog belonged to the occupier of the land on which the livestock were injured. The obvious case is that where the owner of the dog is also the occupier of the land strayed upon. It is more difficult to determine the meaning of 'belonged to', especially in light of the fact that a keeper of a dog for the purpose of section 3 may be either the owner or the possessor.[52] This has the effect that any keeper may rely on the defence provided by section 5(4), even though he is not the occupier of the land where the livestock were injured. If one may borrow, by analogy, the definition of 'belonged' from section 4(2),[53] a dog would belong to the person in whose possession it is. Such a person would always be a keeper, but not necessarily the only keeper, of the dog. For example, if a dog is owned by A and is in the possession of B, then both are keepers **7.15**

---

[46] *Grange v Silcock* (1897) 77 LT 340. It may have been a defence that the animals were injured in the course of use by the occupier and his dog of reasonable force to expel such trespassing animals: *Grange v Silcock,* above, at p 341.

[47] Law Commission Report, para 73; Williams, pp 356–7; and see *Trethowan v Capron* [1961] VR 460.

[48] And see Art 8(3) of the Animals (Northern Ireland) Order 1976, SI 1976/1040, as amended by Sch 1 of the Dogs (Northern Ireland) Order 1983, SI 1983/764.

[49] This subsection was modelled on the defence to a criminal charge under the Dogs (Protection of Livestock) Act 1953, s 1(3).

[50] Animals Act 1971, s 5(6).

[51] See ch 4, above, para 4.12; cf *Dobbie v Henderson* 1970 SLT (Sh Ct) 27.

[52] Animals Act 1971, s 6(3).

[53] Where it relates to liability for straying livestock. The definition in s 4(2) is expressed to be for the purpose of s 4.

of it and both may rely on the protection of section 5(4), provided that the dog 'belongs' to whichever of them is the occupier of the land strayed upon. It would be sensible to regard the dog as belonging to both, so that whichever occupies the land, both are protected. If, however, the analogy is drawn with section 4(2), the dog would only belong to its possessor. This would have the curious effect, in the above example, that if B occupied the land where the livestock strayed, both he and A would be protected by section 5(4); but if A occupied the land, then it would appear that neither would be protected. The dog belonged to B who was not the occupier, while the land was occupied by A to whom the dog did not 'belong', even though he was its owner. This is, it must be admitted, a most unlikely factual situation.

7.16 What is the result if 'belong to' is defined as meaning 'owned by'?[54] If, in the earlier example, A occupies the land, then both he and B are protected, because the dog belongs to the occupier and this brings section 5(4) into operation, whichever keeper is the defendant. This is an unlikely circumstance, for it would mean that the dog caused injury while on the owner's land, although not in the owner's possession. The more likely case is the converse, where B occupies the land and possesses the dog. Here neither B nor A appear, on this hypothesis, to be protected by section 5(4), as the dog does not 'belong' to the occupier.

7.17 The alternative element, and one which ought to resolve most of the problems posed by the varied possible definitions of 'belong', is that the defence provided by section 5(4) is satisfied if the presence of the dog on the land was authorized by the occupier, even though the dog does not belong to him. This will deal with the difficult case provided by a definition of 'belong to' as 'owned by', ie the situation where the dog is possessed by the occupier but owned by someone out of occupation. There is no doubt here that the occupier would authorize the presence of the dog on his land. This alternative provision also accommodates the situation where there is only one keeper, and so no problem as to whom the dog belongs, but that keeper is not the occupier of the land. So long as the occupier has authorized the dog's presence, then the keeper is protected from liability. If, for example, a shepherd is working with his dog on land occupied by someone else, then if the dog injures sheep that have strayed onto the land, the shepherd will be protected from liability under section 3 if the presence of his dog on the land is authorized by the occupier.

7.18 It might be mentioned, finally, that the three defences which have been considered are the only defences provided by the Animals Act 1971 to liability for dogs under section 3.[55] It is no defence, for example, that the dog has not escaped from control,

[54] The Dogs (Protection of Livestock) Act 1953, s 1(3) speaks of a dog 'owned by, or in the charge of, the occupier'.

[55] It has been argued with regard to similar legislation in other jurisdictions that all common law defences apart from the need to prove *scienter* applied: *Wilkins v Manning* (1897) 13 WN (NSW) 220; *Simpson v Bannerman* (1932) 47 CLR 378; *Trethowan v Capron* [1961] VR 460; F Trindade, P Cane, and M Lunney, *The Law of Torts in Australia,* 4th edn (2007), para 12.4.1; *Chittenden v Hale*

or that the injury has been caused by the act of a third party. Furthermore, although it is a defence to liability under section 2 of the Animals Act 1971 that the damage is suffered by a person who has voluntarily accepted the risk thereof,[56] there is no such defence of 'consent' to liability under section 3.[57]

(5) Joint liability

7.19 There are two main problems to consider here. The first is where damage is done by more than one dog. If two dogs act together in causing damage to livestock, then it is suggested that the keepers of both dogs will be liable. They are to be treated as either concurrent or joint tortfeasors, so that each will be liable for the whole of the damage caused,[58] subject to contribution between them under the Civil Liability (Contribution) Act 1978. If the two dogs do not act together, but each separately causes injury to the claimant's livestock, then each keeper is liable only for the damage done by his own dog.[59]

7.20 The second problem arises from the fact that there may be more than one keeper of the same dog. Both the owner and possessor of the dog may be liable under section 3 of the Animals Act 1971, as keepers, for damage caused by the dog. It is suggested that they will be classed as joint tortfeasors, and each will be liable for the whole damage, although this may, again, be apportioned between them in accordance with the Civil Liability (Contribution) Act 1978. Such apportionment will be on the basis of what is 'just and equitable having regard to the extent of that person's responsibility for the damage in question'.[60] It may well be that, in cases of strict liability, where neither of the keepers of the dog is to blame, the apportionment can only be an equal division; although the courts should look both to the relative blameworthiness of the defendants and to the extent to which each contributed to the cause of the damage.[61]

(6) Breach of statutory duty

7.21 No provision for civil actions for breach of statutory duty is made in the legislation[62] providing for criminal offences relating to the keeping of dangerous dogs.[63]

[1933] NZLR 836; and see *Christian v Johannesson* [1956] NZLR 664; *Knowlson v Solomon* [1969] NZLR 686; S Todd, *The Law of Torts in New Zealand*, 5th edn (2009), para 6.10.03.

[56] Animals Act 1971, s 5(2); see above, paras 2.129–2.139.

[57] cf *Chittenden v Hale* [1933] NZLR 836, 848.

[58] *Arneil v Paterson* [1931] AC 560; and see *Piper v Winnifrith* (1917) 34 TLR 108, 109.

[59] *Piper v Winnifrith*, above; and see *Popp v Hoffman* (1953) 10 WWR 337; cf *Lankshear v Farr* [1930] NZLR 347.

[60] Civil Liability (Contribution Act) 1978, s 2(1).

[61] M Jones and A Dugdale, *Clerk & Lindsell on Torts*, 20th edn (2010), paras 4.28–4.29.

[62] eg the Dogs Act 1871, the Dogs Act 1906, the Guard Dogs Act 1975, the Dangerous Dogs Act 1989, the Dangerous Dogs Act 1991, and the Dangerous Dogs (Amendment) Act 1997.

[63] One effect of the repeal, by s 13(2) of the Animals Act 1971, of various provisions of the Dogs Acts 1906–1928 was to repeal s 1(3) of the Dogs Act 1906, which empowered a court of summary

Indeed, the Guard Dogs Act 1975[64] expressly provides that that Act is not to be construed as conferring any civil right of action.[65] However, a rather different approach has been adopted in Northern Ireland, where provision is made by Article 8(2) of the Animals (Northern Ireland) Order 1976[66] for the recovery of damages, up to a prescribed limit, as a civil debt. Furthermore, Article 53 of the Dogs (Northern Ireland) Order 1983[67] provides a right of action for breach of statutory duty, under Articles 22, 25, 26, 28, and 29, for the causing of damage by a dog, including death or personal injury. These provisions cover damage from dogs straying, being out of control, the use of guard dogs, and various attacks by dogs. So, for example, the occupier of land where a guard dog was kept was held liable when it bit a visiting child;[68] but any defence to the criminal liability under the Order will also provide a defence to civil liability under Article 53;[69] so an occupier would not be liable to a trespassing child.[70] Furthermore, civil law defences such as contributory negligence or *volenti* will also be available.[71]

2. Protection of Livestock against Dogs

(1) Introduction

7.22 Although there was no liability at common law in cattle trespass for the incursions of dogs, there were circumstances where such trespassing dogs might be shot.[72] Such action could be justified as reasonable defence of property. The best statement of the common law rules applicable to this type of case is that of Scott LJ in *Cresswell v Sirl*:[73]

> The relevant rules of law may be thus stated: (1) The onus of proof is on the defendant to justify the preventive measure of shooting the attacking dogs. (2) He has, by proof, to establish two propositions, but each proposition may be established in either of two ways: *Proposition No.* 1: That at the time of shooting, the dog was either (a) actually . . . attacking the animals in question, or (b) if left at large would renew the attack so

jurisdiction to award damages of up to £5, as a civil debt, for injury caused by a dog to livestock. A suggestion that a similar jurisdiction, up to £25 damages, should be conferred on magistrates' courts by the Animals Act 1971 was not accepted: 306 HL Deb (1969), cc 72–4; HC Standing Committee A, 16 March 1971, cc 3–13; 815 HC Deb (1971), cc 596–600.

[64] See *Hobson v Gledhill* [1978] 1 WLR 215.

[65] Guard Dogs Act 1975, s 5(2).

[66] SI 1976/1040.

[67] SI 1983/764.

[68] *Canavan v Scott* [2001] NI 48; and see *Taylor v O'Hare* [2002] NIQB 59; *McGivern v Green* [2006] NIQB 53.

[69] *Morrison v Miller* (1987) Unreported, 16 December; *Hampton v Cranston* (1998) Unreported, 10 September.

[70] Art 29; *Beattie v McConnell* [2005] NIQB 47.

[71] *Beattie v McConnell*, above; *Neeson v Acheson* [2008] NIQB 12.

[72] This was, of course, apart from any civil liability under the Dogs Acts 1906–1928 or criminal liability under the Dogs (Protection of Livestock) Act 1953.

[73] [1948] 1 KB 241, 249; approved in *Ramage v Evans* [1948] VLR 391.

that the animals would be left presently subject to real and imminent danger unless renewal was prevented. *Proposition No.* 2: That either (a) there was in fact no practicable means, other than shooting, of stopping the present attack or preventing such renewal, or (b) that the defendant, having regard to all the circumstances in which he found himself, acted reasonably in regarding the shooting as necessary for the protection of the animals against attack or renewed attack.

It would appear that such action against the dog had to be taken by the owner of the animals being attacked or, presumably, by someone acting on his behalf.

Applying these rules, the owner of animals has been considered to have acted law- **7.23**
fully when he shot a dog attacking chickens[74] or worrying sheep.[75] It must be emphasized that there was no right to shoot the dog unless there was a real or imminent danger to the animals in question.[76] There would appear to have been no right to shoot a trespassing dog attacking wild animals, such as pheasants, even though the person shooting the dog had sporting rights over the land in question.[77]

The Law Commission considered that the rules laid down in *Cresswell v Sirl* to **7.24**
govern the circumstances in which measures might be taken against trespassing dogs were inadequate in two respects.[78] First, they required that the measures be taken against the dog during an attack or when there was a likelihood of an imminent renewal of an attack; they did not apply to the imminence of the first attack. Second, they gave no right to take the measures against the dog after the attack and when it was escaping. The Law Commission, therefore, reformulated the rules governing the right to take action against marauding dogs. These rules are to be found in the Animals Act 1971, section 9[79] of which provides:

(1) In any civil proceedings against a person (in this section referred to as the defendant) for killing or causing injury to a dog it shall be a defence to prove—
  (a) that the defendant acted for the protection of any livestock and was a person entitled to act for the protection of that livestock; and
  (b) that within forty-eight hours of the killing or injury notice thereof was given by the defendant to the officer in charge of a police station.

---

[74] cf *Goodway v Becher* [1951] 2 All ER 349. The rules have also been considered applicable to the case of the right to shoot homing pigeons eating one's crops: *Hamps v Darby* [1948] 2 KB 311; and see *Taylor v Newman* (1863) 4 B & S 89. In Queensland, it has been doubted whether there is a right to shoot turkeys which are injuring crops: *Kelly v Nufer* [1918] Qd WN 13; or whether there is a right to shoot a trespassing bull to protect property: *R v Rogers* [1916] Qd SR 38. The suggestion in the former case that 'the more valuable the class of animal trespassing, the more difficult such a defence would be' might be compared with the comment of Blackburn J in *Taylor v Newman*, above, at p 91, that 'a person might shoot even a valuable greyhound which is chasing a hare, if the hare was in peril'.

[75] *Cresswell v Sirl* [1948] 1 KB 241; and see *Stephenson v Auton* [1934] LJCCR 423; *Raine v Temple* [1943] LJCCR 99; *Thayer v Newman* (1953) 51 LGR 618.

[76] *Workman v Cowper* [1961] 2 QB 143.

[77] *Gott v Measures* [1948] 1 KB 234.

[78] Law Commission Report, para 85.

[79] There is provision to similar effect in Art 30 of the Dogs (Northern Ireland) Order 1983, SI 1983/764.

(2) For the purposes of this section a person is entitled to act for the protection of any livestock if, and only if—
  (a) the livestock or the land on which it is belongs to him or to any person under whose express or implied authority he is acting; and
  (b) the circumstances are not such that liability for killing or causing injury to livestock would be excluded by section 5(4) of this Act.

(3) Subject to subsection (4) of this section, a person killing or causing injury to a dog shall be deemed for the purposes of this section to act for the protection of any livestock if, and only if, either—
  (a) the dog is worrying or is about to worry the livestock and there are no other reasonable means of ending or preventing the worrying; or
  (b) the dog has been worrying livestock, has not left the vicinity and is not under the control of any person and there are no practicable means of ascertaining to whom it belongs.

(4) For the purposes of this section the condition stated in either of the paragraphs of the preceding subsection shall be deemed to have been satisfied if the defendant believed that it was satisfied and had reasonable ground for that belief.

(5) For the purposes of this section—
  (a) an animal belongs to any person if he owns it or has it in his possession; and
  (b) land belongs to any person if he is the occupier thereof.

7.25 The basic effect of this section is that anyone who kills or injures a dog in protection of livestock which belongs to him or is on his land will not be liable in civil proceedings for the death of or injury to the dog. Before considering the elements of this defence in further detail, three general points might be made. First, the defence applies only to civil proceedings brought against the person who killed or injured the dog.[80] It does not apply to criminal proceedings. Any defence to criminal proceedings for killing or injuring a dog, for example, a prosecution for discharging a firearm so as to cause unnecessary suffering to a dog,[81] or for criminal damage,[82] must rest either on specific statutory defences thereto,[83] or on the common law rules as laid down in *Cresswell v Sirl*.[84] Second, section 9 of the Animals Act 1971 applies to all cases of killing or injuring dogs, and not just to the shooting of them. As the Law Commission said:

> What are being discussed are the circumstances in which measures taken against a dog, which would normally give cause for a civil action, may be excused.[85]

[80] These are most likely to be proceedings for trespass to goods.
[81] *Isted v CPS* (1997) Unreported, 16 October.
[82] See Criminal Damage Act 1971.
[83] Criminal Damage Act 1971, s 5.
[84] [1948] 1 KB 241.
[85] Law Commission Report, para 85, n 144.

The defence provided by section 9 will apply, therefore, whether the dog is shot or hit with a stick or any other weapon, such as stones thrown at it. Third, section 9 applies only to action taken against dogs. The common law rules will continue to apply to causing the death of, or injury to, other animals in protection of one's property, as in the case of the depredations of pigeons.

(2) Scope of the defence

The various elements of the defence provided by section 9 must now be examined. **7.26**

(a) Livestock

The purpose of section 9 is to protect 'livestock'. It must be proved that the defendant acted for the protection of livestock. This means that it is only when animals within the definition of livestock are threatened by a dog that it may, under section 9, be killed or injured. 'Livestock' is defined, as has been seen, by section 11 as: **7.27**

> cattle, horses, asses, mules, hinnies, sheep, pigs, goats and poultry, and also deer not in the wild state and, in sections 3 and 9, also, while in captivity, pheasants, partridges and grouse.

Poultry is itself defined as 'the domestic varieties of the following, that is to say, fowls, turkeys, geese, ducks, guinea-fowls, pigeons, peacocks and quails'. Therefore, if a dog has been injured by the owner of livestock he may resist an action for trespass to goods where the dog was attacking sheep,[86] a horse,[87] domestic fowls,[88] or deer in a deer-park.[89]

There are, however, two particular comments to be made on the definition of livestock. The first is that, for the purposes of the defence provided by section 9, a dog may be killed or injured when threatening pheasants, partridges, or grouse, but only when they are in captivity.[90] There will be no such right in the case of such birds when wild, even though they are attacked on the defendant's land or on land over which he has shooting rights.[91] So, such birds will be protected when they are young birds in pens, but not when released onto a shooting estate. Second, if the animal threatened by the dog falls outside the definition of livestock, no defence will be provided by section 9. It will not apply, for example, to injuries inflicted on a dog in protection of a cat, another dog,[92] or rabbits kept either as pets or for commercial purposes. In all such cases, reliance will have to be placed on the common law rules **7.28**

---

86 cf *Cresswell v Sirl* [1948] 1 KB 241; see above, para 7.22.
87 cf *Quigley v Pudsey* (1894) 26 NSR 240.
88 cf *Janson v Brown* (1807) 1 Camp 41.
89 cf *Barrington v Turner* (1681) 3 Lev 28; *Protheroe v Matthews* (1833) 5 C & P 581.
90 As in *Miles v Hutchings* [1903] 2 KB 714.
91 cf *Gott v Measures* [1948] 1 KB 234.
92 cf *Wright v Ramscot* (1667) 1 Saund 84.

as to defence of property.[93] It will not be sufficient, at common law, to justify shooting a dog on the basis that it was merely trespassing. It is wrongful, for example, to shoot another's dog when it has just come onto your land to play with your dog;[94] but it is lawful to shoot a trespassing dog which is killing your rabbits. If, however, there is no property in the rabbits[95] or in hares[96] then there is no right to shoot the dog which is attacking them, even if it is doing so on your land. There is no property in the animals in whose defence you are acting.[97]

(b) Notice to the police

7.29 The defendant in the civil proceedings who has killed or injured the dog must, in order to avail himself of the protection of section 9, have notified the police of the killing or injury within 48 hours thereof.[98] There is no need to give notice to the owner of the dog. Failure to give notice will only deprive the defendant of the protection of section 9. There is no reason to believe that he would be unable to rely on his, admittedly less extensive, common law rights.

(c) Defendant entitled to act for the protection of livestock

7.30 The person who injured or killed the dog must have been someone who, within the terms of section 9, was entitled to act for the protection of livestock.[99] Two requirements must be satisfied. First, the livestock or the land on which it is must belong to the defendant or to a person under whose authority he is acting.[100] Livestock belongs to its owner or possessor.[101] Therefore, a man may shoot a dog which is injuring his livestock, even though the livestock are not on his own land. He may also so act even though he has merely possession of them without ownership. Furthermore, the occupier of the land where the livestock are has the same rights against threatening dogs, even though he is neither possessor nor owner of the livestock, for land is taken to belong to its occupier.[102] Anyone authorized by the owner or possessor of the livestock, or the occupier of the land where the livestock are, may act against a dog within section 9. This authorization may be either express or implied. It will mean, therefore, that no action will lie against an employee of such a person for killing or injuring a dog which is threatening his employer's livestock,

[93] eg *Cresswell v Sirl* [1948] 1 KB 241.
[94] cf *Barnard v Evans* [1925] 2 KB 794.
[95] cf *Wadhurst v Damme* (1604) Cro Jac 45, in the light of *Sutton v Moody* (1697)1 Ld Raym 250.
[96] cf *Vere v Lord Cawdor* (1809) 11 East 568.
[97] *Gott v Measures* [1948] 1 KB 234, 239.
[98] Animals Act 1971, s 9(1)(b). A suggestion that the period should be 6 hours was not accepted in the House of Lords: 312 HL Deb (1970), cc 905–9.
[99] Animals Act 1971, s 9(1)(a).
[100] Ibid, s 9(2)(a).
[101] Ibid, s 9(5)(a). The subsection actually talks of 'an animal' belonging to its owner or possessor, but the relevant animals are those which constitute livestock. It is assumed that poultry may be classed as animals for this purpose.
[102] Ibid, s 9(5)(b).

for there can be little doubt that such employees will be impliedly authorized to protect their employer's livestock.

A corollary of the definition of the person entitled to rely on the defence provided by section 9 is that there is no requirement that the dog be trespassing on the defendant's land when it is killed or injured. It does not matter whether the dog is on or off the defendant's land or whether the livestock are or not, subject to qualification where they are trespassing on the dog keeper's land.[103] If livestock are worried by a dog while on the highway, the defendant who kills or injures the dog will fall within the protection of section 9 if he owns or possesses the livestock or acts under the authority of such a person. Equally, it may be a defence to a civil action for killing or injuring a dog that it was worrying livestock, even though the dog was lawfully brought onto the land where the livestock are.[104] **7.31**

The second requirement is that 'the circumstances are not such that liability for killing or causing injury to the livestock would be excluded by section 5(4)'.[105] The object of this provision is to deal with the case where livestock have strayed onto another's land and they are threatened by a dog which belongs to the occupier of that land or whose presence on the land has been authorized by the occupier. If, therefore, livestock owned or possessed by A stray onto B's land and are worried there by B's dog, there will be no statutory right in A to kill or injure B's dog in order to protect his livestock. This is because had B's dog killed or injured A's livestock, section 5(4) would have prevented A from successfully claiming damages under section 3 for harm done by the dog, as the livestock had strayed onto B's land. **7.32**

One problem, which has already been considered,[106] is that section 5(4) merely talks of livestock which have 'strayed', and it may be that they have strayed as a result of the failure of the person onto whose land they have strayed to fence them out. If they are then attacked by that person's dog, there would not appear to be any right, under section 9, for their owner to kill or injure the dog in protection of his own livestock. **7.33**

(d) Defendant acted for the protection of livestock

The person who injured or killed the dog must not only have been someone who is entitled to act for the protection of livestock, but he must also have actually acted for the protection of that livestock.[107] He must act in protection of the livestock that **7.34**

[103] Ibid, s 9(2)(b), below.

[104] Subject to the requirement, discussed below, para 7.39, that there were no other reasonable means (such as the owner calling the dog off) of ending the worrying.

[105] Animals Act 1971, s 9(2)(b). Section 5(4), which has been discussed above, paras 7.13–7.17, provides that: 'A person is not liable under section 3 of this Act if the livestock was killed or injured on land on to which it had strayed and either the dog belonged to the occupier or its presence on the land was authorised by the occupier.'

[106] Above, para 7.14.

[107] Animals Act 1971, s 9(1)(a).

he is entitled to protect. If he is the owner or possessor of sheep, he may only kill or injure a dog which is worrying his sheep. He may not take action against the dog, under section 9, if it is worrying someone else's sheep, unless they are on his land, or unless, perhaps, the fact that it has worried other sheep causes him to believe that it is about to worry his sheep.[108]

7.35 Section 9 specifies the only two circumstances where a person who kills or injures a dog is deemed to act for the protection of livestock. The first is where 'the dog is worrying or is about to worry the livestock and there are no other reasonable means of ending or preventing the worrying'.[109] The first element of this requirement to be considered is the meaning of 'worry'. No definition is provided in the Animals Act 1971, although it is defined in the Dogs (Protection of Livestock) Act 1953[110] as:

> (a) attacking livestock, or
> (b) chasing livestock in such a way as may reasonably be expected to cause injury or suffering to the livestock or, in the case of females, abortion, or loss of or diminution in their produce or
> (c) being at large (that is to say not on a lead or otherwise under close control) in a field or enclosure in which there are sheep.[111]

While this definition cannot be regarded as necessarily authoritative for the purposes of different legislation, it does indicate the type of conduct which might be thought to fall within the term 'worry' for the purposes of the Animals Act 1971. If livestock are stampeded by a dog without their being attacked, then if there is no reasonable danger of injury to them, there will be no 'worrying'. The passage of a pack of hounds down a road might frighten livestock nearby, but this should not justify the killing of the hounds.[112]

7.36 The meaning of 'worry' has fallen for consideration in other jurisdictions with legislation similar to that of section 9 of the Animals Act 1971. In South Australia, in *Hanlin v O'Sullivan*,[113] it was pleaded in defence to a prosecution for unlawfully killing a dog that the dog had been worrying sheep and that this was a defence both at common law[114] and by statute.[115] There was no evidence that the dog had attacked the sheep, bitten them, or caused them any external injury. It had chased them into a corner of the paddock where they were kept. The court was prepared to interpret 'worry' as being substantially wider than its etymological meaning of 'seize by the

---

[108] Animals Act 1971, s 9(3)(a), below, paras 7.35–7.39.

[109] Ibid.

[110] Section 1(2), as amended by the Wildlife and Countryside Act 1981, Sch 7, para 3.

[111] Although subs (c) does not apply to a dog owned or authorized by the occupier of the land or the owner of the sheep; nor does it apply to a police dog, guide dog, trained sheep dog, working gun dog, or a pack of hounds: s 2(A) of the 1953 Act.

[112] cf *Bond v Belville* [1963] Crim LR 103.

[113] [1954] SASR 286.

[114] Relying on *Cresswell v Sirl* [1948] 1 KB 241.

[115] Registration of Dogs Act, 1924–1948, s 21 (South Australia).

throat'. It was not to be confined to 'mangled or lacerated by the teeth'. It was considered that 'worrying' is a 'comprehensive term, which connotes or includes an attack, which the common law would accept as a justification for preventive measures'.[116] Furthermore, the court held that:

> chasing by dogs, which causes any real and present danger of serious harm to the animals chased—as it must when the animals are 'ewes heavily in lamb'—constitutes an attack which, at common law, entitles the owner to take effective measures of prevention.[117]

On this definition, the dog in question was held to have been worrying sheep. It is suggested that this interpretation accords with the definition in the Dogs (Protection of Livestock) Act 1953 and provides a reliable guide to the meaning of 'worry' in section 9 of the Animals Act 1971.[118]

A difficult type of case is that where a dog runs out at a horse, frightening it, and causing it to run off in fear. If this is likely to cause injury to the horse, then it is suggested that the horse is being 'worried' and the dog may be shot with impunity.[119] It might be thought strange if there was not such a right to kill the dog, for if the horse is in fact injured, then there would appear to be liability imposed on the keeper of the dog by reason of section 3 of the Animals Act 1971.[120] It should be the case that all conduct which would involve liability under section 3 ought to justify the killing or injuring of the dog under section 9. If the conduct of a dog puts the rider of a horse in jeopardy, then he has a common law right to act in self-defence,[121] although such conduct falls outside the scope of section 9. He cannot be said to be acting for the protection of livestock, unless he acts to protect his horse as well as himself. **7.37**

Under section 9(3)(a) the dog need not be actually worrying livestock. It is sufficient that it 'is about to worry the livestock'. This will enable a farmer to take precautionary measures to protect his livestock. If he thinks that they will be attacked or otherwise worried, he can prevent the dog from doing this. This is wider than the common law rule for that dealt only with an actual attack or the threat of a renewed attack. Section 9 permits action against the dog to prevent the first attack. **7.38**

Before a dog which is worrying or about to worry livestock may be killed or injured, there must be no other reasonable means of ending or preventing the worrying. If it is reasonable to call the dog off before shooting it, then this must be tried first.[122] This requirement would also suggest that it might be reasonable to act in a way **7.39**

116 [1954] SASR 286, 295.
117 Ibid.
118 And see *Stephen v Milne* 1960 SLT 276.
119 See *Quigley v Pudsey* (1894) 26 NSR 240.
120 Above, paras 7.05–7.08; and see *Cowell v Mumford* (1886) 3 TLR 1.
121 *Morris v Nugent* (1836) 7 C & P 572; *Quigley v Pudsey*, above.
122 Nevertheless, a dog may be killed or injured, under s 9(3)(a), even though it is under the control of another person, as where it is set on the livestock by its keeper.

likely to injure, rather than likely to kill. It might be reasonable to throw stones at a dog, thereby injuring it, rather than shoot it dead outright.[123] On the other hand, where a dog is actually worrying sheep, it is probable that shooting is the only practicable remedy. It will not matter that the defendant in killing or injuring a dog has been mistaken as to the dog's behaviour. The requirements of section 9(3) are regarded as satisfied if the defendant believed that they were satisfied and had reasonable ground for that belief.[124] If he reasonably thinks that the dog is worrying or is about to worry livestock, or if he reasonably believes that there is no other way to prevent it so doing or of ending the worrying, then he will be justified in killing or injuring it. Finally, there is no requirement under section 9(3)(a) that the defendant should be unaware of to whom the dog belongs.[125] He can kill or injure a dog even though he is well aware of whose it is.

7.40 The second circumstance where a person who kills or injures a dog is deemed to act for the protection of livestock is laid down in section 9(3)(b), namely where:

> the dog has been worrying livestock, has not left the vicinity and is not under the control of any person and there are no practicable means of ascertaining to whom it belongs.

This is an extension of the common law which was limited to the type of circumstance covered by section 9(3)(a).[126] This second case could be characterized, in part, as an act of vengeance against a dog for what it has already done. It is only preventative in the long term. If the dog is about to worry livestock, then action is justified on that basis, rather than on the ground that it has already worried. The justification for killing the dog which has already worried is that it might do it again, even though it is not just about to do so, and that the defendant does not know to whom it belongs so that he is unable to take steps against the owner to prevent any future worrying.

7.41 This second circumstance is defined more narrowly than that where the dog is actually worrying or about to worry, and a number of conditions have to be satisfied. The first is that the dog has been worrying livestock,[127] or that the defendant reasonably believes that it has.[128] The one difficulty raised here is as to whether the livestock

[123] This requirement of reasonableness ought to be adequate to deal with cases of brutal killing or maiming of dogs. Such conduct would not be a reasonable means of ending or preventing the worrying; cf *Wilgress v Ritchie* [1920] 2 WWR 421. Would castration be reasonable to prevent future worrying? See *Robinson v Wagner* (1910) 30 NZLR 367.

[124] Animals Act 1971, s 9(4).

[125] cf Animals Act 1971, s 9(3)(b).

[126] See *Cresswell v Sirl* [1948] 1 KB 241; *Ramage v Evans* [1948] VLR 391; and see *Wells v Head* (1831) 4 C & P 568; *Crow v Palmer* (1888) 6 NZLR 408; *Sommers v Sandilands* (1910) 13 WALR 53; *O'Leary v Therrien* (1915) 27 DLR 701; *Austin v Laking* [1933] GLR 543; cf *Deep v Cook* (1938) 55 WN (NSW) 115.

[127] 'Worrying' will have the same meaning as in s 9(3)(a), above.

[128] Animals Act 1971, s 9(4).

which has been worried must have belonged to the defendant who shot the dog. There seems to be a difference in this respect between the wording of section 9(3)(a) and section 9(3)(b). In the first case, the defendant is deemed to act for the protection of *any* livestock if the dog is worrying or about to worry *the* livestock. The words italicized would indicate that the livestock to be protected is, naturally, that which is being or is about to be worried. On the other hand, section 9(3)(b) provides that a person is deemed to act for the protection of *any* livestock if the dog has been worrying livestock. There is no indication that, in this case, the dog must have been worrying the same livestock as its killing or injuring is meant to protect. This becomes of some importance when one looks also at the question of who may act in protection of livestock.[129] If the dog is about to worry, or is actually worrying, livestock, then the only people who are entitled to injure it are the owner or possessor of that livestock, the occupier of the land where it is, or any person acting with their authority.[130] If the dog has actually worried livestock and the other requirements of section 9(3)(b) are satisfied, then anyone who owns or possesses livestock or occupies land on which there is livestock may kill or injure the dog in protection of their livestock, even though the livestock which has been worried or the land where the worried livestock was kept does not belong to them.[131]

The second requirement under section 9(3)(b) is that the dog has not left the vicinity. There would seem, from this, little doubt that the dog need not still be on the land where it worried the livestock. It must still be in the neighbourhood, and it is not sufficient that it has been away and has later returned, unless the defendant reasonably believes that it has not been away. The problem here is to know how large an area 'the vicinity' is. The narrower the courts choose to define it, the greater will be the defendant's difficulty in escaping liability for shooting a dog which has undoubtedly worried the defendant's sheep, but which he has had to track down in order to kill it and thereby protect his flocks in future. **7.42**

The third requirement is that the dog is not under the control of any person.[132] The defendant may not shoot a dog which has worried livestock and is still in the vicinity if it is under the control of its keeper. Furthermore, he may not do so if *any* person has it in his control. This would seem to include himself. If he catches the dog, he is then prevented from killing it. He is only allowed to kill or injure it while it is at large. The defendant will be protected if he kills a dog which is under the control of some person if he reasonably believed that it was not under control. No definition of 'control' is given in the Animals Act 1971. No doubt a dog which **7.43**

[129] Discussed above, paras 7.30–7.33.

[130] Animals Act 1971, s 9(2)(a), s 9(5).

[131] It would clearly seem to have been the intention of the Law Commission that the person who could rely on s 9(3)(b) was to be only the person to whom the livestock which had been worried belonged, or the occupier of the land where it was kept: Law Commission Report, para 88.

[132] cf *R (Mino) v Corliss* (1957) 120 Can Crim Cas 341.

is on a lead or under some form of physical control may not be killed or injured. It is suggested that also included is the situation where the dog, if trained, is 'subject to disciplinary control'.[133] If a dog is responding to its keeper's commands, it is under his control and may not be shot or injured.

7.44 Finally, the defendant may only kill or injure a dog which has been worrying livestock if there are no practicable means of ascertaining to whom the dog belongs, or if the defendant reasonably believed that there were no such means. The object of this condition is to allow action to be taken against an apparently ownerless dog which has already worried livestock, but not against one where it is known to whom it belongs. A dog is held, for these purposes, to belong to any person who owns it or has it in his possession.[134] There must also be no practicable means of discovering to whom it belongs. In many cases, it will be impossible to discover to whom it belongs without catching it, which may be very difficult; but, once it has been caught, then it cannot be killed or injured within section 9. Just as the scope of phrases such as 'the vicinity' or 'under the control of any person' are essentially factual questions for the court in each case, so also is the determination of whether there were, or the defendant reasonably believed that there were, no practicable means of ascertaining to whom the dog belonged.

7.45 There is one problem which is concerned with the interrelation of section 9(3)(a) and section 9(3)(b). It will be apparent that the right to kill or injure a dog is wider when it is actually worrying livestock than when it has been worrying them. In the former case, it does not matter that the defendant knows to whom the dog belongs, nor does it have to be out of anyone's control. These differences mean that it is important to know when the scope of one subsection ends and the other takes over. When can it be said that a dog ceases to worry and must be regarded as 'having been worrying'? If the dog has made off and is several fields away when shot,[135] then it is suggested that the dog must be treated as one which 'has been worrying'. This type of problem has arisen in other jurisdictions which also have had statutory provisions relating to the shooting of dogs. In New Zealand, where legislation provided that a dog which was 'biting or attacking' any person or livestock, might be destroyed,[136] it was held that a dog which had been worrying and attacking sheep had ceased to do so when chased into another field and shot 10 minutes later while lying down.[137] In New South Wales, it was provided that it was lawful to destroy a dog which was 'attacking any person or animal'.[138] Where a dog which was

[133] *Jolliffe v Dean* (1954) 54 SR (NSW) 157, 159.

[134] Animals Act 1971, s 9(5)(a).

[135] eg *Wells v Head* (1831) 4 C & P 568.

[136] Dogs Registration Act 1955, s 25 (New Zealand); and see now the Dog Control Act 1996, s 57, as substituted by s 35 of the Dog Control Amendment Act 2003.

[137] *Crow v Palmer* (1888) 6 NZLR 408, decided under the Dog Registration Act 1880, the forerunner of the 1955 Act.

[138] Dog and Goat Act 1898, s 20 (NSW), since repealed.

attacking sheep was shot as it ran away from the sheep at the approach of the defendant, it was held to be lawful to kill it.[139] Jordan CJ was 'disposed to think that, even if a dog when detected in the act of killing sheep attempted to escape when it saw that it was detected, it could, nevertheless, be killed so long as it was killed at once and incidentally to the actual detection'.[140] It is suggested that this dictum might provide a guide line for an English court in order to determine when a dog has ceased to worry livestock for the purposes of the interrelation of section 9(3)(a) and section 9(3)(b).

139 *Deeps v Cook* (1938) 55 WN (NSW) 115.
140 Ibid, at p 117. See also *Hanlin v O'Sullivan* [1954] SASR 286.

APPENDIX

The marginal notes to the sections are printed in bold type after each section number

Animals Act 1971
(1971 c. 22)

Strict liability for damage done by animals

An Act to make provision with respect to civil liability for damage done by animals and with respect to the protection of livestock from dogs; and for purposes connected with those matters.

[12th May 1971]

Strict liability for damage done by animals

1. New provisions as to strict liability for damage done by animals

(1) The provisions of sections 2 to 5 of this Act replace—

(a) the rules of the common law imposing a strict liability in tort for damage done by an animal on the ground that the animal is regarded as ferae naturae or that its vicious or mischievous propensities are known or presumed to be known;

(b) subsections (1) and (2) of section 1 of the Dogs Act 1906 as amended by the Dogs (Amendment) Act 1928 (injury to cattle or poultry); and

(c) the rules of the common law imposing a liability for cattle trespass.

(2) Expressions used in those sections shall be interpreted in accordance with the provisions of section 6 (as well as those of section 11) of this Act.

2. Liability for damage done by dangerous animals

(1) Where any damage is caused by an animal which belongs to a dangerous species, any person who is a keeper of the animal is liable for the damage, except as otherwise provided by this Act.

(2) Where damage is caused by an animal which does not belong to a dangerous species, a keeper of the animal is liable for the damage, except as otherwise provided by this Act, if—

(a) the damage is of a kind which the animal, unless restrained, was likely to cause or which, if caused by the animal, was likely to be severe; and

(b) the likelihood of the damage or of its being severe was due to characteristics of the animal which are not normally found in animals of the same species or are not normally so found except at particular times or in particular circumstances; and

(c) those characteristics were known to that keeper or were at any time known to a person who at that time had charge of the animal as that keeper's servant or, where that keeper is the head of a household, were known to another keeper of the animal who is a member of that household and under the age of sixteen.

3. Liability for injury done by dogs to livestock

Where a dog causes damage by killing or injuring livestock, any person who is a keeper of the dog is liable for the damage, except as otherwise provided by this Act.

4. Liability for damage and expenses due to trespassing livestock

(1) Where livestock belonging to any person strays on to land in the ownership or occupation of another and—

(a) damage is done by the livestock to the land or to any property on it which is in the ownership or possession of the other person; or

(b) any expenses are reasonably incurred by that other person in keeping the livestock while it cannot be restored to the person to whom it belongs or while it is detained in pursuance of section 7 of this Act, or in ascertaining to whom it belongs;

the person to whom the livestock belongs is liable for the damage or expenses, except as otherwise provided by this Act.

(2) For the purposes of this section any livestock belongs to the person in whose possession it is.

5. Exceptions from liability under sections 2 to 4

(1) A person is not liable under sections 2 to 4 of this Act for any damage which is due wholly to the fault of the person suffering it.

(2) A person is not liable under section 2 of this Act for any damage suffered by a person who has voluntarily accepted the risk thereof.

(3) A person is not liable under section 2 of this Act for any damage caused by an animal kept on any premises or structure to a person trespassing there, if it is proved either—

(a) that the animal was not kept there for the protection of persons or property; or

(b) (if the animal was kept there for the protection of persons or property) that keeping it there for that purpose was not unreasonable.

(4) A person is not liable under section 3 of this Act if the livestock was killed or injured on land on which it had strayed and either the dog belonged to the occupier or its presence on the land was authorised by the occupier.

(5) A person is not liable under section 4 of this Act where the livestock strayed from a highway and its presence there was a lawful use of the highway.

(6) In determining whether any liability for damage under section 4 of this Act is excluded by subsection (1) of this section the damage shall not be treated as due to the fault of the person suffering it by reason only that he could have prevented it by fencing; but a person is not liable under that section where it is proved that the straying of the livestock on to the land would not have occurred but for a breach by any other person, being a person having an interest in the land, of a duty to fence.

6. Interpretation of certain expressions used in sections 2 to 5

(1) The following provisions apply to the interpretation of sections 2 to 5 of this Act.

(2) A dangerous species is a species—
- (a) which is not commonly domesticated in the British Islands; and
- (b) whose fully grown animals normally have such characteristics that they are likely, unless restrained, to cause severe damage or that any damage they may cause is likely to be severe.

(3) Subject to subsection (4) of this section, a person is a keeper of an animal if—
- (a) he owns the animal or has it in his possession; or
- (b) he is the head of a household of which a member under the age of sixteen owns the animal or has it in his possession;

and if at any time an animal ceases to be owned by or to be in the possession of a person, any person who immediately before that time was a keeper thereof by virtue of the preceding provisions of this subsection continues to be a keeper of the animal until another person becomes a keeper thereof by virtue of those provisions.

(4) Where an animal is taken into and kept in possession for the purpose of preventing it from causing damage or of restoring it to its owner, a person is not a keeper of it by virtue only of that possession.

(5) Where a person employed as a servant by a keeper of an animal incurs a risk incidental to his employment he shall not be treated as accepting it voluntarily.

Detention and sale of trespassing livestock

7. Detention and sale of trespassing livestock

(1) The right to seize and detain any animal by way of distress damage feasant is hereby abolished.

(2) Where any livestock strays on to any land and is not then under the control of any person the occupier of the land may detain it, subject to subsection (3) of this section, unless ordered to return it by a court.

(3) Where any livestock is detained in pursuance of this section the right to detain it ceases—

(a) at the end of a period of forty-eight hours, unless within that period notice of the detention has been given to the officer in charge of a police station and also, if the person detaining the livestock knows to whom it belongs, to that person; or—

(b) when such amount is tendered to the person detaining the livestock as is sufficient to satisfy any claim he may have under section 4 of this Act in respect of the livestock; or

(c) if he has no such claim, when the livestock is claimed by a person entitled to its possession.

(4) Where livestock has been detained in pursuance of this section for a period of not less than fourteen days the person detaining it may sell it at a market or by public auction, unless proceedings are then pending for the return of the livestock or for any claim under section 4 of this Act in respect of it.

(5) Where any livestock is sold in the exercise of the right conferred by this section and the proceeds of the sale, less the costs thereof and any costs incurred in connection with it, exceed the amount of any claim under section 4 of this Act which the vendor had in respect of the livestock, the excess shall be recoverable from him by the person who would be entitled to the possession of the livestock but for the sale.

(6) A person detaining any livestock in pursuance of this section is liable for any damage caused to it by a failure to treat it with reasonable care and supply it with adequate food and water while it is so detained.

(7) References in this section to a claim under section 4 of this Act in respect of any livestock do not include any claim under that section for damage done by or expenses incurred in respect of the livestock before the straying in connection with which it is detained under this section.

Animals straying on to highway

8. Duty to take care to prevent damage from animals straying on to the highway

(1) So much of the rules of the common law relating to liability for negligence as excludes or restricts the duty which a person might owe to others to take such care as is reasonable to see that damage is not caused by animals straying on to a highway is hereby abolished.

(2) Where damage is caused by animals straying from unfenced land to a highway a person who placed them on the land shall not be regarded as having committed a breach of the duty to take care by reason only of placing them there if—

(a) the land is common land, or is land situated in an area where fencing is not customary, or is a town or village green; and

(b) he had a right to place the animals on that land.

Protection of livestock against dogs

9. Killing of or injury to dogs worrying livestock

(1) In any civil proceedings against a person (in this section referred to as the defendant) for killing or causing injury to a dog it shall be a defence to prove—
  (a) that the defendant acted for the protection of any livestock and was a person entitled to act for the protection of that livestock; and
  (b) that within forty-eight hours of the killing or injury notice thereof was given by the defendant to the officer in charge of a police station.

(2) For the purposes of this section a person is entitled to act for the protection of any livestock if, and only if—
  (a) the livestock or the land on which it is belongs to him or to any person under whose express or implied authority he is acting; and
  (b) the circumstances are not such that liability for killing or causing injury to the livestock would be excluded by section 5(4) of this Act.

(3) Subject to subsection (4) of this section, a person killing or causing injury to a dog shall be deemed for the purposes of this section to act for the protection of any livestock if, and only if, either—
  (a) the dog is worrying or is about to worry the livestock and there are no other reasonable means of ending or preventing the worrying; or
  (b) the dog has been worrying livestock, has not left the vicinity and is not under the control of any person and there are no practicable means of ascertaining to whom it belongs.

(4) For the purposes of this section the condition stated in either of the paragraphs of the preceding subsection shall be deemed to have been satisfied if the defendant believed that it was satisfied and had reasonable ground for that belief.

(5) For the purposes of this section—
  (a) an animal belongs to any person if he owns it or has it in his possession; and
  (b) land belongs to any person if he is the occupier thereof.

Supplemental

10. Application of certain enactments to liability under sections 2 to 4

For the purposes of the Fatal Accidents Acts 1846 to 1959,[1] the Law Reform (Contributory Negligence) Act 1945 and the Limitation Act 1980[2] any damage for which a person is liable under sections 2 to 4 of this Act shall be treated as due to his fault.

[1] See the Fatal Accidents Act 1976, s 6(1), Sch 1, para 1(1); Sch 2.
[2] Amended by the Limitation Act 1980, s 40(2), Sch 3, para 10.

11. General interpretation

In this Act—

'common land' means–

(a) land registered as common land in a register of common land kept under Part 1 of the Commons Act 2006;
(b) land to which Part 1 of that Act does not apply and which is subject to rights of common within the meaning of that Act;[3]

'town or village green' means land registered as a town or village green in a register of town or village greens kept under Part 1 of the Commons Act 2006;[4]

'damage' includes the death of, or injury to, any person (including any disease and any impairment of physical or mental condition);

'fault' has the same meaning as in the Law Reform (Contributory Negligence) Act 1945;

'fencing' includes the construction of any obstacle designed to prevent animals from straying;

'livestock' means cattle, horses, asses, mules, hinnies, sheep, pigs, goats and poultry, and also deer not in the wild state and, in sections 3 and 9, also, while in captivity, pheasants, partridges and grouse;

'poultry' means the domestic varieties of the following, that is to say, fowls, turkeys, geese, ducks, guinea-fowls, pigeons, peacocks and quails; and

'species' includes sub-species and variety.

12. Application to Crown

(1) This Act binds the Crown, but nothing in this section shall authorise proceedings to be brought against Her Majesty in her private capacity.
(2) (2) Section 38(3) of the Crown Proceedings Act 1947 (interpretation of references to Her Majesty in her private capacity) shall apply as if this section were contained in that Act.

13. Short title, repeal, commencement and extent

(1) This Act may be cited as the Animals Act 1971.
(2) The following are hereby repealed, that is to say—
   (a) in the Dogs Act 1906, subsections (1) to (3) of section 1; and
   (b) in section 1(1) of the Dogs (Amendment) Act 1928 the words 'in both places where that word occurs'.
(3) This Act shall come into operation on 1st October 1971.
(4) This Act does not extend to Scotland or to Northern Ireland.

[3] Amended by the Commons Act 2006, s 52, Sch 5, para 2.
[4] Ibid.

INDEX

References are to chapter and paragraph number. Footnotes are denoted by 'n', eg 3.02n